Praise for *Agile Management for Software Engineering*

"At last! While software engineers will design systems around the common principles of software engineering, the same level of rigor has not been paid to the management principles. I highly recommend this book to anyone who is looking to bridge current thinking on management and process control to the management of software development. If you are accountable for not just software development but also making your business a success."
    —**Craig Hayman**, VP Development, I...

"Finally, a book that takes Theory of Constraints and Critical Chain thinking and applies them to software development. Reading this book will change how you think about software projects."
    —**Mike Cohn**, Director of Articles, Agile Alliance

"In 2001 Sprint PCS faced the challenge of how to literally invent the systems and applications necessary to launch the first nation-wide high speed wireless data service, PCS Vision. With "Agile Management. . ." David Anderson does a good job of describing the methods employed at Sprintpcs.com in Kansas City to deliver on that challenge—over 250 people practicing Feature Driven Development and reporting their progress to me at the monthly operations review. Through a lean and agile approach Sprint delivered in August 2002—introducing more than a million people to a color-screen, Java-capable phone with PCS Vision service."
    —**Scott B. Relf**, Chief Marketing Office, Sprint PCS

"Examining a subject from a different perspective can result in new insight. In this book, David does exactly this for the agile software development process phenomenon."
    —**Stephen R. Palmer**, co-author "A Practical Guide to Feature Driven Development"

"A tremendous contribution to the literature of the field. This should be required reading for all development teams going forward."
    —**John F. Yuzdepski**, VP & GM Openwave Systems

The Coad Series

Peter Coad, *Series Editor*

———■———

- David J. Anderson
  Agile Management for Software Engineering:
  Applying the Theory of Constraints for Business Results

- David Astels
  Test Driven Development: A Practical Guide

- David Astels, Granville Miller, Miroslav Novak
  A Practical Guide to eXtreme Programming

- Andy Carmichael, Dan Haywood
  Better Software Faster

- Donald Kranz, Ronald J. Norman
  A Practical Guide to Agile Unified Process

- James McGovern, Scott W. Ambler, Michael E. Stevens,
  James Linn, Vikas Sharan, Elias Jo
  A Practical Guide to Enterprise Architecture

- Jill Nicola, Mark Mayfield, Michael Abney
  Streamlined Object Modeling: Patterns, Rules, and Implementation

- Stephen R. Palmer, John M. Felsing
  A Practical Guide to Feature-Driven Development

About the Series

The Coad Series is a growing collection of practical guides "from the trenches." The series focuses on key "must be addressed" IT pain points, felt by leaders around the globe. The series is especially suited for CIOs, IT department managers, technology leaders, and change agents. The Coad Series addresses the four dimensions of successful IT: technology, process, people, and vision. For the series, Peter Coad personally selects authors and topics and then mentors the authors at a strategic level along the way.

About the Series Editor

Peter Coad (pronounced "code") is senior vice president and chief strategist of Borland (http://www.borland.com) Software Corporation. Coad collaborates with fellow Borland execs in formulating long-term business and product strategies. Peter also represents Borland worldwide as a thought leader, industry luminary, and evangelist among CXOs, technical department managers, and developers.

Peter is globally recognized as an accomplished business strategist, model builder, and thought leader. As business strategist, Peter formulates long-term competitive strategies for Borland. Previously, as Chairman, CEO, and President of TogetherSoft, he led in growing that company 11.6 times revenue in the span of two years, overall profitably. As model builder, Peter has built hundreds of models for nearly every business imaginable, fully focused on building-in strategic business advantage. As thought leader, Peter writes books (six to date) on building better software faster; he speaks at industry events worldwide; and he is the Editor-in-Chief of The Coad Series, published by Prentice Hall; in addition, Peter was an invited speaker on business strategy at the 2003 "Future in Review" conference.

Coad attended the Stanford Executive Program for Growing Companies and received a Master of Science in Computer Science (USC) and a Bachelor of Science with Honors in Electrical Engineering (OSU).

Agile
Management
for Software
Engineering

Applying the Theory of Constraints for Business Results

David J. Anderson

Foreword by Eli Schragenheim

PRENTICE HALL
PTR

PRENTICE HALL
Professional Technical Reference
Upper Saddle River, NJ 07458
www.phptr.com

Library of Congress Cataloging-in-Publication Data

Anderson, David J. (David James)
  Agile management for software engineering / David Anderson
    p. cm
  Includes index
  ISBN 0-13-142460-2.
  1. Software engineering. 2. Computer software--Development--Management. I. Title

QA76.75 .A48 2003
005.1--dc22

2003017798

Editorial/production supervision: *Carlisle Publishers Services*
Cover art: *Jan Voss*
Cover design director: *Jerry Votta*
Art director: *Gail Cocker-Bogusz*
Interior design: *Meg Van Arsdale*
Manufacturing manager: *Alexis R. Heydt-Long*
Manufacturing buyer: *Maura Zaldivar*
Executive editor: *Paul Petralia*
Editorial assistant: *Michelle Vincenti*
Marketing manager: *Chris Guzikowski*
Full-service production manager: *Anne R. Garcia*

PRENTICE
HALL
PTR

© 2004 by Pearson Education, Inc.
Publishing as Prentice Hall Professional Technical Reference
Upper Saddle River, New Jersey 07458

Prentice Hall PTR offers excellent discounts on this book when ordered in quantity for bulk purchases or special sales. For more information, please contact: U.S. Corporate and Government Sales, 1-800-382-3419, corpsales@pearsontechgroup.com. For sales outside of the U.S., please contact: International Sales, 1-317-581-3793, international@pearsontechgroup.com.

Company and product names mentioned herein are the trademarks or registered trademarks of their respective owners.

Printed in the United States of America

Second Printing

ISBN 0-13-142460-2

Pearson Education LTD.
Pearson Education Australia PTY, Limited
Pearson Education Singapore, Pte. Ltd.
Pearson Education North Asia Ltd.
Pearson Education Canada, Ltd.
Pearson Educación de Mexico, S.A. de C.V.
Pearson Education–Japan
Pearson Education Malaysia, Pte. Ltd.

About Prentice Hall Professional Technical Reference

With origins reaching back to the industry's first computer science publishing program in the 1960s, and formally launched as its own imprint in 1986, Prentice Hall Professional Technical Reference (PH PTR) has developed into the leading provider of technical books in the world today. Our editors now publish over 200 books annually, authored by leaders in the fields of computing, engineering, and business.

Our roots are firmly planted in the soil that gave rise to the technical revolution. Our bookshelf contains many of the industry's computing and engineering classics: Kernighan and Ritchie's *C Programming Language*, Nemeth's *UNIX System Adminstration Handbook*, Horstmann's *Core Java*, and Johnson's *High-Speed Digital Design*.

PH PTR acknowledges its auspicious beginnings while it looks to the future for inspiration. We continue to evolve and break new ground in publishing by providing today's professionals with tomorrow's solutions.

PRENTICE
HALL
PTR

For Nicola and Mikiko—the agile Andersons

Contents

Contents

Contents

Foreword

It is so good to finally have a book targeted at the software industry that challenges some of the basic business assumptions behind software engineering, and particularly those behind managing software organizations. At the time these words are written, the software business is facing huge difficulties worldwide. I hope that these difficulties also generate a willingness to look afresh at the business and to have the courage to contemplate changes. Other industries, particularly in manufacturing, went through such conceptual changes in their business processes during the 1980s and the 1990s. It is certainly not easy, but as I've personally experienced, it is highly desirable.

In 1985 I managed my own software company in Israel and was quite proud with my new package for certified public accountants. But, even though my package competed very nicely in the market, I noticed an on-going business problem: More and more development was needed to keep the package alive. In such a case, how do I justify the on-going investment? Eventually, I was not sure that a small software company, focused on a specific market niche, could be a good business—even when the product itself was enthusiastically accepted by the market. I felt that even though I already had my MBA, I needed a better perspective to understand the business.

Then I met Dr. Eli Goldratt.

I had heard a lot about Dr. Goldratt's international software company, Creative Output, Inc., which was seen as much more than just an excellent and innovative software company. It challenged some of the most sacred norms of business, such as the concept of product cost. I could not understand how anyone could challenge the basic concept that a unit of a product has a certain cost associated with it. I was intrigued enough to be open to an offer: Join Creative Output in order to develop a video game for managers that would deliver some new managerial ideas. At the time, computerized games were focused on fast fingers and perfect coordination. They were certainly not something of interest to adults. How could a computer game be readily accepted by grown-up managers and deliver new managerial ideas?

This was the start of a mental voyage into a new management philosophy that does not lose its grip on reality. I turned myself into a management consultant with a focus on improving whatever is the particular goal of the organization. Software became an important supporting tool, but not the focus of the change efforts.

The relevance of the Theory of Constraints (TOC) to the software industry is twofold:

1. Vastly improving the flow of new products to the market.
2. Determining the real value of a proposed project, or even just a feature, to the final user. The underlying assumption is that if we know the real value to the user, it is possible to develop the right marketing and sales approach to materialize the value to the user and to the software organization.

David Anderson focuses mainly on the first aspect in this book, which includes looking at the business case and ensuring the ability to make it happen. Software organizations can definitely be improved with the help of the new generic managerial insights that have already changed traditional western industries. David does a great job in bringing together the generic managerial ideas and rationale and combining them with software-focused approaches to come up with a coherent approach on how to improve the business.

Read this book carefully with the following objective: **Learn how to make more with less.** Don't accept every claim David raises just because he says it is so. If you truly want to make more with less, you need to be able to internalize the claim. All I ask is you give it a chance. Dedicate time in order to rethink your environment, and then see for yourself what to do. Overcoming inertia is the biggest challenge of any really good manager in any organization. Of course, rushing to implement new fads can be even worse. Keeping an open mind and confronting new ideas that invalidate basic assumptions are what I suggest you strive for. This book is for you to struggle with. It is not trivial, and it is not a fad. If you like what you do now, it should be your responsibility to check out new ideas that might yield huge improvements.

Here are some brief insights regarding the assessment of the value to a potential customer of a new feature, particularly to a new software package.

A new Feature can bring value to the user only if it eliminates, or vastly reduces, an existing limitation. The amount of the value depends on the limitation removed—not on the sophistication of the feature itself. Let us take a simple example. At a certain time in the history of word processors, somebody had an idea: Why not add a spell checker to the package?

What is the value of the spell check we now have as a routine feature? What limitation does it eliminate or reduce? For people with a very good knowledge of the language, spelling mistakes are caused by writing too fast. So, without a spell checker, those people need to read carefully what they just wrote. People who are not in full command of the language (for example, me, as an Israeli) need to look at the dictionary very often, which is quite time consuming.

This need leads us to recognize two additional insights.

People developed some rules to help them overcome the limitation. People who used word processors had to go over whatever they just wrote before sending the document to others. People without good command of the language needed to be supported by a dictionary.

Once the limitation is vastly reduced, people should replace the old rules with new ones that take full advantage of the removal of the limitation. If this does not happen, then there is no added value to the Feature.

Now we can see whether adding a spell checker to an existing word processor brings value. Suppose you have perfect command in the language, would you now refrain from carefully reading your recent document before sending it away? Spelling mistakes are hardly the main reason to go over any document that I want other people to read. So, for people with perfect knowledge, the spell checker offers no real value. But, for me as a person in good command of Hebrew, but not good enough in English, spelling mistakes in English are a nuisance. But, could I really avoid them just by the use of a spell checker? As long as the spell checker does not suggest how to write the word correctly—the limitation is only marginally reduced and thus not much value is produced. This means that if we want to generate significant value for the specific user group that has not mastered the language, we need to add good suggestions of what should be written instead.

In this simplified example, we already see the need to check the behavior rules both before the limitation is eliminated and after. Is it always clear what the new behavior rules should be? Assuming the user is well aware of what the new rules should be is a very common trap for too many software features.

Suppose that a new Feature is added to a sales-graph display module in which the trends shown by the graph are analyzed for statistical significance. The limitation is lack of knowledge on whether market demand is really up or down or just part of the normal statistical fluctuations. The current behavior of the management is: If sales are up, the sales agents are complimented and get appropriate bonus; if sales are down, there are no bonuses and some hard talk from management.

What should the new management rules be once management knows whether the rise in sales is significant? I'm afraid that in the vast majority of the cases the behavior will be exactly the same. Hence, the newly added Feature will not add value to the customer, even though some customers might ask for it and even exert a lot of pressure to have the Feature developed. Eventually, the value to the software company of developing the Feature will be negative.

Of course, for a good managerial consultant assisting in the formation of better decision processes, a specific Feature can bring immense value both to the consultant and the client. In this case, a strategic partnership between the consultant and the software company can be a win-win for all, including the client.

Improving the flow of the Features that truly bring value to the customer and also have a good chance of generating revenues for the software organization is what this unique book is all about. The Agile Manifesto principle of "Our highest priority is to satisfy the customer through early and continuous delivery of valuable software" is fully in line with the Theory of Constraint's objectives. To be more precise, TOC strives to generate more of the organization's goal. But, in order to do so, the organization has to generate more value to its customers. The means of early and continuous delivery of software that truly generates value should assist both the software organization and its clients in achieving more of their respective goals.

Please bear in mind that improvement has only one criterion: Achieving more of the goal. The path to truly improving the performance of your software organization may well start with this book.

Eli Schragenheim

Introduction

*"Poor management can increase software costs more
rapidly than any other factor."*

Barry Boehm[i]

As Barry Boehm points out, bad management costs money [1981]. These days it also costs jobs. Senior executives, perplexed by the spiraling costs of software development and depressed by poor results, poor quality, poor service, and lack of transparency are simply shrugging their shoulders and saying, "if the only way this can be done is badly, then let me do it badly at a fraction of the cost." The result is a switch to offshore development and layoffs. With the state of the economy in 2003, what was a trickle has become a positive trend. If the trend isn't to become a flood, management in the information technology business needs to get better. Software development has to cost less and produce better results—more reliably, with better customer service, and more transparency. This book will teach **the Agile manager** how to achieve that.

Why Agile Management?

Building software costs a lot of money because it is labor intensive knowledge work.

Software engineers and their colleagues in project management and related functions are very well paid. It's a basic supply versus demand problem. Throughout most of my life, demand for IT workers has exceeded supply. The rates of pay have risen accordingly. Most software engineers under the age of 40 earn more than their peers who entered traditional professions such as medicine, law or accountancy. In many American firms, software engineering pays better than marketing.

Recently, with the global economic downturn, large corporations and many smaller ones are focused on trimming costs to improve profits or reduce losses. The high dollar line item for IT is under pressure. CIOs are having their budgets cut. The result is that jobs are moving offshore to outsource firms in Asia, Australia, and Eastern Europe. Knowledge work is moving out of rich countries and into poorer countries. Typically, an Indian outsource supplier can offer a labor rate of 25% of the rate for an equivalent U.S. software developer.

The Economic Imperative

---

[i] [Boehm 1981] Software Engineering Economics

If software knowledge work is to remain in the rich, developed countries of the world and software engineers in America, Europe, and Japan are to maintain the high standard of living to which they have become accustomed, they must improve their competitiveness. There is a global market for software development, and the rise of communications systems such as the Internet, have made it all too easy to shrink the time and distance between a customer in North America and a vendor in India or China.

Jobs are at stake! Just as western manufacturing was threatened by the rise of Asia in the latter half of the 20th century, so too is the knowledge worker industry threatened by the rise of a well-educated, eager workforce who can do the same work for between one tenth and one quarter of the cost.

The answer isn't that software developers must work harder if they want to keep their jobs. Software engineers aren't the problem. The answer is that management techniques must improve and working practices must change in order to deliver more value, more often, in order to improve competitiveness.

The Thesis for Agile Management

This is a book about software engineering management. It is also a book about business. It is a book about managing software engineering for the purpose of being successful at business. It will offer proof that Agile software development methods are better for business.

The information technology industry hasn't been good at managing software engineering and hasn't shown an aptitude for management and process control. As a result, information technology businesses are often run by seat-of-the-pants intuition and rough approximations. It is common, to the point of being accepted as industry standard practice, for information technology projects rarely to follow the plan, to be late and over budget and fail to deliver what was promised.

Software engineering management is traditionally a poorly practiced profession. This may be because it is poorly (or rarely) taught. Only recently has my local college, the University of Washington, begun offering an MBA program in high technology management. Such programs are rare. As a result, there is little management expertise in the industry.

However, many techniques do exist that can improve the competitiveness of software development businesses. These techniques have been proven in other industries. The challenge has been figuring out how to apply them to software development. Techniques such as the Theory of Constraints [Goldratt 1990a], Lean Production [Womack 1991], Systems Thinking [Senge 1990], and new ideas evolving out of the recent science of Complex Adaptive Systems are providing insights that unleash the latent ability of knowledge worker talent.

The secret to economically viable software engineering is new working practices based on new management science. The Agile manager must construct an Agile learning organization of empowered knowledge workers. When this is achieved the results will be dramatic. Improvements of 4 times are easily achieved. 10 times is definitely possible. Imagine if your software engineering organization could do 5 times as much work in half the time it currently takes. What would it mean for you, your job, and your organization?

Knowledge work isn't like manufacturing. Stamping out car bodies can be performed with a high degree of certainty. It is dependable to within a very low tolerance. Failures and errors are rare. The time to stamp two car bodies is almost precisely twice the time to stamp a single car body. The time to stamp 100 bodies is probably precisely derived from the time to stamp a single car body multiplied by 100. Manufacturing is in many ways predictable, linear, and, in the case of chemical processes, defined by scientific rules.

Knowledge work is neither linear nor defined. So it isn't like manufacturing. The assumption has been that because it isn't like manufacturing and isn't predictable and linear, it just can't be managed the same way. In fact, attempts to bring traditional management to software engineering processes have tended to fail. Software projects rarely if ever run to plan, and estimating is generally a black art with the resultant estimates often a complete fiction. Software development, from the perspective of the boardroom, has been out of control.

This book will show that dismissing software engineering as an uncontrollable process is wrong. It can be managed like other parts of a business. The secret is to manage the right things and to do so with transparency. Just because software engineering has greater uncertainty associated with it than manufacturing production does not mean that management methods are invalid. It simply means that those methods must accommodate greater uncertainty. The Theory of Constraints teaches managers how to buffer for uncertainty and this book will explain how to apply that technique to software development. It is important that value chain partners, management, and shareholders understand the correct model for managing software development, a model that accommodates uncertainty, and learn to trust the techniques of the Agile manager.

The Agile manager's new work becomes a study in setting the governing rules for controlling the system of software production. The Agile manager needs to learn what to track, how to track it, how to interpret the results, and what to report to senior management. This book explains what, why, and how to do this.

Some high technology workers on the west coast of the United States are giving up the profession and changing careers. All around the world, high tech workers are disillusioned. They are beginning to realize that a job in high technology is not worth sacrificing family life, social life, or health. They are realizing that their hourly rate doesn't look so good, considering all the unpaid overtime they are expected to work. They are realizing that there must be more to life.

One former colleague, from my time in Singapore, recently trained as an artist and photographer. Another, with whom I worked in Kansas City, quit the business and moved to Paris, France, where he works in the non-profit sector. Another colleague recently resigned in order to start an auto-tuning business. Yet other colleagues, who work as contractors, are only prepared to work part time. One prefers to work in a shoe store, and another does flower arranging. I hear similar anecdotes from people I meet all over the industry. What is happening?

Accept Uncertainty, Manage with Transparency

A Trend of Frustration

IT workers turn up for work for four reasons: the cause (the vision and leadership of the organization), the love of technology (usually a specific choice in which an almost religious fervor is aroused), the money (and it is usually pretty good), and the boss (people really do work for people). Let's consider these in turn.

The cause and the technology can often be grouped together. They include the mission of the business, the vision of the future, the technology being used, and the industry into which all of this is being deployed. There are IT workers who will simply never work in the defense business, for example. Creating a great cause that will draw people to it is a matter for great leadership. There has been much written about leadership in recent years. Perhaps there is a yet-to-be-written great book about IT industry leadership but teaching leadership is not within the scope of this book.

The money is important. IT workers are in demand. Demand exceeds supply. Even in hard times, demand for IT workers remains strong. Often a recession strengthens demand because automated systems can replace other workers and reduce cost. Consider the recent trend in automated machines for airline check-in, for example.

The boss is very much the scope of this book. If the boss doesn't get it, the staff will get disillusioned and leave. High staff turnover in IT businesses is usually an indication that the management "doesn't get it." Management is important. People like to work in well managed, properly organized environments. They like to have clear objectives and an environment in which to do great work.

This book will give IT industry bosses a new set of tools for managing. It will show them how to assess the IT parts of their businesses, as they would any other part of the business. It will show how to demonstrate whether or not IT delivers true value-add and produces a suitable return on investment.

Running software engineering as a proper business actually produces effects that result in more optimal use of resources, more efficient production of code, and a better creative and professional environment for the staff. When the boss really "gets it," the staff knows it and like it. The key to low staff turnover and high performance from a software development organization is better management.

The Agile Manifesto

Recently, there has been a rebellion in the industry against the growing tide of poor performances, long lead times, poor quality, disappointed customers, and frustrated developers. It is a rebellion against poor management. A passionate body of software developers has declared that there must be a better way—delivering software should be more predictable. These passionate people espouse a number of new software development methods, which they claim will enable faster, cheaper, better software development with on-time, on-budget delivery of the agreed scope. These new methods are known collectively as Agile methods.

The word "agile" implies that something is flexible and responsive and in a Darwinian sense has an innate ability to cope with change. An agile species is said to be "genetically fit." By implication, Agile software development methods should be able to survive in an atmosphere of constant change and emerge with success.

The accepted definition of Agile methods was outlined in February 2001 at a summit meeting of software process methodologists which resulted in the Manifesto for Agile Software Development.[ii] It was created by a group of 17 professionals who were noted for what, at the time, were referred to as "light-weight" methods. Lightweight methods started with Rapid Application Development (RAD). The RAD approach sought to time-box software releases to strict delivery dates, subordinating everything else in the project, including budget, scope, and staffing levels to achieve the delivery date. The term "rapid" came from the suggested nature of the time-boxes—much more frequent than traditional software development, that is, 2 weeks to 3 months.

Agile methods are mostly derived from the lightweight approach of RAD. They add extra dimensions, primarily the recognition that software development is a human activity and must be managed as such.

Manifesto for Agile Software Development

We are uncovering better ways of developing
software by doing it and helping others do it.
Through this work we have come to value:

Individuals and interactions *over processes and tools*
Working software *over comprehensive documentation*
Customer collaboration *over contract negotiation*
Responding to change *over following a plan*

That is, while there is value in the items on
the right, we value the items on the left more.

Kent Beck, James Grenning, Robert C. Martin, Mike Beedle, Jim Highsmith, Steve Mellor, Arie Van Bennekum, Andrew Hunt, Ken Schwaber, Alistair Cockburn, Ron Jeffries, Jeff Sutherland, Ward Cunningham, John Kern, Dave Thomas, Martin Fowler and Brian Marick

© 2001, the above authors
this declaration may be freely copied in any form,
but only in its entirety through this notice.

The Agile Manifesto, as it has become known, is a very simple and concise declaration that seeks to turn the traditional view of software development on its head. The manifesto is based on 12 principles[iii]:

Our highest priority is to satisfy the customer through early and continuous delivery of valuable software.

[ii]http://www.agilemanifesto.org/.
[iii]http://www.agilemanifesto.org/principles.html. Kent Beck, James Grenning, Robert C. Martin, Mike Beedle, Jim Highsmith, Steve Mellor, Arie Van Bennekum, Andrew Hunt, Ken Schwaber, Alistair Cockburn, Ron Jeffries, Jeff Sutherland, Ward Cunningham, John Kern, Dave Thomas, Martin Fowler, and Brian Marick.

Welcome changing requirements, even late in development. Agile processes harness change for the customer's competitive advantage.

Deliver working software frequently, from a couple of weeks to a couple of months, with a preference to the shorter timescale.

Business people and developers must work together daily throughout the project.

Build projects around motivated individuals. Give them the environment and support they need, and trust them to get the job done.

The most efficient and effective method of conveying information to and within a development team is face-to-face conversation.

Working software is the primary measure of progress.

Agile processes promote sustainable development. The sponsors, developers, and users should be able to maintain a constant pace indefinitely.

Continuous attention to technical excellence and good design enhances agility.

Simplicity—the art of maximizing the amount of work not done—is essential.

The best architectures, requirements, and designs emerge from self-organizing teams.

At regular intervals, the team reflects on how to become more effective, then tunes and adjusts its behavior accordingly.

There are a number of Agile methods. In Section 2, this book looks closely at three of them—Extreme Programming (XP), Feature Driven Development (FDD), and Scrum. Though other Agile methods are not explored, the book will provide the basic guidelines and metrics for making an appropriate assessment of each in comparison to more traditional software development methods.

The Problem with Agile Methods

Agile methods propose some unusual working practices. Extreme Programming, as its name suggests, has some of the more radical. They often go by names that sound as if they belong in the skateboard park or amongst the off-piste snowboarding community. The strange language and the strange practices scare management in large companies. Are they ready to stake their careers, reputations and fat bonuses on pair programming and stacks of filing cards?

Agile methods introduce scary counter intuitive working practices. If managerial fears are to be overcome, it is necessary to provide management methods that allay those fears. This requires methods that report believable and familiar statistics and have meaning to the business. It is necessary to demonstrate the economic advantages and focus on real business benefits. Software development is about making more profit, not about making great code. By leading with the financial arguments, senior managers in large companies can gain confidence that the expensive knowledge workers understand the true goal. This book will show how to mature a software engineering organization to the point where it can report believable financial metrics. It will also show what those metrics should be and how to calculate them.

Agile methods promise a lot, but where is the proof? Agile methodologists will reply that, "the proof is in the pudding." In other words, give it a try and find out for yourself. These claims have been heard before. Who can recall 4GL (so-called "fourth generation languages") that promised to eliminate developers and allow ordinary workers to create labor saving tools for themselves? Or perhaps you were sucked into the world of visual software assembly from components? Did the arrival of Visual Basic really eliminate developers? The IT world has been full of promises. Why should Agile methods be any different?

Are Agile methods a genuine trend in changing working practices or are they just another fad that lets software people "goof off" at work? This book will show that Agile methods echo the techniques of Lean Production and the Theory of Constraints which revolutionized manufacturing industry.

Agile software development is really about a change in working practices and a change in management style. Agile methods understand what management truly is. They understand that management is more than economics and engineering, that it is very much about people. "Rightly understood, management is a liberal art, drawing freely from the disciplines that help us make sense of ourselves and our world. That's ultimately why it is worth doing" [Magretta 2002, p.3]. Because of this basis in existing experience, I firmly believe that the Agile approach is a genuine trend, a change in working practices and paradigm shift in how software is produced. It is not a fad.

Agile Methods— A Fad or a Trend?

In order to adopt Agile methods in a large corporation, it is not enough to go before the board and say, "Gee, people say this works. Why don't we give it a try?" The CIO is likely to be a pragmatist, not prone to early adoption or risk taking. It will be necessary to argue a business case based on hard numbers indicating better profitability and higher return on investment. Doing so is the only way to make Agile methods look attractive and to fight against the short-term thinking that is driving decisions to outsource software engineering offshore.

This book will arm the Agile manager with the material to make a business case for agility. Agile methods can be justified on improved value-added and ROI. This book will teach the Agile manager to manage up and lead with a financial argument.

A framework for scientifically measuring and assessing Agile methods is presented. The metrics involved are used to determine the level of added value and the received return on investment. Much of the work that made this possible was developed by Eli Goldratt and his colleagues. It is a body of knowledge known as Throughput Accounting [Corbett 1997]. Throughput Accounting, based on the applications of the Theory of Constraints to manufacturing production, is used as the basis for the financial arguments presented.

The Business Benefit

**Toward a
Software
Economic
Miracle**

While the West during the 1970s and 1980s was focused on increased automation through the use of robots on the assembly line, the Japanese produced far better results through management techniques that changed working practices. These working practices originated at Toyota and are known as the Toyota Production System or Kanban Approach.

The technology industry has for the last 30 years, like western manufacturing, also been focused on technology solutions. There have been third and fourth generation languages, modeling and abstraction tools, automated integrated development environments, and automated testing tools. To some extent, the Agile community rejects this ever increasing technology approach and instead embraces new management techniques and changes to working practices. In this respect, Agile methods resemble the principles first advocated by Toyota and now known in the West as Lean Production.

The techniques of Lean Production created an economic improvement of twenty to fifty fold during the second half of the 20th century. For example, Womack and colleagues [Womack 1991] report that in one recent year Toyota built half as many cars as General Motors using less than 5% of the people. In other words, Lean Production at Toyota had produced a ten fold improvement over its American mass production competitor. Some Agilists are reporting four fold economic improvements [Highsmith 2002; Schwaber 2002]. This is equivalent to the improvements made in automobile manufacturing in Japan in the earlier part of that half century—for example, those at Mazda between the 1960s and 1980 when productivity was improved by four fold. During the most recent twenty years, some of these manufacturers have gone on to make improvements of five times or greater. This produced a cumulative economic improvement of twenty times or more. It is precisely these types of gains that created the Asian economic miracle of the latter 20th century and provided vast wealth across the globe.

If Agile software development can provide a four fold improvement within 9 months, why would a company outsource to an Indian supplier that promises a four fold cost reduction over 3 to 4 years?

The software industry now employs over 30 million people worldwide[iv] and can list the world's richest company, Microsoft, amongst its number. What if it were possible to create another economic miracle? What if software development resembled the manufacturing efficiency of 1925? It is just possible that Agile methods represent the beginning of an understanding of how to build software better, faster, and cheaper. Is it just possible that there is a latent economic improvement in the order of 95% waiting to be unleashed? Agile methods are a step down the road to a leaner knowledge worker industry. They really do produce financial benefits, and this book will demonstrate how to calculate them.

[iv]Estimates taken from figures by Gartner Group and IBC suggest that there are around 15 million software developers. It is reasonable to assume that those employed in other related functions, such as project, program, and product management, will account for 15 million more.

"Most management books are only for managers. This one is for everyone—for the simple reason that, today, all of us live in a world of management's making. Whether we realize it or not, every one of us stakes our well-being on the performance of management,"[v] said Joan Magretta introducing her book "What Management Is" [2002, p.2]. As Tom DeMarco observed in his book "Slack,"[vi] the Dilberts[vii] of the world have abdicated responsibility. It suits them to blame the manager. Dilbert fails to see it as his duty to help his manager be more effective. Management is a task that concerns everyone involved in a business from the stockholders to the most junior of employees. Hence, this book is intended for a wide audience—an audience of anyone who cares whether or not a software business is well run.

The text is intended for anyone who is interested in changing the working practices of software development to make them more effective and more competitive. The book is primarily aimed at all levels of management in all software-related disciplines and those who aspire to senior individual contributor or line manager positions in the foreseeable future. It should also appeal to Masters degree and MBA students looking for a management career in a software-related industry. Every CEO, CFO, COO, and CIO who runs a business with significant expenditures on software development activity needs to understand the new paradigm and theory presented in Section 1. Lou Gerstner, writing in his IBM memoir pointed out that cultural change must be led from the top if it is to be effective [Gerstner 2002]. If change is to be led from the top, the boss must adopt the correct mental model of Agile development practices in order to frame decisions and understand the counterintuitive activity happening beneath.

This book defines 4 basic management roles and describes a set of practices for each role. Those roles are development manager, program manager, project manager, and product manager. Each is described in Chapter 8, "The Agile Manager's New Work." Specific details for the development manager's role are defined in Chapters 5 and 9. The program manager's role is defined in Chapter 10. The project manager's role is defined in Chapter 7. The product manager's role is defined in Chapter 16.

The thesis of the book is that the development manager is responsible for running an on-going system of software production. This must be managed with metrics based on fine grained units of production activity. However, programs and projects must be measured at a coarse grained level that reduces the uncertainty through aggregation of fine grained tasks. How to buffer against variability is explained in Chapter 4. The product manager must define the groupings of fine grained functionality which have meaning as valuable deliverables, that is, the coarse grained items to be tracked by the program and project manager.

Together, all 4 roles interact to define a 2-tiered management system that sets the governing rules for the system, but allows highly delegated,

---

[v][Magretta 2002] What Management Is, page 2.
[vi][Demarco 2001] Slack
[vii]Dilbert is a registered trademark of United Feature Syndicate. Dilbert, a cartoon character created by Scott Adams, suffers under a pointy haired boss who just doesn't get it!

self-organization within. Successful Agile management requires a highly delegated system of empowered knowledge workers. The essence of Agile management is self-organizing production, framed within the planned assembly of valuable components, and delivered frequently to generate a the required ROI for the business.

An Agile Maturity Model

Chapter 11 introduces the notion that Agile methods can mature in an organization as it learns to use them better. This book leads with the financial metrics. It focuses on the true goals of a business and then examines how management must organize and report the day-to-day workings of the software production system in order to deliver the desired financial results. This approach has been taken to demonstrate the compelling reason for switching to Agile software development.

In practice, the approach to delivering a failure-tolerant, agile, learning organization will happen inside-out. The working practices will come first, then the traceability, then the metrics, then learning, and eventually the financial metrics and results. The Agile Maturity Model describes this progression.

How to Read This Book

Section 1 is intended as general reading for anyone interested in running a software development business for better results. It is suitable reading for all levels of management from team lead developers to CIOs, CEOs, CFOs, and GMs. Section 1 explains Agile management, its practices and theory. It explains how to apply the Theory of Constraints and Lean Production methods to software engineering as a general practice. For many readers Section 1 will be sufficient.

Section 2 is intended for readers who need to manage the change to Agile software development in their organization and for those who need to understand why they are making a change and how to implement what they are changing to. Chapters 19 and 20 give an outline of traditional software development methods and will help an agile manager explain the current reality and create a baseline from which to measure improvement. The remainder of Section 2 surveys a subset of Agile software development methods. This survey is not meant to be exhaustive. It shows, by example, how to relate specific Agile methods to the theory presented in Section 1. Chapters 21 through 30 lay out possible future realities for an Agile software development organization and demonstrate how to measure them to show an economic improvement. FDD, XP, Scrum, and RAD are compared against the theory from Section 1. The emphasis is on explaining these methods rather than comparing them against each other. Relative comparisons are left for Section 3.

Section 3 is for those who need to choose one method over another and those who seek to understand Agile methods and develop the future of Agile software development management. It seeks to understand the similarities and differences and the varying foci of currently available Agile methods. The applicability of these methods is considered against their appropriateness for different types, sizes, and scales of software projects. Section 3 is intended primarily for Agile methodologists and those who wish to further the debate about the future of Agile software development.

Acknowledgements

No book is ever the work of only one person. I am fortunate to have been the one who was in the right place at the right time and who undertook to write the material down. For me personally, this book could not have happened were it not for coincident circumstances over a 7 year period that gave me unique perspectives with which to "see" the relationship between the Theory of Constraints and Agile software development methods. There are many people to thank.

I owe a great deal to the team that created Feature Driven Development—especially, Jeff De Luca, Peter Coad, Stephen Palmer, Philip Bradley and Paul Szego. Were it not for the experience I gained working with them and later running FDD projects in other parts of the world, this book would not have been possible.

In addition, Mac Felsing pointed out the significance of the S-curve and how it could be anticipated by the development manager. Mike Watson provided much of the insight that led to a formal explanation of the S-curve effect. Jason Marshall helped me to "discover" that Cumulative Flow Diagrams were the ideal method to visually report the flow of value. Ken Ritchie was a continual inspiration and provided many early review comments. His knowledge of both FDD and TOC was immensely helpful both before and during the writing of the manuscript. Daniel Vacanti helped me understand daily stand-up meetings by running them with my team every morning. He also provided the arguments for the "generalist versus specialist" Vanishing Cloud diagram in Chapter 31. Vahid Nabavizadeh and Chris Bock provided the project tracking evidence to show that FDD Features converge on a mean with a low standard deviation. Martin Geddes contributed much of the thinking behind the notion of "perishable requirements" as well as pushing me to develop the ideas and discussion in Section 3. Without the insights from Mac, Mike, Ken, Jason, Dan, Vahid, Chris, and Martin, I wouldn't have had much to say in this text.

I'd like to thank Peter Coad for giving me the chance to write such an unusual book and Paul Petralia at Prentice Hall for his advocacy and help throughout. Both of them had faith that this would be a worthwhile project. I'd also like to extend special thanks to Anne Garcia, Production Editor at Prentice Hall and Ann Imhof, Production Coordinator at Carlisle Communications.

John Yuzdepski inadvertently instigated the outline for this book when he gave me a copy of *The Goal* in March 2001. I read it on a flight to Japan and created a 36-slide presentation during the return journey that later became the basis for the formal proposal to the publisher.

The official reviewer team of Martin Geddes, Mike Cohn, Ken Ritchie, Luke Hohmann, and Eli Schragenheim persevered with difficult early draft and provided guidance, corrections and reassurance that insured the final book communicated this complex material in a straightforward fashion.

I must express my immense gratitude to all the unofficial reviewers who gave of their time freely in order to make this a better book. Some of their smallest comments led to big changes in the structure and communicability of the text. Thanks to Keith Mitchell, Alana Muller, Pujan Roka, Les Novell, Mary Poppendieck, John Resing, Frank Patrick, Keith Ray, R.A. Neale, Anthony Lauder, Hal Macomber, Alan Barnard, Lawrence Leach, Steven Holt, Ken Schwaber, Pawel Pietrusinski, Chris Bock, Daniel Vacanti, Vahid Nabavizadeh, Greg Wilson, Stephen Palmer, Mac Felsing, Cliff Gregory, and Tom Werges.

A number of senior executives in the software and telecommunications businesses have been supportive of my efforts and provided encouragement. They included Scott Relf, Jonathan Prial, Craig Hayman, Greg Post, Joe Gensheimer, and John Yuzdepski.

Finally, I must thank my wife, Mikiko, for her patience and assistance throughout what seemed like a very long year whilst this book was written and produced.

David J. Anderson,

Seattle, Washington, May 2003

Agile Management

"The best companies in an industry build process that allows them to outperform their competitors"

Louis V. Gerstner [2002]

Section 1 uses Peter Senge's fifth discipline [1990]–*Systems Thinking*–to approach the management of software engineering as a holistic business problem. The profitability and investment return from software engineering is treated as a "limits to growth" system archetype. "Limits to growth" systems archetypes can be addressed and improved using Eli Goldratt's *Theory of Constraints* [1990]. Each constraint will be identified and a suitable investment proposed to elevate the system and increase the profit and return on investment possible from software engineering. Proposed improvements to the system of software engineering will be made using techniques proven in *Lean Production* [Womack 1991] and the *Toyota Production System* [Ohno 1988].

Briefly, the underlying theory of project management as it is currently taught is examined. Then, a better model based on Lean Production principles that track the flow of value through a series of transformations is suggested.

Traditional cost accounting leads to poor quality management decisions, leading to lower profits and lower return on investment. The use of Throughput Accounting can reverse this trend. Chapters 2, then 15 through 17 will show how to apply *Throughput Accounting* to software engineering.

The use of a few carefully chosen metrics, delivered as feedback at a regular operations review can turn a software engineering organization into what Senge called a "learning organization" [1990] where a culture of continuous improvement delivers ever improving financial results.

The combination of *Systems Thinking*, *Theory of Constraints* and *Lean Thinking* [Womack 1996] will show that core tenets of Agile software methods–a motivated, empowered workforce, quality first, small batch sizes, constrained release dates, and use of best practices to reduce variance and uncertainty–combine to produce improved financial results.

chapter 1

Theories for Agile Management

The Theory of Constraints (TOC) was introduced in 1984 in Eli Goldratt's business novel, *The Goal*. Initially unavailable in stores, Goldratt described the book as a marketing brochure for his consulting business. It was later available in book stores and sold over 2 million copies. Described as a love story, *The Goal* follows Alex Rogo on his personal journey as he gradually turns around his ailing and unprofitable manufacturing plant. Facing closure of his plant, and the breakup of his marriage, everything seems to be going wrong. Then he meets Jonah. Jonah is a master in the application of the Theory of Constraints, and he coaches Alex to better understand how his own manufacturing plant works.

TOC, applied to manufacturing, seeks to identify bottlenecks in the production line. The underlying assumption is that a production facility is only as fast as the slowest process in the chain. As a general rule, TOC assumes that a value chain is only as strong as the weakest link in the chain. The capacity of the weakest link is the current system constraint.

TOC improves manufacturing profitability by first identifying the constraint, then maximizing the exploitation of the constraint. The rate of throughput on the constraint—the capacity of that process stage or machine—is used to regulate the throughput of the whole assembly line or system. New material is only introduced into the system at the rate that it

The Theory of Constraints

3

can be consumed by the bottleneck. In TOC, this technique is known as Drum-Buffer-Rope. (It is fully explained in Chapter 3.) Applying this basic TOC principle to a manufacturing plant has the effect of reducing the inventory of material throughout the system.

Just-in-Time Inventory

In the early 1980s, another theory—this one from Japan—was also catching on in western manufacturing. The Japanese were at that time significantly outperforming their western competitors. Their products were often cheaper and better. One of the most successful Japanese companies was Toyota. It used the Toyota Production System, or Kanban Approach, devised by Taiichi Ohno [Ohno 1988]. This system sought to minimize inventory in the factory and ensure that required inventory was delivered to the point where it would be consumed, just before it was needed. Ohno had based the technique on methods used by American grocery store chains, which he had observed stacking shelves on an as-needed basis, just as consumers were ready to buy products. Generically, Ohno's technique was known as just-in-time (JIT) manufacturing.

Chapter 2 shows that reduction of inventory and of the sums invested in the inventory have a significant effect on the profitability of a manufacturing business. Hence, reducing inventory through use of JIT was one critical way to compete with the Japanese. Reduced inventory was also seen in the early 1980s as a side effect of TOC's focus on bottlenecks. There was little association between TOC and JIT in the published literature.

Reducing inventory reduces the level of investment. The Return on Investment (ROI) for a plant practicing JIT, or inventory control from TOC's Drum-Buffer-Rope, will increase. Japanese manufacturers were thus enjoying significantly better ROI than their western competitors during much of the 1960s, 1970s, and 1980s.

$$(\text{more}) \ \text{ROI}[1] = \frac{\text{Throughput (T)} - \text{Operating Expense (OE)}}{(\text{less}) \ \text{Investment in Inventory}}$$

Western competitors had assumed that Asian firms simply had lower labor rates and failed to fully comprehend the competitive advantage of lower inventory levels. As reducing inventory also reduced the financing charges and the cost of storage space, the Operating Expense (OE) was lower, too. Reducing operating expense increases profitability. In industries where margins are tight, these small variations can mean the difference between profit or loss.

$$(\text{more}) \ \text{Net Profit}[2] \ (\text{NP}) = \text{T} - (\text{less}) \ \text{OE}$$

[1]This Throughput Accounting definition of ROI will be explained in Chapter 2.
[2]Throughput Accounting definition for Net Profit.

The Japanese had also realized that better quality was important. They learned the importance of quality assurance (QA) from the American statistician Edwards Deming. Deming had visited Japan in the 1950s and taught Statistical Process Control (SPC) theory, specifically how to interpret the control charts of Walter Shewhart [Wheeler 1992]. Control charts show whether a process is under control. Control is defined by whether or not the output is within the acceptable tolerance for the specification. If something is within specification, it is of good quality. Hence, adoption of SPC led the Japanese to focus on product quality. As explained in Chapter 9, improved quality improves the throughput of a system. Hence, the Japanese were enjoying improved profitability from quality assurance, as well as improved ROI from just-in-time inventory control.

Another theory that caught on in the west in the early 1980s was Total Quality Management (TQM). It sought to bring repeatability, control, and predictability to manufacturing through traceability. TQM espoused the notion that manufacturing could be more efficient (read "profitable") if quality were improved. Quality could be improved through improved traceability, which would provide audit trail information for verification and validation of quality. TQM gave rise to ISO-9000, Tick-IT, and other quality-related initiatives. TQM used a mental model in which the upstream process was the "supplier" and the downstream process the "customer." Everyone had an "internal customer" for their work. TQM was based on the notion that locally optimal quality would lead to a global optima. It was not based on the ideas of systems thinking.[1] However, it did have a positive effect on many organizations. As quality improved, so did throughput and, consequently, profitability.

Quality improves production because it reduces rework. Rework means less waste, less OE, and a higher Production Rate (R). Assuming sales is not a constraint and all increases in production lead to increases in sales, it can be shown that investment in quality pays for itself. Increased Throughput (from sales) leads directly to higher profits and better return on investment:

$$(\text{more) Net Profit (NP)} = (\text{more) T} - \text{OE}$$

$$(\text{more) ROI} = \frac{(\text{more) Throughput (T)} - \text{Operating Expense (OE)}}{\text{Investment}}$$

In the late 1980s, western industrialists recognized that JIT and QA had related parts to play in the overall improvement of the manufacturing industry. The term "Lean" was first coined by Womack and colleagues in their book, *The Machine That Changed the World*, which documented the superior ability of the Japanese automobile manufacturing processes in comparison to western mass production pioneered by Henry Ford at Ford and Alfred Sloan at General Motors [Womack 1991]. What Womack and colleagues were actually documenting was the combination of Ohno and Shingo's [Shingo 1989] low

---

[1]O'Connor, Joseph & McDermott, Ian, *The Art of Systems Thinking: Essential Skills for Creativity and Problem Solving* Thorsons, San Francisco, California 1997.

Table 1-1
Management theory and its focus areas.

Theory	Focus
JIT	Inventory
TQM/QA	Quality & Conformance
TOC	Bottlenecks
Lean	Inventory, Quality, & Conformance
Six Sigma	Quality & Variance

inventory, just-in-time system with Deming's quality system. In Japan it is known as the Toyota Production System (or the Kanban System) and, more recently, "The Toyota Way," because Toyota has recognized that the management method can be applied to more than just production.

Six Sigma

Six Sigma is a quality-related term that specifically refers to a defect level of less than four per million. This level is considered in many industries to represent perfection. However, the term has grown in meaning to define a management method for implementing manufacturing systems that lead to improved quality and focused investment to eliminate errors. It is most notably associated with General Electric and Motorola.

Six Sigma as a process focuses on two areas: quality assurance and reduction of variance. It takes the position that it is better to have defects with a repeatable pattern (a low variance) than defects with a random pattern. The assumption is that defects that repeat probably have a common cause. If the common cause can be found, the defect can be removed with a single change or investment. Hence, improved quality is achieved through reduction of variance.

Comparison of Theories

It is now recognized that all these theories—JIT, QA, TQM, Lean, Six Sigma, and TOC—are related. They represent best practices for running a process, system, or value chain. TOC originally focused on bottlenecks. JIT originally focused on reduction of inventory. TQM and SPC were focused on quality and conformance to specification. The concept of Lean is the effective combination of all of them. Six Sigma also focuses on quality and can be seen as complementary to Lean as shown in Table 1-1.

The effect of these theories on the manufacturing industry has produced an immense economic improvement for society. Nowadays, the public expects exceptional quality from consumer products. Very low prices are expected for amazingly complex technical products, such as DVD players. When, for example, was the last time you saw someone take the trouble to repair a broken coffee maker or iron? It simply isn't worth it. A new one can be purchased for less than $20. Economic gains such as these have been possible through application of Lean Thinking [Womack 1996] in manufacturing.

Has Improved Profitability Been the Only Benefit?

Manufacturers will tell you that their business gets more competitive every year. In the last 30 years, competition has gone off the scale and productivity improvements of up to 30 times were common. The truth is TOC, JIT, TQM, SPC, and Six Sigma have done more than just improved profitability. These theories have improved overall competitiveness. That means that manufacturing is now more flexible and faster to react to market conditions. This has been achieved through reduced inventory, reduced lead time, better visibility into inventory levels, better understanding of the processes at work, and better understanding of how to exploit system elements and processes.

In summary, the application of TOC, Lean, SPC, JIT, or TQM has improved the agility of the manufacturing industry. Lean manufacturers are agile manufacturers. Manufacturers who best exploit their capacity constrained resources are agile manufacturers. Manufacturers with better quality assurance systems are agile manufacturers.

With the financial metrics presented in Chapter 2, it can be shown that agility and profitability go hand in hand. In the manufacturing industry, agile processes are better for business. Could this also be true in the software business?

Mary Poppendieck has shown in her work on Lean Programming that the theories of JIT and TQM can be applied to software development [2001]. Poppendieck has suggested that Agile software development methods such as Scrum share common principles with Lean Manufacturing. Others in the Agile community, including Beck & Fowler [Beck 2002a/2002b], have observed that Agile methodologists have a lot to learn from Taiichi Ohno's Kanban approach.

Eli Goldratt has suggested that the sciences evolve in three distinct phases—classification, correlation, and effect-cause-effect [Goldratt 1990].

Three Phases of Scientific Development

Phase 1—Classification

Classification is the phase in which nomenclature is debated and then agreed upon. People discuss what exactly is involved in the field they are pursuing or studying. They then agree on the names for founding elements or principles. The current state of Agile methods for software development would suggest that several of them have an agreed internal nomenclature. This is certainly true of XP, Scrum, and FDD. However, the nomenclature may not yet be complete. Initiatives such as Scott Ambler's *Agile Modeling* suggest that more nomenclature may be necessary [2002]. There is certainly no agreement across Agile methods on a combined or unified nomenclature. Agile methods as a combined science can be considered to be in the classification stage.

Phase 2—Correlation

Correlation is Goldratt's term for the phase in which corroborating evidence is available to show that a method works in practice. Correlation is a

Theories for Agile Management

phase of pattern recognition. The science of astronomy, when it was still known as astrology, spent thousands of years in the correlation stage. It was possible for astrologers to predict astrological events such as the turning of the year, the rise of the planets in the sky, and so forth by pattern matching against observations of recurring patterns.

It could be argued that the science of Object Oriented Analysis has reached the correlation stage. The classification stage ended with an agreement on the Unified Modeling Language—the nomenclature of OO Analysis and Design. The correlation stage actually started prior to this, with the emergence of patterns in the early 1990s. The correlation phase is now in full swing. A considerable body of work is available on OO Analysis. Books which have broken new ground include *Analysis Patterns* [Fowler 1997], *Object Models* [Coad 1996], *JAVA Modeling in Color with UML* [Coad 1999], and *Streamlined Object Modeling* [Nicola 2001]. Similar work has been published in the field of OO Design by a long list of authors, notably *Design Patterns* [Gamma 1995] and *Java Design* [Coad 1997]. Others seek to teach the theory in a more palatable form, for example, *Applying UML and Patterns* Larman [2001].

Individually, then, some Agile methods have entered the correlation phase. That is to say that there is "proof in the pudding." There is corroborating evidence that the techniques work. People from all around the world have run XP, Scrum, and FDD projects and have reported better results. I personally have run (or been involved with) more than 10 FDD projects, and the results are remarkably similar across all of them. This similarity has been true across four geographical locations, with four different teams, each with different cultural, educational, and personal backgrounds, and irrespective of technology or industry involved. Evidence that shows a method or theory to be true in practice means the method or theory is in the correlation stage.

Phase 3—Effect-Cause-Effect

The third and final stage in the emergence of a science is effect-cause-effect. Astronomy became a science after Isaac Newton proved why apples fall down, rather than sideways. This effect was explained through its cause—gravity. The theory was then used to predict another effect—the Earth's orbit of the sun. When it is possible to postulate a theory, measure the effect, and validate the theory, science is being practiced.

If the art of managing software development is to be developed into a science, agreement must be reached on what is to be measured and what those measurements are called. How one measurement affects another must be understood. This would then permit managers to predict the effect of a decision on a new situation based on what is already known.

Many aspects of software development can be correlated against aspects of the manufacturing industry. Within manufacturing, many effect-cause-effect relationships are understood. Manufacturing has grown into a science over the last 30 years. By translating cause-effect relationships from manufacturing to software development, it should be possible to predict the effect. If the effect can be measured and validates the accuracy of the prediction, then software development management will have evolved into a science.

If, for example, the suggestion made in Chapter 2 that ideas can be treated as the inventory in a system of software production is acceptable, then it could be predicted, based on the cause-effect relationship observed in manufacturing, that reducing inventory will improve overall profitability. This is something that can be easily measured.

First, the existing organization must be measured to determine a baseline for the experiment. The current inventory level must be established, along with the production rate. It may be necessary to correlate the existing results against an expectation for the new Agile method to be introduced, that is, map Use Cases to Stories or Function Points to Features. The chosen Agile method should be introduced under controlled circumstances. The results should be measured. If the prediction is correct, a reduction in inventory and an increase in production rate should be observed. If so, there is scientific proof that Agile methods really are better for business.

There has been considerable debate amongst Agile methodologists since Schwaber and Beedle published their book describing the Scrum method. Schwaber observed that traditional software development methods were like defined process control mechanisms and argued that this was the root cause of today's problems with traditional methods [2002, pp. 24–25]. What was required instead was an empirical method, which all Agile methods were. This made them better.

Webster's dictionary defines empirical as "Depending upon experience or observation alone, without due regard to science and theory." In other words, there is no underlying scientific theory that explains the observed phenomena. Control and prediction are based purely on observation of a pattern. To use Goldratt's terminology, the notion of empirical measurement relates to the correlation phase of a science. When it is possible to observe a pattern but not to explain it, then it may be possible to base measurements around observation of the pattern repeating. Astrology, the predecessor of Astronomy, was based purely on empirical measure. Empirical measure gave us the 7-day week and the 365-day year long before Isaac Newton explained why it takes the Earth 365 days to orbit the sun.

Defined measurement, on the other hand, is based on the concept of a known cause-effect relationship. Defined measurement allows a prediction of how long a ball bearing will take to hit the floor after it rolls off a table.

In an interview with Jim Highsmith [Highsmith 2002, p. 242], Schwaber extends his discussion to state that all empirical processes are "chaordic," a term which contains the notion that all software development lives on the edge of chaos. The debate surrounding Agile methods has polarized into one of chaordic versus defined processes—Agile versus traditional methods. The Agilists use the chaordic nature of software development to argue that there is no point in planning software development or trying to predict it. Rather, the only course of action is to observe it and report the results.

This notion is abhorrent to most senior executives of large companies. The notion that a major area of cost—software development—should be allowed to run without planning or defined goals is unlikely to curry favor in the boardroom.

However, I do not subscribe to the assumption that software development is always chaordic and lives on the edge of chaos. Chapter 32 will discuss Wheeler [1992] who has classified four types of process control—one of which is called the "edge of chaos." Software development can exist within each of his four categories. Further, it is not automatically true that empirical processes are chaotic or tend towards chaos. An empirical process may be a convergent process. Its convergence may have been observed through empirical measure, but may not have been explained by science. Hence, an empirical process can produce results with an accuracy normally expected from a defined process, but without the scientific explanation of why. The sun, for example, rises every morning, but for many thousands of years, this regularity was unexplained. As a result, superstitions and religious beliefs were based on the miracle that the sun didn't tend toward chaos, and the sky didn't lie dark for years.

Convergent Versus Divergent Processes

It may be more important to understand not whether a process is empirical or defined, but whether it is convergent or divergent. Convergent implies that under some form of control a process will converge over time on a predictable solution. This applies to both empirical and defined processes. For example, one developer I spoke to said, "In my experience, a good Extreme Programming team becomes adept at assessing their velocity and predicting what they can deliver in a single, 2-week iteration." This would suggest that Extreme Programming is a convergent process.

Divergent processes are processes that refuse to converge under control and consistently produce inconsistent results. In control theory, divergence is usually described as chaotic or out-of-control behavior. Specifically, a process is described as being "outside the envelope" (of control). When a process is not under control and not capable of being brought under control, it is a divergent process.

Chaos Theory and Uncertainty

In the last 20 years, a whole new branch of science has emerged based on chaos theory. For the previous 300 years, science had been grounded in the theories of the mathematician Renee Descartes [1625] who suggested that everything could be gradually decomposed until such time as it was divisible no further and at this point it would be possible to scientifically explain its behavior and composition. Its corollary held that something that was not understood simply had not been sufficiently decomposed.

The principles of Descartes suggest that eventually everything is convergent when it is properly understood—alchemy becomes chemistry, astrology becomes astronomy. Science has taught us to believe that all things converge and do so to a singularity. For example, there is only one precise answer to the time it takes the Earth to orbit the sun. However, study of weather patterns has shown that there are things that do not converge on a singularity. No matter how many weather sensors are added to a weather prediction system, the accuracy will only ever be so good. Adding more sensors does not improve it further. This does not mean that the science of meteorology is divergent. It means that it does not converge on a singularity, rather it converges on an approximation—a value with a measure of uncertainty.

The principle of uncertainty has been known in physics for some time, having been postulated by the nuclear physicist Hiesenberg. The science of physics learned to live with uncertainty. The Theory of Constraints teaches the business systems methodologist how to live with uncertainty in other fields, such as production, project management, and enterprise resource planning.

Philosophically, an effect that is known to involve uncertainty is not necessarily divergent or uncontrollable. It is merely convergent on an approximation. It does not mean that something that is uncertain cannot be classified, codified, measured, or controlled. It simply means that our measurements must always reflect a degree of uncertainty.

Hence, this text is grounded in a basic assumption that planning and prediction are possible within some bounds of uncertainty. Financial predictions for the performance of a software development business are possible, but must always be couched with a degree of tolerance. Agile management is all about being able to cope with uncertainty.

Peter Senge has called systems thinking the "Fifth Discipline" [1990]. He believes that the ability of an organization to understand what it does as a holistic system is the first step in becoming a learning organization. A learning organization is one that constantly improves its competitiveness because it understands what it does and how it actually does it. Software development can be seen as a complex adaptive system. All such systems have feedback loops. Feedback provides the opportunity for improvement. Senge calls this "learning." Feedback is necessary for learning.

Systems Thinking and Learning Organizations

In recent years, science has discovered phenomena that are described as "emergent." This has spawned the new science of Complex Adaptive Systems. Chapter 2 will show that complex systems with feedback loops produce adaptive behavior and exhibit emergent properties. Simple rules govern the internal behavior of the system, which results in the externally observed adaptive behavior. Hence, systems thinking, control theory, and emergence are all related. The study of Complex Adaptive Systems tries to understand what the simple rules are that produce often amazing results. Simple rules are what inspire ants to build great anthills and to work as a team to perform tasks that ought not to be possible for such basic creatures.

Emergence

It has been observed by Agile methodologists that software development is a complex adaptive system, that produces adaptive behavior—working code—and exhibits emergent properties—foosball tables in basements and on-line bug databases.

The argument has been made that if software development is emergent and the outcome is by the nature of adaptive systems unpredictable and uncertain, then software development cannot be planned or predicted. Therefore, software development should not be planned, but should emerge based on last-minute decisions on what to do next.

This notion is suggested in the Agile Manifesto principle, "The best architectures, requirements, and designs emerge from self-organizing teams." The notion of self-organization implies emergence. The argument follows that adaptive systems imply an unknowable outcome. Hence, planning is futile.

Again, among those interested in running a business for profit, the notion that planning and control are impossible is a little daunting. The thesis of this book is that software is not divergent and can be planned and controlled. The proper jobs of executives are to set the goal for the adaptive behavior of the system and to select the method with which the goal is measured and the system feedback delivered. In addition, they may need to create an environment within which the complex adaptive system of software development can exist freely to self-organize at the appropriate level.

The tasks for each manager at each level in the hierarchy of a software development organization are to define the desired output from the part of the system under his or her control, to define the rules for measuring that system, and to create the conditions for the system to operate freely and then to keep out of the way, allow it to self-organize based on feedback, and produce the desired results.

What is important is that those setting the rules set rules that reflect the nature of the system holistically, which leads to delivery of global optima rather than local efficiencies. With the correct rules, the performance of a system is predictable within a degree of uncertainty. For example, it is predictable that a nest of ants will build an anthill. The size of the anthill and the area it will cover can be predicted with some certainty, based on knowledge of the type of ants and the population. What cannot be predicted is the precise shape, the precise time of completion, or the necessary level of effort. Nevertheless, predicting the growth of an anthill is like predicting the weather, it can be done with a degree of accuracy. It is not chaotic.

Summary

Agile management must cope with uncertainty and deliver better business results. To do this, it must incorporate techniques from TOC, JIT, TPS, TQM, QA, Six Sigma, and Lean Production. Specifically, agility is delivered through a focus on quality assurance, reduction of inventory, identification and investment in bottlenecks to increase production, and reduction in variance, which improves estimation and quality assurance.

Agile software development methods are methods of empirical control for software production management. Empirical methods are not necessarily chaotic and can be planned and estimated. The design of a software development method must be such that the method converges and produces repeatable results as often as possible.

Agile software development methods are complex adaptive systems that exhibit emergent properties and adaptive behavior. The desired adaptive behavior from an agile system of software production is working code valued by the customer.

chapter 2

Management Accounting for Systems

"Tell me how you will measure me and
I will tell you how I will behave."

Eli Goldratt [1990b]

Suspend for a moment everything you have already learned about software development lifecycles. Ignore concepts of sequential processes, iterative processes, spiral processes, and their like, and consider the stages of the transformation of an idea into tangible working code.

Figure 2–1 shows a generic simple single loop system. The system receives an input. It performs some operation on the input. The result is compared with some expected result, and an output and feedback are generated. The feedback is reintroduced mixed with the input to the system, and the operation is performed again.

A General System

There are a number of known properties in general systems. All systems are nonlinear. This means that there is no linear relationship between the effort (or energy) expended in the operation of the system and either the input or the output. The nonlinearity is introduced by the feedback loop. All complex adaptive (or closed-loop) systems have feedback loops.

However, the input is usually proportional to the output. The output is derived from a combination of input. For example, four wheels (input) are required for one car (output). Four wheels are always required. It is never five or three or any other number. Hence, the relationship between input and output is both linear and predictable.

The output is predictable because all systems exhibit adaptive behavior. The adaptive behavior is designed into the system. The system is intended to produce an output that is predictable. If the output is not as predicted, the adaptive behavior is described as undesirable behavior. The feedback loop is intended to control the undesirable behavior and correct the system so that the desired adaptive behavior results.

When a system settles down and produces the desired adaptive behavior, it is said to be "convergent," "stable," and "under control." When a system does not settle to the desired adaptive behavior, it can be described as "divergent," "unstable," "out of control," or "chaotic."

Figure 2–1

A general system.

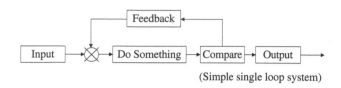

(Simple single loop system)

General systems can be described using the language of emergence by saying that a system is designed with a set of governing rules that determine the desired adaptive behavior.[1] These rules are generally simple in nature, but result in complex and occasionally unexpected adaptive behavior. The operation of the system produces a number of artifacts, by-products, or internally observable behavior. These are known as emergent properties.

Thinking with Systems Is Hard

The human mind is not naturally programmed to think in systems. It does not naturally think nonlinearly. From an early age, we learn to think in simple terms of cause and effect and to speak in a language rooted in linear cause-effect concepts. In addition, we expect the effect to happen immediately after the cause, so that they can be easily associated.

I experience this cause-effect learning first hand with my daughter, who at the time of writing this chapter is a mere seven months old. She is just learning cause-effect relationships. She has discovered that if she throws a toy from her high chair, then Dad will pick it up and give it back to her. He will also talk to her and generally entertain her. From her point of view, she throws the toy (the cause) and Dad shows her immediate attention (the effect). The effect is gratifying to her (feedback), and she throws the toy again. In Systems Thinking, this is known as a reinforcing loop [O'Connor 1997, p. 40]. She can associate the cause with the effect because the time delay is negligible.

What my 7-month-old daughter is too young to understand is the balancing loop, that is, the hidden effect of her action. The balancing loop is that Dad gradually becomes bored with this game—with each iteration his desire to continue decreases. Eventually, he doesn't pick up the toy but passes her another toy. A new game of throw and pick up begins. This time the game lasts for a shorter number of iterations before Dad refuses to pick up the toy and instead gives her another one. A third game begins, but it soon ends when Dad no longer wants to play. There are chores to be done or a book to be written.

In Systems Thinking, this effect is known as a balancing loop. At first, Dad has fun playing the game, but gradually his level of annoyance grows until he doesn't want to play any more. The annoyance is a balancing loop. Due to the obscure nature of the feedback loop and the time delay between the beginning of the game and the balancing effect kicking in, my daughter has no concept of why or how the game came to an end.

[1]Emergence is also known as Complex Adaptive Systems (CAS), a relatively recent field of scientific study.

Systems Thinking is complex! Cause-effect thinking is simple—even a 7-month-old can do it! Systems Thinking must be taught rather than learned naturally. Humans are not programmed to easily comprehend effects that are delayed from, or several derivates from, their original cause.

It is not unusual to meet people who are good at coping with complexity. However, probably only a few of them are systems thinkers. Much of the complexity in life is detail complexity [O'Connor 1997, p. 15]. Detail complexity describes something that has many parts, for example, a project plan with 1,500 tasks has detail complexity. Software analysis has detail complexity. UML class diagrams or database entity-relationship diagrams have detail complexity.

On the other hand, a system with many nested feedback loops, where small variations in the operation of the system can leverage enormous differences in the outcome, is said to have "inherent complexity." Understanding inherent complexity is difficult. It does not come naturally. Understanding inherent complexity means deducing the rules of the system operation, understanding the emergent properties and how varying the rules will leverage effect on the output of the system. If the inherent complexity is properly understood, it should be possible to expend the minimum amount of energy to leverage the maximum amount of improvement in the adaptive behavior (or outcome) of the system. A failure to understand the inherent complexity can result in changes that lead to undesired adaptive behavior or to expending excessive amounts of energy in the system in order to achieve the desired outcome. Expending excessive amounts of energy happens when the leverage point is chosen incorrectly because of a failure to fully comprehend the system.

Detail Complexity Versus Systems Complexity

Throughput Accounting [Corbett 1998] is a management accounting process that grew out of the manufacturing production application of the Theory of Constraints [Goldratt 1984]. Throughput Accounting can be generally applied for the management, control, and reporting of any system. It is a useful technique for management systems based on the Theory of Constraints, Lean Production [Womack 1991], Six Sigma [Tayntor 2002], or the Toyota Production System [Ohno 1988]. Throughput Accounting is appropriate for managing general systems because it focuses on Throughput, which is the desired adaptive behavior of the system.

Figure 2–2 demonstrates how to assign the basic financial measurements of Throughput Accounting to a general system. Throughput Accounting treats the value of the input at the time of arrival as Investment (I). The costs of operating the system are treated as fixed costs. It is assumed that the system is a continuous process and that after it processes an input, it goes on to process another and so on. The only marginal (or direct) costs are those associated with delivering specific units of output as they leave the system, that is, packaging, delivery, and installation. The fixed costs of operating the system are defined as Operating Expense (OE). The value attributable to the output is known as Throughput (T). Throughput is the value of the output less any direct costs. Throughput Accounting isn't necessarily about money. Value

Throughput Accounting for General Systems

Figure 2-2
Throughput
Accounting for a
general system.

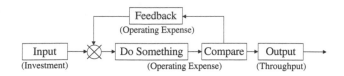

can be measured in other ways, as will be shown in the forthcoming education system example. Value, in the general case, is an abstract term.

$$\text{Value Added} = \text{Value}_{\text{Of Output}} - \text{Investment}_{\text{In Inputs}}$$

Throughput Accounting is at odds with the traditional form of management accounting practiced in western business—cost accounting. The differences between cost accounting and Throughput Accounting will be examined later in this text. At this stage it is sufficient to realize that Throughput Accounting focuses on the desired adaptive behavior of the system (Throughput), while cost accounting focuses on the cost of the energy expended in the system (Operating Expense). As the energy expended in the system has a nonlinear relationship to the desired adaptive behavior, cost accounting is a method that seeks to control the output of a system using an often inaccurate nonlinear mapping of cost against result.

Example: The Education System[2]

Figure 2–3 shows a simplified, but valid, model for the education system. A pupil arrives at a school for a new term (the input). During the term the school expends energy teaching, and hopefully, the pupil learns. At the end of the term, an assessment of learning is made through examinations. The test results are then used to determine the level of learning achieved and whether the pupil can pass to the next grade. The output from the system is a pupil with an enhanced level of knowledge.

The education system can be described using complex adaptive systems language. It can be stated that a higher level of knowledge is the desired adaptive behavior and that test results are emergent properties of the system.

Throughput Accounting the Education System

Figure 2–4 shows the same education system diagram and demonstrates how to assign the basic values for I, OE, and T.

[2]This example in not purely theoretical! On January 23, 2003, the British government announced that in addition to the absolute performance league tables of examination results already in use, a value added metric would be used to assess the performance of secondary schools in England and Wales.

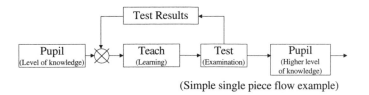

Figure 2–3
The education
system (simplified).

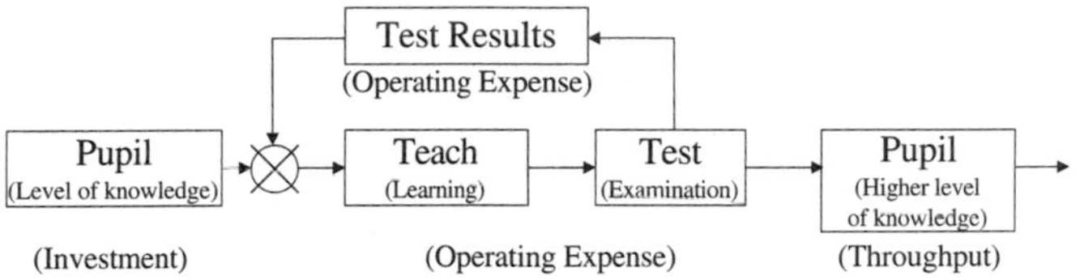

(Simple single piece flow example)

Figure 2–4
Throughput account-
ing for education.

$$\text{Unit of Inventory} = \text{Pupil}$$
$$\text{Value of Inventory} = \text{Knowledge of Pupil}$$
$$\text{Investment} = \text{Knowledge}_{\text{Input}} = \text{Value}_{\text{Input}}$$
$$\text{Value Added} = \text{Value}_{\text{Output}} - \text{Value}_{\text{Input}}$$
$$\text{Throughput} = \text{Knowledge}_{\text{Output}} - \text{Knowledge}_{\text{Input}}$$

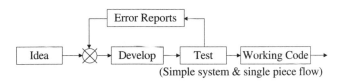

(Simple system & single piece flow)

Figure 2–5
Software develop-
ment system.

In this case, the value of Investment and Throughput and the Value Added by the system are all measured in terms of knowledge. Throughput Accounting does not need to be about money.[3] Throughput Accounting is a method of management reporting that adapts to the units of the desired adaptive behavior of the system.

Figure 2–5 shows a basic system mapping for the process of software development. This example shows how a single idea is transformed in the system into functional code. Anyone who develops software for a living will recognize that this is probably too simple a model to be useful. Software development is a complex adaptive system with many feedback loops.

---

[3]In *Throughput Accounting*, Corbett introduces the notion that TA can measure value-added in education [p. 147].

A System of Software Development

Management
Accounting for
Systems

17

Figure 2–6 shows how a more complex system has more feedback loops. It may still be too simplistic, but it is intended as an example only. Throughout Section 1 all the example system diagrams are intended as templates for the purpose of explaining the theories for Agile management. The examples are also intended to be read as single piece flows, that is, they show the progress of a single idea and do not imply any form of aggregation of ideas or any particular software development lifecycle method.

Figure 2–6 shows that in order to achieve Throughput from the software development system, the idea must pass through three transformations and three sets of tests that can feed back to three different points in the system. It should be obvious from a glance at the diagram that the energy required in the system to produce Throughput from initial Investment is nonlinear with the level of input or output. Loops upon loops of feedback create the nonlinearity.

Stages of Transformation

Figure 2–6 shows a single idea passing through the system. Using Lean Production terminology, it shows a "single piece flow." A single unit of input is shown flowing through a series of transformations until it appears as output.

It is important to recognize that I am talking here about a series of transformations on an idea. I am not talking about phases in the software engineering lifecycle. This is an important distinction.

Much of the debate about which software engineering lifecycle method is best is centered in arguments about how things are done. I would like to suggest that what is done does not vary across different methods of *how*. In the abstract or general case, shown in Figure 2–6, what is done is simply this—ideas are gradually transformed into finished executable code through a series of transformation steps, which are, loosely, analysis, design, coding, and testing.

The debates over software engineering lifecycle methods revolve around:

- How many ideas to aggregate together for transformation at any one time
- Whether or not a single pass of transformations is required, or whether the process needs to be repeated through several iterations
- Whether or not stages of transformation need to be visible or can be hidden
- Whether or not tangible documentation needs to be provided for each stage in the transformation
- What is the best method of performing a transformation
- Which artifacts should be produced
- Which language (written or visual) should be used.

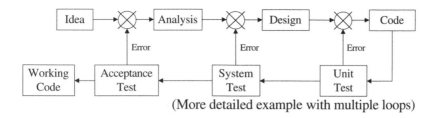

Figure 2–6
Software development system.

(More detailed example with multiple loops)

Despite all of these variations in how to achieve Throughput, I contend that all the transformation stages—analysis, design, coding, and testing—are required and do happen. Sometimes, analysis is explicitly declared. Sometimes it is rolled into the design stage. Almost all methods acknowledge the testing stage. Occasionally, testing is left as an exercise for the customer. However, all the stages of transformation are present.

Methods that suggest that stages of the transformation are skipped are really saying that stages of the transformation are invisible. In the case in which a programmer simply writes some code, is analysis and design missed, or does the programmer simply do it in her head before typing in the code? Is it possible to just type in code, without first thinking the problem through? Would such random code lead to a properly finished product? The reality is that software developers must think things through. Whether or not they write it down, discuss it with colleagues, or simply do it, that process of thinking involved the transformation of an idea through several stages.

Section 2 will survey alternative software development methods and examine the economics of each. Regardless of the method used, the work presented here is built on the premise that finished code cannot be delivered without each idea being processed through a series of transformations. Whether or not the ideas are all processed through each stage together, that is, the Waterfall method or they are processed in small batches, that is, Feature Driven Development, or the number of ideas processed is bounded by a fixed time, that is, Rapid Application Development, is interesting and affects the economics of software development. However, it doesn't undermine the notion that all software starts as individual ideas that are transformed through stages in a system of software development.

Throughput Accounting Software Development

For the purposes of illustration, I return to the simpler model in Figure 2–7 that shows how to assign the basic attributes of I, OE, and T to software development.

Figure 2–7
Throughput
accounting software
development.

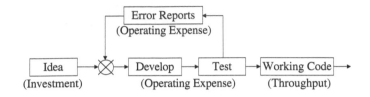

$$\text{Unit of Inventory} = \text{Idea}$$
$$\text{Value of Inventory} = \text{Investment to Create the Idea}$$
$$\text{Investment} = \text{Value}_{Input}$$
$$\text{Value}_{Output} = \text{Sales Price} - \text{Direct Costs}^4$$
$$\text{Value Added} = \text{Value}_{Output} - \text{Value}_{Input}$$
$$\text{Throughput}^5 = \text{Value}_{Output}$$

The System Goal

Throughout the rest of this text, I will refer to the desired adaptive behavior of the system as The System Goal. Undesired adaptive behavior is failure to meet the system goal. In other words, it is energy needlessly expended. Lean Production has a different term for this—waste! The Toyota Production System uses the original Japanese term—*muda*! Waste can be the generation of by-product or simply energy expended that produces no positive value-added in pursuit of the system goal.

Expending energy costs money. Undesired adaptive behavior, or waste, means that the OE is higher than it needs to be. The same T can be achieved with less OE if waste is reduced or eliminated.

The goal of a business, with the exception of not-for-profit and charitable foundations, is to make a profit. In other words, the desired adaptive behavior of a software development system is to make a profit—not produce working code! Working code alone is not enough. The code delivered as Throughput must be of customer value. The greater the value, the greater the Throughput! Throughput in software development is measured in units of currency ($).

A profit implies that the value of the output from the business is greater than the value of the input to the business. The input to a software development business is the Investment (I) made in product ideas and the cost of expending energy (OE) developing the software. The output from the business is the sales value of working code less any direct costs of sale, such as installation, training, delivery, hardware, operating systems, or middleware. The elementary metrics Throughput, Investment, Operating Expense and Inventory are defined in Figure 2–8.

---

[4]Direct Costs are marginal costs directly associated with the sale of working code. These could include packaging and delivery, but more likely cover installation, training, and support.

[5]Assumes a constant level of Investment, that is, the system is an on-going process; when the project is complete, another will start. If the project is a one-off and the development team (system) will not be maintained after completion, the Investment will not be replaced. In which case, the value of the Investment must be subtracted out of the Value Added figure. As this is not considered the normal case, it is ignored for the purposes of this text.

THROUGHPUT	INVENTORY
Rate of cash* (gross margin) generated through sales, not production or design *assuming a constant level of investment	Quantity of material queuing for input to, in-process through, or waiting for output, from the system
INVESTMENT	OPERATING EXPENSE
The sum of money invested in (or value expressed by) the Inventory and the system used to transform it into Throughput	The sum of money spent in the system to produce Throughput from Inventory

Figure 2–8
Summarizing Throughput Accounting for general systems.

Profit and Return on Investment

Having defined the basic units of measure (metrics) for Throughput Accounting of general business systems, it is possible to define the calculations for Net Profit and Return on Investment.

$$\text{Net Profit}^6 = \text{Throughput} - \text{Operating Expense}$$

$$\text{Return on Investment} = \frac{\text{Net Profit}}{\text{Investment}}$$

It is obvious from these two simple equations that in order to make more profit, Throughput must be increased and/or Operating Expense decreased. In order to improve ROI, Investment must be decreased or Net Profit increased. Investment includes the amount of money sunk in Inventory. Hence, reducing Inventory levels will reduce Investment levels.

To put this in the language of Lean Production, more value must be delivered and/or waste must be eliminated, and Inventory levels must be reduced.

To summarize, all businesses must focus management attention on three things to make greater profits and have higher ROI:

- Increase Throughput (T)
- Decrease Investment (I)
- Decrease Operating Expense (OE)

[6]Assumes a constant level of investment.

THROUGHPUT	INVENTORY
Rate of cash* generated through delivery of working code into production, not merely code complete *Assuming a constant level of Investment	Quantity of ideas for client-valued functionality queuing for input to, in-process through, or waiting for output, from the system
INVESTMENT	**OPERATIONAL EXPENSE**
The sum of money invested in the system of software production plus the sum spent to obtain the ideas for client-valued functionality input to the system	The sum of money spent in the system to produce working code from ideas for client-valued functionality

Figure 2–9
Summarizing throughput accounting for software development.

More Profit From Software

Figure 2–9 summarizes the definition of the elementary metrics for Throughput Accounting of software development. In order to make greater profit and have greater ROI from software, Throughput (T) must be increased. This means more client-valued functionality must be delivered more often. The rate of delivered value must increase.

The amount of working capital required for Investment (I) must decrease. That means that the costs of gathering requirements must be reduced by finding better ways of identifying and gathering truly client-valued ideas and communicating those ideas to the software engineers.

The Operating Expense (OE) involved in the development of software must be decreased. This means that waste must be eliminated. Energy must not be wasted on undesirable adaptive behavior or production of by-product. Only truly client-valued functionality should be built—energy expended building features the client doesn't value is waste! Due to the acutely labor intensive nature of software development, ways must be found to achieve more with less, to produce more client-valued Throughput (T) using fewer people. The cost of people is the biggest contributor to OE.

To summarize, software development businesses must focus management attention on three things to create greater profits and higher ROI:

- Increase Throughput (T)
- Decrease Investment (I)
- Decrease Operating Expense (OE)

Working Capital Requirements

The figures for T, I, and OE can be used to predict the working capital requirements for a software business. If the rate at which units of inventory (V) are converted into working code (Q), that is, client-valued functions delivered in a given time, is known and the OE for the same amount of time is also known, the average cost to transform a single unit of inventory from input to output can be calculated. The quantity of client-valued functions delivered is shown as Q. An average unit of Q would require the mean amount of OE in order to transform it from an idea into working code—the average cost per Function (ACPF).

$$\text{Average Cost per Function (ACPF)} = Q_{\text{time period}}/OE_{\text{time period}}$$

If the ACPF is known and the total units of inventory (V) for a given project is known, then the estimated cost to convert the requirements into finished code can be expressed as:

$$\text{Estimated Cost of Project Delivery (D)} = V_{\text{project}} \times ACPF$$

The value for D will be accurate if the definition of an average unit of V does not change during the life of the project. Getting a precise value for D would require understanding the complexity of each unit of inventory and being able to accurately calculate the amount of OE expended in the system to convert the idea into working code. As I will show, trying to work with precise estimates has been a contributing factor in the systemic failure of traditional software development methods. Hence, it is actually better to work with this imprecise measure and to accommodate the imprecision in calculations using it.[7]

With an approximation for D and using I as the value of the inventory plus the capital invested in the system of software production, that is, in equipment and tools for the development and test teams, the working capital requirements to complete a single project will be the cost of acquiring the requirements plus the cost of providing the software developers with all the equipment they need and the cost to convert those requirements into working code.

$$\$ \text{ Working Capital Requirements} = \$I + \$D$$

It is easy to run a business with hindsight. Reporting the past is useful for describing what actually happened, but it is more useful to be able to predict the future and to make decisions to influence the future outcomes of the business. The real question to be answered isn't "How well did we do last quarter?" but "Which decisions should we make in order to do better next quarter?"

Predicting the Future

---

[7]A whole field of statistics has grown up around the concept of working with numbers that have a degree of imprecision (or uncertainty) built into them. In engineering, imprecision is known as tolerance or variance. Coping with variance and uncertainty is a major factor in Agile software development methods and is discussed later in this text.

The problem with trying to predict the profitability of a software business is the unpredictability of the OE figure. OE is hard to predict because estimation of software projects is notoriously poor. If it is not possible to estimate how much time it will take and how many resources are needed to complete a software project, it is impossible to calculate a figure for OE. It is bad enough that marketing departments can only forecast sales, but without a firm grasp of OE, both variables are unknown and unpredictable. Hence, the profit prediction could look more like this:

$$\text{Net Profit} = \text{Unknown (T)} - \text{Pretty hard to guess (OE)}$$

Calculating an expected return on investment for a future software product has been next to impossible. If profit is hard to predict, then ROI presents a problem with three unpredictable variables. Sales, and hence T is almost impossible to predict. OE is difficult to calculate. In addition, the cost of acquiring the requirements is also unknown. Calculating a cost of input to create requirements has been notoriously difficult because organizations don't try to measure it—When was the last time you saw a marketing manager fill out a time sheet? Accounting departments have been unaware that it is important and hence haven't been focused on recording the investment made in ideas for new software. However, unless the true cost for I is known, it is impossible to calculate an ROI. Management must start to gather data on the cost of acquisition of the ideas being input into the software development system.

$$\text{ROI} = \frac{\text{Unknown (T)} - \text{Pretty hard to guess (OE)}}{\text{Didn't bother to measure (I)}}$$

Framing the Problem

It is now possible to construct a framework for the problem on how to run a software development organization like any other business that is accountable to its officers and its stockholders. This framework will elevate software development to the point where practical, fact-based, executive decisions can be made about investment in new products, investment in people, and investment in tools, equipment, and facilities for those people.

Using General Systems Thinking and Throughput Accounting to calculate Net Profit and ROI, only three metrics are required from the business: Throughput, Investment, and Operating Expense. Two of those variables are under direct control of the software development business—Operating Expense and Investment. However, the value of Throughput (T) must also be known before proper decisions can be made. Determining the value of Throughput for different types of software businesses is explained in Chapters 15, 16, and 17. The remainder of Section 1 explores and explains how to go about metering a software development organization to report the three metrics, T, I, and OE, and how to use these to accurately control software development, that is, deliver working code on time, within budget, and with agreed function whilst meaningfully reporting progress to senior management, that is, demonstrating delivery of the desired financial results for NP and ROI.

The financial metrics presented are a numerical construction. They are designed to allow a normalized view of the value added by the software engineering activity in the full value stream of the business. For the purposes of devising useful management metrics, the sum of money spent on creating ideas and communicating those ideas is being treated as an investment. All upstream activity is treated as an investment, and all downstream activity as a direct cost against Throughput.

It is important not to get carried away with whether this is real. For example, worrying about whether the software development business would pay the marketing department for requirements or sell the output to the field service organization for deployment is not a useful exercise. These are not important issues. The purpose of management accounting is to produce numerical data that can be used to make appropriate management decisions for investment and operation of the business. The financial metrics serve this purpose, and they create a normal form that can be used to assess different types of software production systems against one another. This mechanism will be used in Section 2 to demonstrate how Agile software development methods financially outperform traditional software development lifecycle methods.

Understanding Software Production in the Value Chain

From the earlier equation for Net Profit, it is possible to deduce that Throughput and Operating Expense are of equal importance. As I have shown, T is very intangible, but OE, though difficult to predict, is calculable in more mature organizations or historically measurable. This fact tends to focus managers on reducing OE in order to improve Net Profit.[8] For this reason, developers fill out time sheets every week.

Cost control is at the heart of the management accounting method known as cost accounting. Cost accounting was created in order to manage assembly lines designed using Taylor's Theory of Scientific Management [Taylor 1911]. Cost accounting was devised in order to accurately measure the efficiency of the men and machines used in the assembly lines of scientific management—the efficiency of energy expended. Cost accounting focuses on cost efficiency, that is, units of production per dollar for each man or machine in the system. This seems intuitively valid until you consider that cost accounting treats labor and machinery operation as a variable cost. The assumption is that men or machines that are inactive do not incur costs. As there is a direct relationship between cost and man or machine hours, efficiency is expressed in those terms.

$$\text{Cost Efficiency} = dQ \,/\, \text{man hour (or machine hour)}$$

Cost accounting assumes that local efficiency leads to global efficiency. The problem with this is easily exposed. Because inactive men or machinery are not truly variable, the costs they incur are placed in a bucket known as "overhead." Overhead is cost assigned to the system as a whole. Hence, local efficiency is no indicator of global efficiency.

Throughput Accounting Versus Cost Accounting

[8]Corbett discusses the alternative focus of cost accounting and Throughout Accounting and the effect that each has on the adaptive behavior of the system—the output of the business [1998, pp. 145–150].

In comparison, Throughput Accounting focuses on delivered value. It seeks to maximize the efficiency of the flow of value through the system. In other words, it wants the latent value added in an investment to be released as quickly as possible as Throughput. Throughput Accounting measures how effectively the system moves the Investment value through the system and converts it to Throughput. This is more usually described as "effectiveness." The business press likes to report the competitiveness of businesses such as auto manufacturing. These days they report the cost efficiency (sic) as the number of hours it takes to build a car. Ironically, we seem to be stuck with the language of cost accounting when the metric being reported is a Throughput Accounting metric.

$$\text{Production Efficiency (Effectiveness)} = dt / dQ$$

Throughput Accounting assumes that men and machines are not easily removed, and the costs associated with them are fixed. Hence, efficiency cannot be expressed in terms of cost. It must be expressed in terms of value delivered.

$$\text{Value Efficiency} = dt / (\text{Value}_{Output} - \text{Value}_{Input})$$

We can express these metrics in more common language by saying that value efficiency or effectiveness is more easily measured as the Lead Time from system input to system output.

Value efficiency answers the question, how many hours or minutes to earn a dollar of value added? Cost efficiency, on the other hand, answers the question, how many units can be transformed for a dollar of local expenditure?

Cost accounting is only applicable in a world where true direct (marginal) costs greatly exceed fixed costs [Corbett 1998, p. 20]. Proponents of modern cost accounting methods such as Activity Based Costing (ABC) argue that Throughput Accounting is only applicable over short time periods, and that ABC is applicable when the time period under consideration is longer. Over a long time period, it is argued, all costs are variable, that is, it is possible to close down a whole division of a company or lay off hundreds of IT workers.

A manager must decide which facts to use in order to make intelligent management decisions that will result in more profits now and in the future. In a world where the business environment is constantly changing, changes that result in ever fluctuating software requirements, it only seems appropriate to evaluate management decisions using a short time window. Ideas for software systems and products are extremely perishable in nature due to the constantly changing nature of the business environment. Such requirements could be obsolete in one year—perhaps less. Hence, the management accounting method used must reflect the fact that the time window is short.

The reality is that labor costs are fixed over a short time window. Software developers are paid every day they come to work, whether or not they are actively involved in the production of working code. Hence, Throughput Accounting is the correct choice for managing software development.

Relative Importance of T, I, and OE

For the same reason, cost accounting has become obsolete as a management tool in Lean Manufacturing, even though it is still in common usage and the basis on which General Accepted Accounting Practices (GAAP) accounts are prepared. Companies have been forced into using one management method for making globally optimal business decisions and another for reporting their accounts to both governments and owners.

The problem with focusing on reducing cost in order to improve the profitability of a business is that it is bounded by zero, that is, below zero it is impossible to reduce costs any further. Achieving zero is impossible. Hence, focusing on costs is limiting. It limits the vision of the business, and it has the psychological effect of focusing managers on internal matters, not customers.

Alternatively, if a focus on delivering customer value is taken as more important, the limits are unbounded. Focusing a business on increasing Throughput leads to outward thinking managers worried about customer satisfaction and to unbounded ideas for continuous improvement. Hence, T is of the greatest importance. In Lean Production, this is referred to as "focusing on value."

If T is of greatest importance, is OE or I the second most important? The answer is that Investment is greater. Reducing I increases ROI and decreases OE through reduced carrying costs of borrowing. However, it is the effect on reducing Lead Time (LT), through reduced inventory that is the more important effect. If a business is to be agile and to deliver customer value faster, then inventory must be reduced. Hence, I is the second most important. In Lean Production, this focus on reducing Lead Time is referred to as "focusing on flow."

By implication, OE is least important in a world of business systems designed to optimize the system goal—increased profits now and in the future.

Figure 2–10 shows the differences in the importance of T, I, and OE between cost accounting and Throughput Accounting.

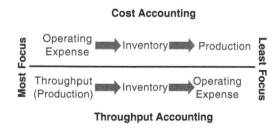

Cost Accounting

Throughput Accounting

Figure 2–10
Alternative focus of accounting models.

Summary

This chapter has shown that very few financial metrics are needed in order to run a software business: Investment, Throughput, Operating Expense, Net Profit, and Return on Investment.

The business must be capable of measuring the cost of acquiring requirements. This cost should be treated as Investment for the purpose of evaluating the effectiveness of the software production system. Ideas for products, captured as requirements, are considered assets in Throughput Accounting for software development.

All costs for operating the system of software production should be treated as Operating Expense, including labor, amortization, cost of financing investments, taxes, and write-downs on perishable assets such as requirements that become obsolete.

In order to calculate Throughput, the direct costs should be deducted from the sales figure. Direct costs include only costs that are strictly variable in relation to the sale. These would include the costs of salesmen's commissions, costs of deployment or installation, and costs of any hardware or software components such as database licenses or application server middleware.

The order of importance of Throughput Accounting metrics T is first, then I, and last OE. The order is selected to focus management attention on outward facing matters and customer value. Focusing on Throughput encourages the development of a learning organization with an unbounded ever-increasing objective.

chapter 3

TOC in Software Production

The Theory of Constraints can be explained with a simple five-step process that needs little explanation.

1. Identify the System Constraint.
2. Decide how best to exploit the System Constraint.
3. Subordinate everything else to the decision in step 2.
4. Elevate the Constraint.
5. If steps 1 through 4 have created a new constraint, return to step 2.

TOC is founded on the notion that a value chain is only as strong as its weakest link. The conjecture is that there is only one weakest link at any given time. This weakest link is known as the constraint. In a process or system that takes input and produces output under some control mechanism, the constraint is described as the capacity constrained resource (CCR).[1] In other words, the value chain is a chain of processes or systems that add value to a raw material and turn it into a finished product. The rate of production of the finished product is constrained by the rate of production of the slowest (or weakest) element in the value chain.

If TOC is to be used to improve a system, constraints must be identified, one by one. Physical constraints are also known as bottlenecks. Hence, identifying bottlenecks is a good place to start looking for the current constraint. It is generally assumed that there is only one global system constraint at any given time. There may be several bottlenecks, but only one will be constraining the overall Throughput.

Figure 3–1 shows a software production system that is constrained by the capacity of System Test, which is only capable of processing 30 units of production per month. The capacity of Acceptance Test at 80 units per month is irrelevant. At most, only 30 units will be passed to Acceptance Test every month.

Once the constraint has been identified, a decision must be made on how to minimize its constraining ability on the system. The utilization or

---

[1]The term CCR is an abstraction. Constraints can take many forms.

Figure 3–1

Software production
system showing rates
of production.

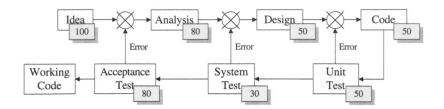

capacity of the constraint must be maximized. The CCR must be fully utilized. It must never be idle. Every unit of production (Q) lost on the constraint is a unit of Q lost to the whole system. The constraint can be
protected from idleness by providing a buffer (or queue) of work for it to perform. As a generalization, constraints are protected by buffers—a queue is
just a type of buffer, a physical buffer of inventory. Protecting a constraint
is a necessary part of exploiting a constraint to the full. Achieving maximum exploitation of a resource means that whatever can be done should
be done to utilize the CCR optimally. This is best explained with a couple
of examples.

Consider a manufacturing machine that cuts silicon wafers into individual chips. Assume that this is the CCR for a chip fabrication plant. How can
the wafer cutter be protected and exploited as a CCR?

It can be protected from starvation by provision of a buffer of completed
wafers. It can be protected from power outage with a provision of uninter-
ruptible power and a backup generator. It can be exploited fully by running
three shifts and utilizing the machine up to 24 hours per day. It can be exploited
by performing a prior quality control check on wafers to insure that only good
quality wafers are processed through the cutting machine.

Exploiting the Software Developer as a Capacity Constrained Resource

Consider a software development constraint. A software developer is
paid to work 8 hours per day. Strictly speaking, 8 hours per day is the constraint. Of course, software developers tend to be flexible in their working
hours, so it might be more accurate to state that the constraint is the period
of time during which the developer shows up in the office. How can the software developer as a resource be protected and exploited?

She can be protected from idleness by always having a pool of development tasks ready to be done. She can be protected from interruptions by
providing a communication structure that minimizes the lines of communication.[2] She can be protected from distraction by providing a quiet envi-

[2]Harlan Mills wrote about the "Surgical Team" in 1971 as an example of a structure designed
to minimize lines of communication and maximize the Throughput of software developers.

ronment for working. She can be further exploited by providing her with the best software development tools available. She can be exploited by providing support staff for nonproductive activities, such as progress reporting and time-tracking, or tools to automate such nonvalue-added work. Nonvalue-added work is waste. She can be exploited by providing adequate training in the technologies being used. She can be exploited by providing a team of colleagues to support her and help resolve difficulties. She can be exploited by ensuring that the requirements she is given are of good quality. This represents just a short list of possible protection and exploitation mechanisms to maximize the completed working code produced by a software developer.

Subordinating to the Exploitation of a Constraint

Step 3 in TOC requires subordination of all other things to a decision to protect or exploit a constraint. Step 3 has profound implications for any business. The effect of step 3 can produce results that are counterintuitive and go against the existing management policies.

To continue with the fabrication plant example, assume that the capacity of the wafer cutting tool has been determined. It has also been determined that the Throughput of the whole plant is constrained by the capacity of the wafer cutter. A decision is made to protect and exploit the wafer cutter to its maximum capacity. In order to subordinate all else to this decision, there must be agreement to regulate the flow of inventory from the factory gate to the wafer cutter at the same speed as the wafer cutter can process it. This is the Drum-Buffer-Rope application of TOC. The rate of the cutter is the drum. The inventory from the factory gate to the cutter is the rope and a buffer in front of the cutter to prevent it becoming idle is the buffer. A similar process in Lean Production (or TPS) is known as "balancing" and results in the determination of Takt time. Takt time plays the same role as the drum in Drum-Buffer-Rope. What this can mean in practice is that other machines earlier in the process may lay idle. Part of the manufacturing plant may be idle because it would produce too much inventory were it to run 24 hours per day. Other parts of the system must only produce as much as can be consumed by the wafer cutting machine.

The psychological effect of this subordination approach when first introduced can be overpowering. If the business is run using traditional cost accounting methods, then the idle machines appear to be very inefficient because efficiency is measured locally as the number of units processed per day/hour/minute. However, if the machines are not permitted to be idle, if there is no subordination of the rest of the plant to the decision to feed inventory at the speed the wafer cutter can cope with it, then inventory will be stockpiled in front of the wafer cutter. The result will be that total inventory will grow and so will investment. Consequently, operating expense will grow, too. The business will become less profitable and return less on the invested capital. Leaving machines idle can be good for business, but it is counterintuitive.

Perishable Requirements

Producing and holding too much inventory is much worse in software because of the perishable nature of the inventory—requirements can go stale because of changes in the market or the fickle nature of the customer. There is a time value to requirements, and they depreciate with time, just like fresh produce, that is, requirements have a time to market value. As time goes by, the potential Throughput from the transformation of the requirement into working code decreases. Increasingly often requirements become obsolete, and they are replaced by change requests for new requirements with a current market value.

Staleness is a very profound problem in software development. Although a requirement (unit of V) may be written down, there is an implicit body of knowledge on how to interpret it. If it isn't being actively processed, that knowledge atrophies—people forget things! Even worse, people leave projects or companies and take the knowledge with them.

For proof of this, ask a developer to explain how some code written 12 months ago actually works, and see whether he can recall from memory or a brief analysis of the source code. Vital details never get captured, and people forget. Loss of memory and loss of detail incur extra costs. Such extra costs can be classified as waste.

Requirements that become stale are pure waste. Such requirements have a $0 potential Throughput value. When this happens, the cost of acquiring the requirement must be written off as operating expense.

Idleness Might Breed Contempt

It ought to be possible to measure the average Production Rate (R), of a developer for any given week, or month, or quarter. For a team of developers, it should be possible to guess approximately how many requirements can be processed for a given time period. If they are to be fully exploited, developers should not be loaded with any more than they can reasonably handle. So the rest of the system of software production must be subordinated to this notion. Requirements should be fed into development at the same pace as the developers can process them into completed code.

Again, the psychological effect of this decision when first introduced could be devastating. If the requirements are generated by analysts who interview subject matter experts and business owners, management must realize that those analysts no longer need to work flat out producing requirements. If development is the constraint, then by implication, analysis must not be the constraint. It could be that the analysts will spend time idle. They are not required to create requirements constantly. In TOC language, this stop-go effect is often called "Road Runner Behavior" after the Warner Bros. cartoon character who only has 2 speeds—full speed and stop. Road Runner behavior may be bad for morale amongst the analysts. Hence, the Agile manager must be aware that the subordination step in TOC is dangerous and needs careful management attention during introduction.

Probably the best way to deal with this is to ensure that everyone understands the Drum-Buffer-Rope principles and that they are aware of the current system constraint. If they know that they do not work in the CCR, they should be comfortable with their new role being only partially loaded. This technique of sharing an understanding of the system process and gaining buy-in to changes has been called "Fair Process" [Kim 1997].

Step 4 requires the elevation of the constraint. In plain English, this means that the constraint must be improved to the point where it is no longer the system constraint. This is best explained by example.

If the wafer cutting machine is the constraint in the fabrication plant, everything has been done to protect and exploit that machine, and everything else in the system has been subordinated to those decisions, but still there is insufficient Throughput from the plant, the constraint must be elevated. With a machine, elevation is simple—buy and commission another machine. With the introduction of the second machine, the wafer cutter may no longer be the constraint. The constraint within the system may have moved elsewhere. Management must now move to step 5 and identify the new constraint. If the constraint has moved outside the system, then (arguably) they are done.[3] For example, if the plant can now produce more than the company can sell, the constraint has moved to sales. Managers at the fabrication plant no longer control the constraint. Hence, there is nothing they can do to improve the Throughput of the business. If, however, the fabrication plant still has an internal constraint, then the managers must return to step 1 and start again.

Elevating the Software Developers Capacity Constraint

How is the developer elevated from a constraint? The most obvious method of elevation used in the software industry is unpaid overtime. The developer is asked to work longer hours. The constraint is stretched. Weekend work may also be requested. Again, the constraint is being stretched. The manager could also choose to hire more developers or to introduce shift working. Another very powerful method is to use a better developer.

It has been known for over 30 years [Weinberg 1971/1998] that some software developers produce much more output than others. Performance differences between the average and the best of 10 to 20 times have been documented [Sackman 1968]. The difference between poor and best is possibly fifty fold. Hence, one way to truly elevate a software development organization is to hire better people.

Good people are hard to find. In a large organization, management must accept that over the statistical sample, the engineering team will tend to be average. Hence, it is important that managers identify top performers, reward and keep them, and apply them judiciously to projects where development is the constraint. By using a top performer on a capacity constrained development project, management elevates the constraint and moves it elsewhere in the value chain.

---

[3]Lepore & Cohen merged the Theory of Constraints with Edwards Deming's Theory of Profound Knowledge and devised a 10-point scheme they call "The Decalogue" [Lepore, 1999]. Stage 9 involves "bringing the constraint inside."

Increasing Throughput by Elevating the Constraint

In Figure 3–1, the System Test process is a bottleneck. It is constraining the Throughput of the system to only 30 units per month. The equations in Chapter 1 demonstrated the best way to be more profitable is to increase Throughput. Figure 3–1 shows that it would be possible to raise the Throughput to 50 units per month if the System Test process was elevated. At 50 units per month, System Test ceases to be the constraint. At that point, Design, Coding, Unit Test, and System Test are all joint constraints. Raising production higher than 50 units per month would require investment to elevate all four of them. The business question to be answered is how much is it worth to increase the capacity of System Test from 30 to 50 units per month?

Focus of Investment

If TOC was to be summarized in a single word, it would be *focus.* TOC teaches managers where to focus investment. Whether it is investment of time, resources, or money, the largest ROI will be gained from investing in the currently identified system constraint.

The financial equations for cost justification are simple. The existing equation for ROI is:

$$ROI_{Pre\text{-}Investment} = \frac{Throughput\ (T) - Operating\ Expense\ (OE)}{Investment\ (I)}$$

If the current constraint is eliminated through an Investment (dI), then Throughput will increase by an amount (dT). The equation post-investment would look like

$$ROI_{Post\text{-}Investment} = \frac{(T + dT) - OE}{I + dI}$$

If $ROI_{Post\text{-}Investment}$ is greater than $ROI_{Pre\text{-}Investment}$ the investment to remove the constraint is worth doing. In fact, the officers of the company, being aware of the option to invest and elevate the constraint, are legally obliged to the shareholders to make the investment—assuming funds are available.

Is the 8-Hour Day the Best Choice of System Constraint?

It seems attractive to decide that there will be only one CCR in the system and that it will be the working day. To simply assume that 8 hours is a constraint and that all personnel are constrained by it seems to provide a convenient option for managers—they don't have to look for other constraints.

Goldratt argues that the 8-hour work day is not a useful constraint because it is not a bottleneck [1994, chs. 30 & 31]. Rather, he would call this an insufficiently buffered resource, that is, demand may outstrip supply. However, in the system of software production, a bottleneck would be a capacity constrained resource (CCR) in front of which a stockpile of inventory is apt to accumulate and beyond which resources may starve for input. This definition of a constraint satisfies the definition required for the Critical Chain [1997].

The capacity constrained resources (CCRs) that are most likely to represent the bottlenecks are not generalist developers and testers but the specialists such as UI designers, architects, data modelers, DBAs (performance tuning wizards), visiting consultants, and maybe even subject matter experts (SMEs). Resources related to expert skills such as usability laboratories, staging environments for performance tuning, prototyping laboratories, and testing labs can also be bottlenecks. Such resources are likely to be shared in large organizations and require scheduling. Sharing a resource and scheduling a date for its use introduces uncertainty into project management.

Summary

Bottlenecks in software production are identified by measuring the trend in inventory at each step in the process. The trend in inventory is affected by the production rate (or capacity) of each process step.

The overall production of the system should be balanced against the capacity of the bottleneck. The bottleneck should be protected and exploited in order to maximize its Throughput.

Management may choose to invest in the bottleneck in order to increase its capacity and hence increase the overall production of code through the whole system. The cost of the investment can be considered against the value of the increased production that will be achieved. The use of TOC provides a focus for management, who may choose to employ Lean Thinking in order to elevate constraints and create improvement.

chapter 4

Dealing with Uncertainty

There are five main constraints in software development management: people, time, functionality, budget, and resources (excluding people). Agile methods recognize these constraints and seek to protect and exploit them [Beck 2000, p. 15].

The Five Constraints of Software Development

Resources must be protected from uncertainty. Uncertainty manifests itself when the unplanned happens. A system can absorb uncertainty with the provision of buffers. Tom DeMarco wrote an entire book *slack*, about buffering resources in software [2001]!

In every case, a constraint can be protected by a buffer. A buffer would normally be allocated in the same unit of measure as the constraint is measured. Hence, people should be buffered with people, schedule with time, budget with money, functionality with requirements, and other resources with similar resources (see Table 4–1).

Protecting the People Constraint

All Agile methods recognize that software development is an innately human activity. It is performed by people. Therefore, people are the single most important potentially capacity constrained resource in software development.

As the single most important resource on a software project, people must be protected. There is more than one way to provide a buffer for the people. The most obvious is to have more developers than needed. The

Table 4–1
Types of constraints and suitable buffers.

Constraint	Buffer with
Scope (Inventory)	Queue
Schedule	Time
Budget	Money
People	People
Resources	Resources

second is to assume that the people are only productive for a subset of the work day. My favorite number is 5.5 hours. This is a personal choice. Others may suggest different numbers. Buffers must also be introduced to accommodate vacations and ill-health. A wise manager will buffer a little more for unpredictable, life changing events such as a death, birth, marriage, terminal illness, and divorce and more esoteric ones such as fire at home, flood, earthquake, automobile accident, sports injury, and, most recently, military service. Typical American high technology employers with whom I have worked seem to assume that they get 48–49 weeks per year of labor from a software developer. Futhermore, they often assume that the employee will work an average of 9 to 10 hours per day when only paid for 8 hours. A good manager who understands that his people constraint must be buffered will assume much less. My personal choice is to allow 15% for vacation and other outage, that is, a 42–43 week work year, coupled to 5.5 hours of productivity each day.

When executives see these hard numbers written down, there is often an adverse psychological effect. Therefore, it is vital that senior management understands that software is an innately human activity and that software developers are not machines that can be switched on and off like the lights.

How big a people buffer is needed? The answer is that buffer size varies with uncertainty. The greater the uncertainty, the larger the buffer must be. There is some possibility that a project will suffer from no downtime or people outage. It is just possible that no one will get sick, get married, have a baby, or suffer a loss of a close family member. It may even be a time of year when no one is interested in taking a vacation. Such times are rare.

It is important that this people buffer is added to the project early.

The so called J-curve effect on the production rate reported by Brooks is discussed in depth in Chapter 31. Brooks suggests that adding people later in a project is not effective; they must be added early [Brooks 1995, p.25].

Brooks' Law: Adding people to a late project makes it later.

Uncertainty will vary with the length of the project. With a very short project, there is little uncertainty about people. With a longer project, there is more scope for things to happen unexpectedly. However, it is better to think of software development as an on-going process where projects are simply inventory passing through a system of software production. In which case, it is reasonable to suggest that people-related uncertainty tends to level out at a predictable level. The numbers I gave above (43 weeks and 5.5 hours) are numbers based on my experience—my own empirical evidence. Others may observe different empirical data.

Protecting the Time Constraint

Every finished product or project has a desired delivery date or a predicted delivery date. A desired delivery date is when the customer asked for delivery. A predicted date is when Engineering (or IT) estimated they could deliver it. The important thing is that a date is agreed upon by the software development organization and the customer. This date is a system constraint. A date gets promised, and it is bad business to break promises.

Sometimes, the delivery date has been set for hard business reasons. For example, a change in government regulations is being introduced, and the new product must be delivered in order for the customer to meet its legal obligations. In other words, the date constraint is imposed from outside the organization and is totally outside the control of anyone in the organization. Such hard delivery dates are common in heavily regulated industries such as investment, finance, banking, tax and audit, telecommunications, power generation, and other public utilities.

If the delivery date is a constraint, it must be protected by a time buffer. The length of the time buffer must be based on the uncertainty involved in the project. The uncertainty must be assessed with respect to the technology, people, subject matter, architecture and delivery environment, the maturity of the organization, and a number of other factors such as the reliability of upstream suppliers.

For example, consider a relatively mature software development organization that might audit as SEI SW-CMM Level 3.[1] With a project that looks similar to one just completed, uses the same architecture, has an existing and experienced team, uses the same technologies, and has subject matter well known and understood by the everyone involved, the company might *just* be 100% certain that the project can be finished on time. In this case, with 100% certainty, I would use my minimum buffer number of 15%.

On the other hand, in a newly formed start-up with a new team, a poor understanding of the subject matter, and a new challenge that requires bleeding-edge technology, it is fairly certain that a lot can and will go wrong. This must be planned for. A good textbook answer for buffering in such a situation would be 200% [Goldratt 1997, p. 46]. In reality, it is only possible to get away with such a buffer, if there is no process maturity and no one making public guesses as to how long the project should take. In many cases, a development manager will find it impossible to gain agreement on 200%. In which case, I would suggest a fallback position of no less than 100%. Table 4–2 shows my rule of thumb numbers for time buffering.

Table 4–2
Certainty and suggested buffer sizes.

Certainty	Buffer Size
100%	15%
90%	25%–30%
80%	50%
50–70%	100%
<50%	200%

---

[1]The Software Engineering Institute (SEI) based at Carnegie-Mellon University has defined a Capability Maturity Model (CMM) for software engineering organizations—Level 1 being chaohie immaturity through to Level 5 representing optimizing performance.

In order to read this table, you must understand the measure of certainty. Certainty is the percentage likelihood that a task will be completed on time. The 100% certainty implies that similar tasks always complete on time. If only one in every two tasks tends to complete on time, then the certainty would be 50%. In reality, certainty is the gut feeling of the developers who are on the spot. If they feel confident, they may estimate 90% certainty. If they've never seen something before and have no idea how to do it, they are more likely to estimate <50% certainty. For example, if a developer estimates a job as 1 month, with a 40% certainty of completion, then the estimate should ideally be inflated by 2 to 3 months.

Protecting the Scope Constraint

The functionality of the system represents another constraint. Once again, the agreed scope represents a promise. Failing to deliver the agreed functionality means a broken promise. Broken promises are bad for business.

If the scope constraint is to be protected, it must be buffered with more scope. In essence, the manager must gain agreement with the customer that some of the scope would be "nice to have" but doesn't need to make it into the currently agreed deliverable.

In other words, if the scope constraint is to be protected, then the scope of required functionality must be prioritized. The customer (or product marketing) must determine the ranked order of importance for the functionality in the scope. This could be as simple as assigning a value on a 3-point scale to each required function, for example, "must have," "preferred," and "nice to have."

Functionality priority is actually a two-dimensional problem. When a customer is asked how important any given feature in the scope might be, the answer is likely to be, "It depends." What the customer means is that the importance varies according to the delivery date. This is best explained with an example.

With an investment banking application, a new feature is required to meet new government legislation. The feature must track stock trading activity of "insiders" within periods shortly before public announcement of trading results. The new law takes effect at the beginning of the fourth quarter. If the customer is asked how important the feature is, they will say it is a "must have" feature. The company stands to be heavily fined if the feature is not delivered on time. However, if the question is rephrased to ask how important the feature is for delivery by the end of the first quarter of the same year, the answer will be different. Naturally, the feature is useless at that time. Early delivery makes everyone feel comfortable about the new regulations, but it is not necessary for the business. The new feature will not be used until October 1. There is no Throughput value in early delivery.

Hence, it is important to gather the time-varied priority for each requirement in the scope. The program manager should plan to agree on a scope with the customer that includes a number of "nice to have" requirements that perhaps later become "must have." Engineering would agree to schedule these requirements in the plan, but the customer agrees to let them slip, in the event of unplanned events disrupting the schedule. This concept of prioritizing requirements is addressed in greater depth in Chapter 16, Agile Product Management.

I can hear a chorus of people shouting, "Wait! You can never get agreement on such a scope buffer." Why not? This is caused by a lack of trust. The customer will assume that buffered requirements will never be delivered. This is based on experience with poor software development organizations who never deliver what they promise and would certainly never overdeliver. Hence, the scope is nonnegotiable.

As a precursor to ever being able to buffer scope, a development organization must provide end-to-end traceability, transparency, and repeatability. It must be capable of building trust with its customers and showing that it can deliver on promises. Only when the customer learns to trust the software development organization, through an understanding gained from visibility into the software process, will the customer agree to prioritize and buffer scope.

Hence, it should be taken de facto that scope buffering is not available to the immature software production system as a protection mechanism against uncertainty. Trust must be earned through a series of deliveries that met expectations. After this, it is possible to negotiate a scope buffer.

Trust

Establishing trust is the most important goal for any development manager. Trust is the most valuable weapon in a development manager's arsenal. Trust is gained through a combination of transparency and delivering on promises. Show people how the system works, what is involved, how long it takes, and what went wrong when it does go wrong, and trust will grow. Lack of trust is usually a symptom of lack of understanding. The organization doesn't need to run like a well-oiled machine. It doesn't need to perform like an automaton in order to win trust. It is all right for things to go wrong. Customers understand human frailty. In fact, they often like it. What they want to see is honesty. They will accept problems occurring when they can see and understand the reason for them.

It is possible to build a customer relationship where buffering scope is a regular occurrence. It requires a mutual trust. Trust must be earned. Managers can earn trust by delivering on a few promises.

Hence, it may be easier initially to use buffers in time and people, to insure that the agreed scope is delivered. It may not be possible to buffer scope until a mutual trust is established. After two or three projects or product deliverables which were on time, and on budget, the customer may be willing to discuss prioritizing requirements and buffering scope.

Protecting the Budget Constraint

The budget for a development project is very important. If it is underestimated, money may run out and the project will fail to deliver. Failure to have enough money may result in a broken promise. Exceeding the budget represents another broken promise. Broken promises are bad for business.

Budget is buffered with money. It is that simple. How much money is needed? Once again, the size of the buffer will depend on the uncertainty. General operating expenses have a low uncertainty. Generally, the cost of the developers and their immediate overheads for office space and other costs are relatively predictable. A buffer will be needed to cope with technology and subject matter uncertainty. In other words, the larger the time buffer, the larger the budget buffer must be.

A budget buffer is needed to cope with time overrun, that is, use of the time buffer. More may be needed to cope with unforeseen costs related to technology or subject matter.

For example, if it is discovered that the team will have to invent a whole new class of middleware in order to meet the requirements, the project has been landed with some unforeseen work to meet nonfunctional (architectural) requirements. Perhaps, it is discovered that the team will need a new, expensive development tool, or the team chooses to buy components or middleware to save time and reduce risk. Technology uncertainty or risk reduction can result in extra budget demands.

When the subject matter for a new software product is poorly understood, the estimate of its complexity may be in error. As the scope is investigated during analysis and design, an area of the requirements may prove to be much more involved than previously thought. This may result in the estimate of the inventory in the system increasing. I call this discovering of unseen inventory, the revealing of scope "dark matter." Dark matter is the stuff of the universe that is known to exist, but cannot be seen or measured. Every project has a degree of dark matter. The newer the subject matter, the more dark matter there is likely to be. If the project is a Human Resources Management system with a team that has done it all before, the chance of a significant mistake in the scope and inventory estimate is unlikely. However, if the project (writing in 2003) is a leading edge wireless, enterprise resource planning system designed to run over a public packet data network delivering ERP to mobile employees in a distributed B2B value chain, then it is new territory. The need for a budget buffer to cope with uncertainty is very important.

Protecting the Resource Constraints

Other resources for a software development organization include desktop computers, all servers, network, backup systems, printers, disk storage capacity, paper, meeting rooms, wall space, tables, chairs, desks, water fountains, vending machines, and toilets, to name just a few.

It is important to remember that because software is an innately human activity, the majority of the costs are incurred by the people. If a day is lost from a developer's time because a PC broke down, it is possible that Throughput for the whole system may have been lost. It is, therefore, vital to know where the constraint is within the system of software production. If a developer works in the constraint and produces a unit of production per day and the software production system averages $10,000 of Throughput per unit, then the cost of losing one developer for only one day could be $10,000.

It doesn't make sense to lose development or test resources because of a failure in equipment. It is essential to have enough equipment for everybody and a buffer stock. The team must not lose efficiency because there is no water in the fountain or tissue paper in the toilets.

How many resources are needed in the buffer? Again, this depends on the uncertainty. These days PCs are very reliable. Perhaps you only need one or two spares for a whole business unit. Servers do not seem to be so reliable. Disk drives seem to wear out. Networks can be unpredictable, too. So can the power supply. Is the organization located somewhere that lost its power due to exceptional weather conditions—flood, snow, or ice-storm? Is the location a place where the power grid is unpredictable and brown-outs are common? It is important to protect the most precious resource and the biggest constraint—developers. In order to do so, resources must be buffered.

Classifying Uncertainty

Meyer and colleagues have classified four types of uncertainty: variation, foreseen uncertainty, unforeseen uncertainty, and chaos [Meyer 2002]. The types of uncertainty encountered will affect more than just the buffer size for project constraints, they may affect the process or system method employed.

Variation

When tasks, activities, or work units can be classified through analysis and empirical data is available for those classifications, planning is straightforward and the degree of uncertainty is firmly bounded. It is bounded by the variance normally associated with that classification. For example, if it usually takes 4 to 8 hours to produce a Servlet to process an HTTP request, then it takes 6 hours +/− 2 hours. This is variance. It can be planned for explicitly.

Over a statistical sample of items of the same classification, the variance should average out. So, to follow the example, in a project with 500 distinct HTTP requests requiring 500 Servlets, the project manager could expect these to take 3,000 hours.

Foreseen Uncertainty

Foreseen uncertainty is identifiable and understood but may not happen. In the example, the user interface design for a website may have specified 500 HTTP requests. However, it is foreseeable that the UI designer will change the design and the total number of Servlets required will change.

There is far greater uncertainty associated with this problem. For example, a relatively mild redesign may involve 10% of the Servlets required. Some of these may have been coded already, in which case they are waste. When work completed is wasted, the effect is to increase the total amount of work required.

There is a greater amount of uncertainty involved in foreseeable uncertainty.

Both variation and foreseen uncertainty were classified by Edwards Deming as "common cause" variation, that is, they are endemic to the process.[2]

---

[2]Walter A. Shewart called this "controlled" variation [Wheeler 1992] page 3.

Unforeseen Uncertainty

This is most likely to occur when a team is pushing the bounds of known technology, such as a team working at the edge of extreme innovation and venturing into research or invention. It is not known, and cannot be known, in advance, if it will encounter a major impediment to its success.

When a team is operating at the edge of the envelope, an even greater buffer for uncertainty will be required.

Chaos

The difference between chaos and unforeseen uncertainty is that a team that encounters unforeseen uncertainty would at least have a firm idea of what it was trying to achieve. Such a team has firm goals and objectives. A team in a land of chaos doesn't necessarily understand what it is doing or where it is going. It could be that the market is not understood and that the potential customers are not even aware they have a need for a product. In this space, everything can change all of the time. Because there is no defined goal, there can be no defined plan.

Deming would classify, unforeseen uncertainty and chaos as "special cause" variation, that is, each event tends to be unique and unlikely to be repeated. Special cause variation is not endemic to the process.[3]

Local Safety

There is a recognized problem with estimating fine grained tasks or deliverables. This problem is known as the "local safety" problem. It can lead to significantly inaccurate estimates caused by explainable human psychology.

If asked how long a small task will take, a developer will naturally not want to deliver it late. After all, this is a small task, it should be on time or the developer wouldn't be professional. Hence, the estimate will include a buffer to absorb the developer's uncertainty about the task.

The estimate given by the developer will depend on how confident that developer is that he has understood the task and knows how to perform it. If there is uncertainty in the understanding of the task, then the estimated time to completion is likely to be significantly longer. No one wants to be late with such a small task.

Consider the graph in Figure 4–1, which shows confidence against the actual time to complete the task. It shows that there are a number of inexperienced developers who will underestimate due to overconfidence. However, most will overestimate, often by as much as 100% or 200%.

---

[3]Walter A. Shewart called this "uncontrolled" variation [Wheeler 1992] page 3.

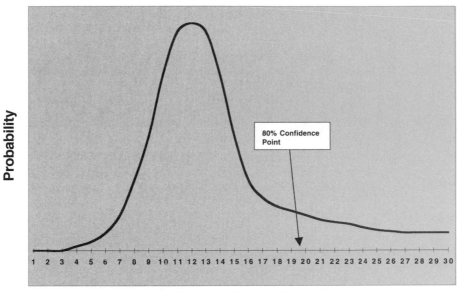

Figure 4–1
Estimated delivery of a 12-day task.

Specifically, Figure 4–1 shows a task that is most likely to complete on the 12th day. Overconfidence can lead to some estimates as little as 5 days. Other estimates will be as long as 30 days. Goldratt predicts that developers with an 80% confidence about the task duration will suggest around 20 days for the task. The difference between 20 and 12 is known as the local safety, that is, 8 days.

So a 12-day task may be estimated as up to 30 days. Imagine if this was to happen across a project with 2,000 tasks. The estimates for the whole project would be wildly inaccurate. In fact, the project might look so costly that it is cancelled before it is even started.

How can this problem be avoided?

Goldratt's first truly astute assertion about project management [Goldratt 1997] is that in an accurately planned project consisting of many tasks, approximately half the tasks will be slightly late, assuming the planning was accurate. This is very counterintuitive, but it is a fact. If a project is accurately planned and delivered on time, statistically approximately half the tasks should be early and half should be late. Accepting this notion is hard, but once accepted, it is possible to consider the solution.

Accurate project planning techniques must avoid asking developers to estimate small tasks based on effort. The tasks to be performed must be broken out based on some form of (relative) complexity and risk. To work best, this requires a codification scheme for assessing the complexity and risk. An analysis method that enables small pieces of client-valued functionality to be codified for complexity or risk is required. This enables the inventory in the system of software production to be estimated without the psychological effect of local safety. By not asking the developer to estimate how long it will take, the local safety problem is removed. In Chapter 33, we will consider how effective various Agile and traditional methods are at codifying inventory to facilitate assessment of complexity in a repeatable fashion.

Hence, complexity and risk analysis of the inventory are the keys to providing estimates without local safety. There are several techniques for doing this: Function Points in structured analysis, Feature Complexity in FDD, and Story Size and Risk Points in XP.

It is possible to correlate the level of effort involved in a given unit of inventory through empirical measure. Historical data for recent projects can be used to estimate the level of effort involved in processing inventory of a given risk or complexity. This data can then be used to estimate how long it will take to process the remaining inventory through the software production system.

Aggregation Reduces Uncertainty

Donald Reinertsen explains the statistical reduction of uncertainty through aggregation of sequential and parallel processes [1997, pp. 93 & 212]. The uncertainty (or variability) in a set of sequential processes reduces as a percentage of the total when the sequential processes are combined. Specifically, for sequential activities the total uncertainty is the square root of the sum of the squares.

$$\sigma_{Total} = \sqrt{(\sigma_1)^2 + (\sigma_2)^2 + (\sigma_3)^2 + \ldots + (\sigma_n)^2}$$

Consider this equation for the 12-day activity shown in Figure 4–1, which had a local safety buffer of 8 days. If there were three such activities to run sequentially, the aggregate uncertainty equation would look like this:

$$13.856 = \sqrt{(8)^2 + (8)^2 + (8)^2}$$

This is a very significant result. The local safety for the three tasks adds to 24 days, but the required uncertainty buffer is approximately 14 days. Hence, the total time required for the three activities is

$$Total\ Time = 12 + 12 + 12 + 13.856 \cong 50$$

The normal plan estimate would have used the local estimations of 20 days for each activity providing a total estimate of 60 days. The overestimation is 10 days or 16.7%. The more activities in the plan, the worse this problem will become.

It is vital that local safety is eliminated from estimates of effort. Inclusion of local safety leads to estimates that are false. False estimates undermine trust. Without trust it is impossible to properly manage a software production system.

For parallel dependent activities, the aggregate uncertainty is the single greatest uncertainty from the activities. For the example given, if all three tasks were undertaken in parallel, the aggregate buffer required would be only 8 days.

Summary

Uncertainty in software production is inevitable. There are five general constraints in software development—delivery date, budget, people, scope, and resources. Uncertainty can apply to any of the constraints.

Uncertainty is addressed through provision of a buffer. The buffer is generally provided in the same form as the constraint, for example, people are buffered with more people.

The provision of buffers on constraints is easier to negotiate under conditions of trust between the supplier and the customer. Trust is built over time with delivery of agreed functionality. Trust is maintained through transparency of process and mutual understanding.

There are four types of uncertainty—variation, foreseen, unforeseen, and chaos. The types of uncertainty encountered in a given software project will affect the size of the required buffers.

Buffers should not be estimated on small tasks. Small tasks suffer from the local safety problem. Aggregating small tasks before estimating the buffer size reduces the total buffer required.

Aggregation of buffers from sequential tasks results in a total buffer that is defined as the square root of the sum of the squares of the local safety buffers.

chapter 5

Software Production Metrics

When selecting metrics for control of a system, it is essential to focus on simplicity and relevance to the system goal. Metrics should ideally be self-generating and should provide leading or predictive indication of the system performance rather than lagging or reactive performance [Reinertsen 1997, pp. 197–217].

Choosing Metrics

In the case of the software production system, it is important that the production metrics reflect and support the financial metrics from Chapter 2. Production metrics must be driven from economics. If the process control metrics do not directly relate to the economics and financial goals of the system, then they are not appropriate.

Agile Software Production Metrics

The quantity of the system input (ideas) relates to the Investment. The Inventory level within the system can demonstrate the current location of the Investment and its progress towards becoming Throughput. The production quantity coming out of the system will directly relate to Throughput. The lead time from input to output will show how long Investment was committed within the system. All of these metrics meet the criteria of being both simple and relevant. They allow the flow of value through the system to be tracked and the value of working code delivered to be recorded.

Inventory-based metrics can also be self-generating based on the stage of transformation of the idea into working code. Records of the transformation as electronic documents can be sourced from the version or document control system.

Inventory-based metrics are predictive. Inventory at the input to the system can be used, based on historical production rate data, to predict the flow through the system.

Tracking Inventory and its flow through the software production system provides metrics that meet all the ideal characteristics for a control system.

Traditional Software Production Metrics

Traditional methods of controlling software production systems have focused on the use of effort-based metrics. The old bellwether has been the line of code (LOC). Almost everyone in the software business will tell you that lines of code is a useless metric. The problem with LOC is that it is an effort-based metric. It is meaningless for measuring the delivery of software value, the output from the system. However, for want of a better metric, lines of code remained popular for a long time.

Another favorite metric is the level-of-effort estimate, generally an estimate in man-hours for the development of a certain piece of requested functionality. The effort expended in hours is then compared with the estimate and adjusted periodically.

Traditional software metrics relate to the Operating Expense (OE) metric from Chapter 2. Traditional software metrics are compatible and perhaps heavily influenced by traditional cost accounting methods. They are focused on cost. Focusing on managing OE is suboptimal in achieving the system goal of more profit now and in the future, with a healthy ROI. It is more important to focus on Throughput and Inventory. Hence, traditional metrics do not meet the criteria for relevance.

Nor do they meet the criteria for simplicity. Brooks [1995] and others have pointed out that the business of software production is nonlinear. As software production is a complex system with feedback loops, it exhibits nonlinear behavior, that is, the effort expended in the system to produce lines of working code is not proportional to the quantity or quality of the output from the system. Hence, tracking effort-based metrics requires the translation through an unknown nonlinear equation in order to communicate client-valued functionality.

Effort-based metrics are not always self-generating. Every developer who has filled in a time sheet can tell you that the time sheet did not self-generate.

Effort-based metrics are not very useful as predictive indicators because of the nonlinear nature of software development and inaccuracy in estimation. The estimate is unlikely to represent the final outcome. Hence, the actual results must be gathered historically. When a developer fills a time sheet, it is an historical record rather than a predictive estimate. Hence, time sheets and effort recoding are lagging indicators.

Traditional software development metrics of lines of code written or time expended do not meet any of the ideal characteristics for system control metrics.

The Inventory in the system of software production must be measured through measures of client-valued functionality. The client of the client-valued functionality is the business owner, or customer, who is paying for the software. The ideas captured as functional requirements or a marketing feature list represent the raw material for the software production system. Requirements represent the ideas being transformed into executable code. These are often referred to as the functional requirements.

Nonfunctional Requirements and Inventory

Are nonfunctional or architectural requirements, for example, performance characteristics, of interest, and should they be tracked?

Nonfunctional requirements should be defined with a minimum requirement. This minimum requirement represents the level below which the functional requirements are not viable in the market. In other words, the functional requirements have no Throughput value unless a minimum level of nonfunctional specification is met. Hence, the base level of nonfunctional requirements does not require individual tracking. If the base level of performance cannot be met, the functional requirement would not be considered as delivered or complete. As functional requirements are being tracked, it is inferred that base level nonfunctional requirements are being tracked along with them.

It is therefore vital to skillfully manage the development of nonfunctional requirements. Excess work on nonfunctional requirements will increase OE, increase lead time, and decrease T.

However, there are preferred levels of nonfunctional performance that could be considered market differentiating, and these have a Throughput value. As they have a Throughput value and extra effort must be undertaken to achieve the additional performance, they should be tracked as Inventory through the system. The idea for the market differentiating performance is the input to the system, and working code that delivers the performance is the output. Architectural features for these ideas should be created and tracked as Inventory in the system.

Software Production Is Development Rather Than Research

There may be product or service concepts that are exceptionally new and are dominated by nonfunctional requirements, for example, on-demand, interactive video streaming broadcast over the Internet. Such projects are probably more rightly classified as research activity and should not be tracked with a management system such as the one described. This system of management is intended for development projects that are mostly infomatic in nature and can be thought of as software production rather than algorithmic research.

Tasks Are Not Inventory

Tasks represent effort that must be expended. They are essentially an internal organization of activity in the software production system. Tasks are not a system input and hence do not represent Inventory. Tasks are actions performed inside the system to move input through the system and generate output. A task list might be an essential project management tool, but it is of no interest to the client. It does not help the customer for the output of the system assess how much value has been delivered. The client does not value a task such as, "Assess the use of the Vitria™ message bus for loosely coupled asynchronous messaging of distributed components." There is no direct correlation between development system tasks and delivery of value. Tasks are interesting only to the internal system. They do not represent the Inventory in the system or the output from the system.

Expressions of Inventory

Inventory can be expressed in different ways depending on the software engineering lifecycle method being used. This will be examined in depth in Section 2. In general, a unit of inventory is an idea for a client-valued function described in a format suitable for use by software developers. In UDP, a unit of inventory is a Use Case. In Extreme Programming, it is a Story Point. In FDD, it is a Feature from the Feature List. In traditional SDLC structured methods, the Function Point is the unit of inventory.

Measuring Production Quantity

Chapter 2 established that Throughput is the most important metric. Production Quantity is the output from the system of production that directly relates to the financial metrics of Throughput. Hence, the production system must track Production Quantity—the output of client-valued functions as working code. In Figure 5–1 production Quantity (Q) is generated by the system of software production from units of Inventory (V) at a rate (R).

Because the system of software production is treated as a continuous process producing a stream of software, it is more interesting to monitor the derivative of Q, the Production Rate (R). R is the quantity of functional requirements, expressed in the same units as the Inventory (V) delivered out of the system in a given period of time.

Figure 5–1
Inventory in the software production system.

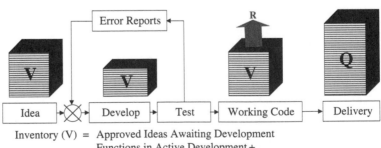

Inventory (V) = Approved Ideas Awaiting Development
Functions in Active Development +
Completed Functions (not yet delivered)

Tracking Inventory with a Cumulative Flow Diagram

The inventory throughout the system can be conveniently tracked using a cumulative flow diagram[1]—a technique borrowed from Lean Production.

In Figure 5–2, the height between the deployment line and the requirements line displays the total inventory in the system. Different software development methods produce different patterns of cumulative flow. The pattern could be thought of as a method signature. Cumulative flow method signatures for each type of software development method will be discussed in Section 2. The pattern shown in Figure 5–2 represents a very Agile process with new material being fed into the system each week and little more than a week of inventory queuing at each step in the system.

Lead Time

There is a derivative measure of Inventory (V) which is important to calculations of OE—Lead Time (LT). Lead Time measures the length of time that Inventory stays in the system. Lead Time is how long it takes a unit of V to pass through the system from input to output. This is sometimes known as cycle time or queue time plus service time.

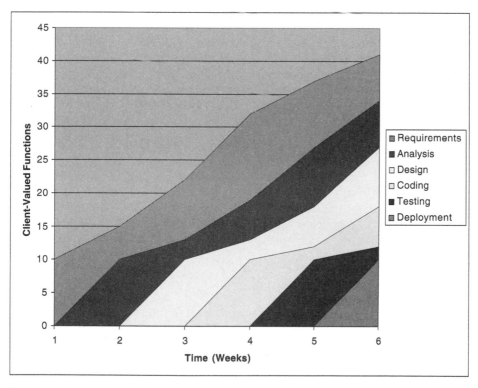

Figure 5–2
Cumulative flow of system inventory.

---

[1]Donald Reinertsen introduced the idea of using cumulative flow diagrams for design activities in *Managing the Design Factory*, p. 50.

Lead Time relates to the financial metrics from Chapter 2 because there is investment sunk in the inventory of ideas. The investment must be financed. The faster ideas can be turned into working code and delivered to a customer, the quicker inventory can be released. Releasing inventory faster has the effect of reducing the overall inventory in the system. Lead Time (LT) and Inventory (V) are related. This relationship is directly proportional as long as the production rate of the system remains constant. This is known as Little's Law.

LT has direct relevance to business. It determines how long it will be before the potential value added, stored in the inventory will be released as Throughput. The value of the Throughput may be affected by LT. The customer may be willing to pay more for shorter LT and hence, T is increased with shorter LT.

OE per Unit

The cost to transform a single unit of inventory through the system is the OE per unit or the Average Cost Per Function (ACPF). This must be determined by examining the global production quantity for a given period of the whole system and dividing it into the OE for operating the system for a period of time.

$$ACPF = \frac{OE_{Quarter}}{Q_{Quarter}}$$

For example, if OE per quarter is $1,350,000 and production is 30 units per month, as shown in Figure 5–2, ACPF will be $15,000.

$$ACPF = \$15,000 = \frac{\$1,350,000}{90}$$

Care must be taken to determine the cost to process inventory through individual steps in the system. If the system has been balanced using a Drum-Buffer-Rope subordination to the system constraint, for example, System Test in Figure 3–1, then there will be idle capacity in many steps in the system. Figure 3–1 showed that steps such as Coding had a capacity of 50 units per month. After subordination there will be 20 units of spare capacity. As all OE is a fixed cost, then production can be increased in nonbottleneck steps without incurring additional OE. Hence, the cost accounting concept of a cost per unit in a local process step is dangerous and misleading. The cost accounting approach shows reduced cost per unit when nonbottleneck capacity is used to increase local production. The local cost per unit is also called "efficiency," which was discussed in Chapter 2.

The only valid and useful cost metric for software production is ACPF; the purpose of which is purely estimation of future OE.

Summary

The software production system must measure the inventory level (V) at each step in the process, including the input. The total inventory held in the system is directly related to the Investment (I) metric from Chapter 1. The rate of delivery of production, the Production Rate, (R), for the whole system is directly related to financial metric Throughput (T). The cost (OE) of moving a single unit of inventory through the system is the Average Cost per Function (ACPF). This can be determined by the OE for a given period of time divided by the Production Quantity (Q), for the same period. Hence, Q, V, and ACPF are the equivalent production metrics to the financial metrics T, I, and OE.

chapter 6

Agile Project Management

The traditional project management model focuses on locking the scope for a project and negotiating or varying the budget (including people and resources) and the delivery date. The PMI and ISO-9000 models for project management are based on this paradigm. In fact, the ISO-9000 definition of quality is derived from the model. Quality here is defined as delivering the scope that was promised, fully functional, on or before the delivery date.

When the scope is defined first, it forces the engineers to estimate the level of effort required to transform the ideas into working code. As discussed in Chapter 4, estimations are prone to uncertainty, and the amount of uncertainty can be very large—resulting in time buffers of as much as 200% of the estimate.

The budget has considerably less uncertainty attached to it. Over a short time window, most or all costs are fixed and the staffing level, resources available, and cost of maintaining them are known. On longer projects, there may be some variance, but it is never likely to be in the order of 200%.

The date has almost no uncertainty attached to it. If the date has been determined by a new law, the constraint is external to the business. If the date has been chosen internally, it is also unlikely to shift by much. Entire marketing programs are arranged around dates, and the cost of missing a date is very high. Marketing dollars are deployed, sales staff and customer care personnel are trained for the new product arrival, stock market analysts have been informed, and customers are told when to expect the new product or system.

Generally, the date has the most certainty, the budget is a close second, and the scope is a distant third. The scope and, more importantly, the estimate attached to it have the greatest uncertainty.

The ISO-9000/PMI model for project management created the worst possible environment for managers. It created a world where the estimate had to be very accurate. The focus in the software engineering world, therefore, has been on achieving greater accuracy of estimates. A reinforcing loop was created where more analysis techniques were required to better understand software development, which would lead to better estimates. However, there was a side effect that created a balancing loop. More and more analysis techniques meant a higher barrier to entry, more and more paperwork, and longer and longer timescales while paperwork was created, read, debated, and agreed. The result was heavyweight, traditional software methods. Lengthening the timescales ultimately limited the ability of estimates to get any more certain.

Traditional Versus RAD Model for Project Management

Figure 6–1

Alternative focus of
PMI and RAD PM
models.

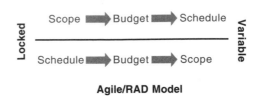

The problem was recognized in the early 1990s by the Rapid Application Development movement (RAD), which turned the traditional model on its head by fixing the delivery date first, then varying the budget and scope to fit the date. However, RAD did not entirely eliminate estimating techniques or achieve negotiable scope buffers, see Figure 6–1.

Most Agile methods, for example, DSDM are derived from earlier RAD approaches. The implication of this is that Agile methods require a negotiable scope and an agreed scope buffer in order to be successful. As discussed in Chapter 4, obtaining the customer agreement for a scope buffer—"optional" or "nice to have" requirements—is difficult. It requires trust between customer and supplier. Such a trust relationship does not generally exist at the initiation of a relationship between a software supplier and the customer for the system. The customer has learned from years of experience that software is always late, always over budget, and does not function properly. The customer has no trust in the software supplier.

One notable standout in the world of Agile methods is Feature Driven Development (FDD), which does not fix the delivery date. Instead FDD allows both the date and the scope to move within some tight bounds.[1] This model provides the flexibility with which to gain the trust required for a fixed date and variable scope.

Task Planning and Effort Tracking

The traditional model created a need for accurate estimating, which led to a management focus on determining the tasks to be undertaken and the effort involved in each task. There were perhaps thousands of years of project management history, and the paradigm was well established. The task and effort paradigm was mixed at the larger grained level with the Scientific Management paradigm to create phases of development and effective gates for partial completion of the project. The combination resulted in the Software Development Lifecycle (SDLC), or "waterfall," model for software production. SDLC is examined more fully in Section 2.

The task planning and effort expended paradigm does not represent a systems thinking approach to management of software production.

---

[1]Jeff De Luca explains this in detail in *Getting Flexible with Planning*, *Feature Driven Development Newsletter*, January 2003, http://www.featuredrivendevelopment.com/node.php?id=508.

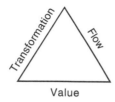

Chapters 1–5 have shown that estimating, measuring, and tracking the effort expended is not useful in determining output from the system of software production—the value delivered to the customer. Task planning and effort tracking have been described as a one-dimensional model of project management [Koskela 2002].

Such a model is also compatible with cost accounting and is OE focused. What is really required is a model of project management that focuses on delivered value and management of inventory. Such a method would be compatible with Throughput Accounting and would be focused on T and I.

Koskela and Howell have proposed a three-dimensional model of project management, as shown in Figure 6–2, that focuses on managing the flow of value through a series of transformations [Koskela 2002]. Such a model would fit nicely with the Systems Thinking and Throughput Accounting-based model for software production proposed in Chapter 2.

Cost Accounting Tracks Value Added

The traditional cost accounting world tracks value added to raw material as it passes along a value chain. In software development, this manifests itself as the measurement of effort expended in tasks that are all assumed to add value. This assumption is probably false. Many tasks in traditional software development do not add value, but produce by-product or waste.

Nevertheless, the completed time sheets from the software developers have been used to determine the value added. The value added to the raw material is determined as the amount of money spent completing the task. Hence, cost accounting values the incomplete inventory by the OE expended on it and not by the potential client value, Throughput (T). This is best explained with a diagram.

Figure 6–3 shows a simplistic example in which an idea is transformed into working code over a 6-week period. As each week goes by, the value recorded for Investment increases as value is added to the partially complete software. The cost of each transformation is booked as value added at the completion of each task.

In Chapter 3, the concept that software ideas are perishable was introduced. The cost accounting approach increases the value of the Investment in the incomplete code, whilst Throughput Accounting would depreciate the value. Throughput Accounting assumes that the Investment is reducing due to the nature of change in the business world, whilst cost accounting reports the opposite. Cost accounting results in senior management believing that

Example Value Flow	Requirements (Investment)	Analysis	Design	Code	Test	Deploy (Value Add)
Week 1	$100	-	-	-	-	-
Week 2	-	$120	-	-	-	-
Week 3	-	-	$140	-	-	-
Week 4	-	-	-	$160	-	-
Week 5	-	-	-	-	$180	-
Week 6	-	-	-	-	-	$200

Time →

Value Added to Inventory →

Figure 6-3
Tracking value added as Investment in Inventory.

they have an asset when they may actually have a liability. The larger the project, the more misleading the numbers will be.

A large project may be due for delivery when it is discovered that it no longer meets the market requirements. The deliverable is of little Throughput value. Change requests will be submitted for new ideas that have current market value, that is, they have a Throughput value. The Investment, in the now worthless, partially complete software, will need to be written off.

The combination of tracking effort expended and recording it as value added produces misleading management information that results in poor quality executive decisions.

Throughput Accounting Tracks the Flow of the Investment Value

Throughput Accounting treats all effort expended in the system as Operating Expense. OE is treated as a cost and never attributed as value added. Throughput Accounting does not recognize the concept of value added. Value is recorded at only two points in the system: the value of the input—Investment (I); and the value of the output—Throughput (T). While the input passes through the system before it is transformed into output, the Investment is depreciated. I is reduced during the system Lead Time (LT). Depreciating I creates an incentive to minimize LT. Cost accounting leads to local optimization by tracking value added. Cost accounting does not discourage the growth of LT. Through tracking the value of working code delivered, Throughput Accounting focuses management attention on the holistic system of software production, leading to global optima.

In Throughput Accounting, there is no need to track tasks and effort expended on each individual task. There is no need for software developers to fill out time sheets.

Example Value Flow	Requirements (Investment)	Analysis	Design	Code	Test	Deploy (Value Add)
Week 1	$100	-	-	-	-	-
Week 2	-	$100	-	-	-	-
Week 3	-	-	$100	-	-	-
Week 4	-	-	-	$100	-	-
Week 5	-	-	-	-	$100	-
Week 6	-	-	-	-	-	$200

Time →

Value →

Figure 6–4
Tracking the flow of Investment value.

Figure 6–4 shows the same example as Figure 6–3, but using Throughput Accounting. An idea is developed into working code over a 6-week period. The flow of the Investment in the idea is tracked through each step of the process, but value is not added. This example does not show any depreciation during the 6-week period. The Throughput value is recognized only in week 6 when the software is delivered.

Tracking investment value in this manner is entirely consistent with tracking the inventory using the cumulative flow diagram presented in Chapter 5. The software production metrics in Chapter 5 are consistent with the financial metrics from Chapter 2, which are both compatible and consistent with the proposed three-dimensional model of Agile project management.

All of this creates the rather uncomfortable conclusion that traditional project management is obsolete in the world of Agile software development.

The Project Manager's New Work

Agile software development creates a paradigm shift for project managers. The job of project management is no longer to create a list of tasks, collect a set of estimates for each task, create a Gantt chart that predicts the end date for the project, and maintain the chart throughout the life of the project. All of that work is obsolete.

The project manager's new work is to assist the flow of value and the continuous generation of Throughput by maintaining the Issue Log and running down issues before they delay the delivery date. Unresolved issues prevent flow and cause Inventory buildup. The project manager monitors the project buffers and reports significant events—events that will impact the delivery date—to the senior management. This role is discussed in Chapter 7, and the full role for the Agile project manager is discussed in Chapter 8.

Example Value Flow	Requirements (Investment)	Analysis	Design	Code	Test	Deploy (Value Add)
Week 1	10	-	-	-	-	-
Week 2	5	10	-	-	-	-
Week 3	7	3	10	-	-	-
Week 4	10	6	3	10	-	-
Week 5	5	8	5	2	10	-
Week 6	4	7	9	6	2	10

Time (vertical axis) · **Value** (horizontal axis)

Figure 6–5
Tracking the flow of inventory.

Tracking the Flow of Value with a Cumulative Flow Diagram

On a day-to-day basis the flow of value can be tracked using the software production metrics from Chapter 5 and the cumulative flow diagram. Figure 6–5 shows the inventory levels for each step in the software production system for a period of 6 weeks. Each unit of inventory represents a single client-valued idea that has reached a particular stage of transformation.

Figure 6–5 can be visualized using the cumulative flow diagram Figure 6–6.

Summary

Donald Reinertsen [1997, ch. 11] stated that the choice of metrics for a design system should be simple, relevant (focused on value-added), self-generating, and leading (predictive). This chapter has shown that a three-dimensional model of project management that tracks the flow of value through a series of transformations can be achieved by using the software production metrics from Chapter 5, R and V, which are simple, relevant, self-generating, and leading. All of this can be easily visualized in a single graph—a cumulative flow diagram. Hence, Agile project management can be achieved by replacing a Gantt chart with a cumulative flow diagram and a plan for the release of inventory into the system.

The existing PMI/ISO model for project management is obsolete. It does not lend itself to a world of constant change and shortening business cycles. Attempts to improve the estimation of software and reduce the variance in order to better improve the results from the traditional model of project management are doomed to failure because of the balancing loop in the system, which creates more paperwork and lengthens lead times.

The existing model of project management was compatible with cost accounting, but generated misleading data that lulled senior management into believing that incomplete software was an asset rather than a liability.

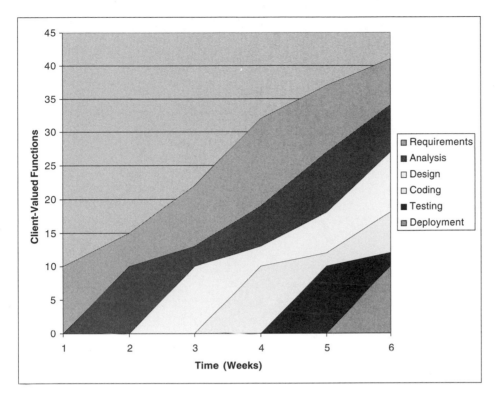

Figure 6–6
Cumulative flow of inventory for Figure 6–5

Throughput Accounting is compatible with a three-dimensional model of project management that tracks the flow of value and does not record value-added on partially complete work. Throughput Accounting records effort expended on transformation as pure operating expense and depreciates the value of the initial investment in requirements. This provides better quality information to senior management who will then become focused on reducing lead times and realizing Throughput earlier.

chapter 7

Agile Project Planning

Once the flow of value through the software production system has been stabilized and the current Lead Time (LT), for the system established, it is possible to estimate the total LT for a release or project. A release or project is simply a collection of feature requests—an aggregation of units of inventory for the software production system.

However, multiplying the Production Rate, (R), by the size of the release, (V), to get a total Lead Time makes a huge assumption—that nothing prevents the continuous flow of transformation through the software production system. The estimate is unprotected. It assumes that the inventory tends towards an average size and that any new project will reflect a similar complexity per unit as a previous one. There is no allowance for uncertainty.

Chapter 4 discussed techniques for dealing with uncertainty and explained how uncertainty is reduced by aggregation. The project delivery date can be protected by creating a buffer of time based on the uncertainty attached to the aggregated set of ideas. Such a buffer is known as a project buffer. It could vary from as little as 15% to as much as 200%.

The Project Buffer

In manufacturing, units of inventory are generally not assembled randomly into finished products. It often makes sense to assemble smaller pieces from raw material and later integrate the small pieces into larger pieces. There may be several layers of logical groupings before the final large assemblies are pieced together into a finished product. The logical groupings that go together to form these interim products may be controlled by the process the material must pass through, the type of machine required, the technology involved, or the physical location of the final product. Manufacturers often talk of four levels—components, subassemblies, assemblies, and products, for example microchips, motherboards, base units, and finished PCs.

It is common in software projects for many things to be done in parallel. A software project with 20 people may have several requirements, all being constructed at any given moment in time. Individual components may be assembled into larger units that can be tested on their own or together with others via integration, system, or product testing.

Logical Collections of Inventory

Table 7–1
Inventory aggregation appropriate for testing.

Inventory	Test Level
Component/Function (idea)	Unit Test
Subassembly/Batch	Integration Test
Assembly	System Test
Product/Release	Product Test/Stress Test/UAT

These various levels of partial deliverables are simply logical groupings of inventory, for example, functions, classes, packages, and complete executable programs. The specific groupings may depend on both the software development method being used and the technology or architecture in use.

Hence, when planning a release, it is not sufficient to assume that an aggregate number of ideas can be assembled randomly. Some planning is required in the assembly.

Group Inventory for Convenient Testing

The logical grouping of functions in an interim product should be grouped according to how they will be tested. Table 7–1 shows some possible groupings of inventory. There will necessarily be dependencies between such interim deliverables, for example, the user interface will be dependent on the business logic, which in turn is dependent on system interfaces and data management (or persistent storage mapping).

It is important that the project is planned so that large aggregations of inventory that are dependent on others are planned to arrive when they are needed. It is not necessary to plan the dependencies for individual units of inventory (functions, features, Use Cases), but merely to determine which grouping they are within and when that grouping is needed.

The Critical Path and Parallel Paths

In project management, the Critical Path is defined as the longest path through real time required for a single chain of dependent tasks to complete in order. By definition, if one item on the Critical Path is delayed, then the project is delayed.

Goldratt's second truly astute assertion about project management is that eventually everything hits the Critical Path [1997]. In plain language, this means that sooner or later every deliverable has the potential to delay the project. If any one feature request gets blocked—any one unit of inventory can't flow through the system—then the project delivery date may be jeopardized.

If it is intended that pieces of a software project be developed in parallel, then a PERT chart for the delivery of the pieces can be drawn. It can be used to signify the Critical Path and indicate the dependencies between the deliverables.

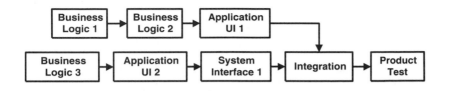

Figure 7–1
Software project with
two parallel tracks.

In Figure 7–1, the path beginning with Business Logic 1 is happening in parallel and is not on the Critical Path. It doesn't hit the Critical Path until System Interface 1 becomes dependent on it. The question arises, at what point must the parallel path be started, in order for it to be delivered when it is needed by the Critical Path? If it is not delivered on time, it will delay the Integration and affect the overall delivery date.

Initially, such a delay would use the available project buffer. Once the project buffer is eaten, every delay in delivering a non-Critical Path item will delay the overall project. Hence, delays in non-Critical Path items can affect the ability to deliver a project on time, if not started at the appropriate time with an appropriate buffer for uncertainty.

The question to be answered is, "When should these non-Critical Path pieces of development begin?" This is normally considered a cost optimization problem. It is not desirable to start the non-Critical Path piece too early because it increases the work-in-process (WIP) inventory in the system. Increasing WIP inventory increases the OE and requires more budget, people, and resources.

Early Start

In a worst case scenario, all parallel pieces would start at the beginning of a project, minimizing the risks by providing the longest possible time for each task. However, it also generates the largest amount of WIP inventory and greatly increases OE.

The early start shown in Figure 7–2 creates extra demand for resources. WIP inventory would be equivalent to the total inventory in the system. There is a very strong correlation between required manpower, budget, resources, and WIP inventory. The correlation between them is nonlinear, that is, a linear increase in WIP Inventory creates a nonlinear increase in staff, budget, and resources and, consequently, a nonlinear increase in OE. Starting everything early increases OE and total required working capital. It might minimize the risks, but it is the most expensive option. It reduces Net Profit and ROI.

Late Start

The obvious alternative is that each parallel path could be started at the latest possible moment. This does two things. It optimizes cash flow by reducing OE, and it maximizes risk. The estimates for the collection of smaller tasks to be started in parallel have no safety built in. They were estimated using an agile technique that eliminates local safety and places all the safety in the project buffer. The project buffer is buffering the Critical Path—the project delivery date, or time constraint (see Figure 7–3).

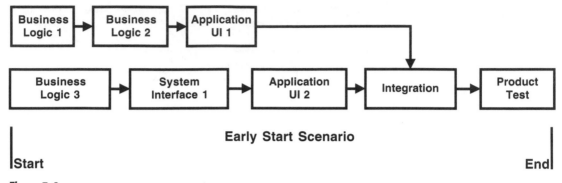

Early Start Scenario

Start   End

Figure 7–2
Early start of parallel path.

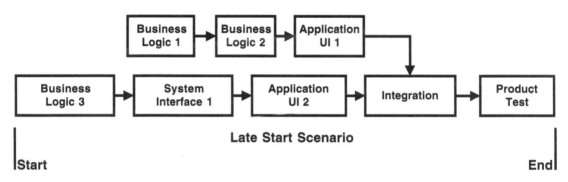

Late Start Scenario

Start   End

Figure 7–3
Late start of parallel path.

Feeding Buffers

The answer is simple. Each parallel path must be treated as its own separate aggregation with its own separate delivery date. The delivery date is the date when the subsystem is needed on the Critical Path. In order to guarantee that the subsystem is delivered on time, its delivery date must be protected by a buffer. A buffer must be calculated for each parallel path or feeding chain. The requirements for each feeding chain must be considered separately, using the same local-safety free method of complexity and risk assessment. The uncertainty associated with this subset of the total requirements should be used to calculate a suitable buffer for the feeding chain. The start date of the feeding chain can then be backed out from the point where the deliverable is needed on the Critical Path.

Buffer Usage

Feeding chains and the Critical Path must all be monitored for buffer usage. The completion of client-valued deliverables in each feeding chain and the Critical Path must be monitored against the original estimate. The rate of delivery, (R), from each feeding chain and the Critical Path must be monitored. The estimated buffer usage, or buffer remaining for each feeding chain must be monitored. As long as the feeding buffers are not used in full, the Critical Path (that is, the project schedule or time constraint) is protected. The project will be delivered on time.

It is worth reiterating Reinertsen's advice for choosing what to measure. Metrics must be simple, relevant, preferably self-generating, and preferably leading or predictive rather than lagging or reactive.

Now that a method for Agile project planning has been described, it is necessary to choose measurements that allow the tracking of the project execution against the plan.

The plan consists of a series of parallel paths for assembly and integration of large grained components for the product or release. Each large grained component is an aggregation of inventory—a collection of client-valued functionality. The Critical Path has been determined, and a delivery date agreed.

Buffer Usage

If the project tracking metric is to be relevant, it must relate directly to the Critical Path and the parallel feeding paths. Each path has a buffer, and buffer usage determines whether or not the Critical Path is affected. The relevant metric is buffer usage.

Each feeding buffer and the overall project buffer should be monitored for usage. There are three possible variations on buffer usage: percentage used, actual days used, and actual days remaining. Experts are divided over which buffer usage mechanism is best. It is generally agreed that the three options produce similar results. The actual buffer usage is important, but if the metric is to be useful and predictive, the rate of buffer usage is also important.

If buffer usage is tracked as a percentage, significance of the percentage used will vary as the project timeline is executed. Figure 7–4 provides an example, a tool for assessing whether or not the buffer usage is critical.

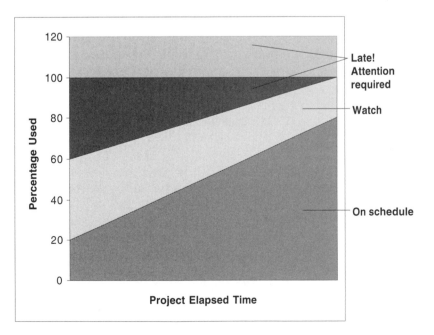

Figure 7–4
Assessing buffer usage.

If a recently started project has already absorbed 40% of its project buffer, it would be shown as "Yellow," or "Watch," status. Attempts should be underway to unblock issues, and negotiation may be taking place, with the intent of recovering some of the lost buffer, for example, some scope reduction.

Later in the project, a 40% buffer usage may not be considered critical, and the project can be reported as "Green," or "On Time." Buffer usage greater than 100% would automatically be "Red," or "Late," status.

Blocked Inventory and Issue Log

The likelihood that the buffer will be used in total and why it is being used are also important. Likely impact on buffers can be tracked by monitoring the individual units of inventory blocked and the trend in blocked inventory. Blocked inventory is a simple and predictive indicator. Blocked inventory may use buffer, and failure to unblock it will eventually lead to an impact on the Critical Path. As Goldratt observed, eventually everything hits the Critical Path.

Each piece of blocked client-valued functionality should have an issue raised against it. The issue should state the reason for the blockage. Hence, the size of the issue log and the trend in issues open will provide a simple and predictive indicator of buffer usage. Both open issues and blocked inventory indicate that the Critical Path (the delivery date and time constraint) is in danger.

Project Management Metrics

To summarize, the project tracking metrics required are the project buffer usage, the usage of each feeding buffer, the quantity of inventory blocked and the trend, and the number of open issues and the trend. Each issue should be related to one or more blocked units of inventory.

Resource Constraints

So far, resource constraints have been ignored in this chapter. There has been an underlying assumption that the system of software production has sufficient developers and testers to complete the work. This assumption is possible if a Drum-Buffer-Rope inventory management mechanism has been implemented [Goldratt 1990a]. If the flow of inventory into the system is regulated at the pace of the system constraint, the estimated delivery dates should be possible based on the current production rate of the system.

The main project planning constraint is the schedule or delivery date. Assuming that this was negotiated based on the capacity of the software production system, the schedule should be achievable under normal circumstances. To ensure that circumstances are normal, the feeding buffers and project buffer can be monitored. Any uncertainty should be absorbed by the buffers. However, this does not make the delivery date completely safe.

There is a hidden assumption that all developers and testers were born equal. If everything is equal, then the production rate should be constant. This is definitely false. It is well documented that skill level and productivity varies wildly across software developers [Sackman 1968].

What if one of the engineers has a particular skill that is in demand, for example, UI design or distributed transaction management? That engineer is needed by every section of the development project in order to provide specialist skills.

In this case, there is an additional constraint—the availability of the specialist resource. Every specialist engineering skill in short supply within the engineering team is a potential additional constraint. Typically, resource constraints will be specialist roles needed to complete client-valued functionality. Hence, user interface designers, database administrators, transaction processing specialists, architects, configuration managers, technical writers, and other critical skills that may not be found in general software developers are all candidates for resource constraints.

Specialist roles that will generally not be resource constraints tend to be horizontal and consultative in nature. These roles include language gurus who advise developers on esoteric or obscure elements in development languages, mentors and coaches, trainers, IT support staff, help desk personnel, program managers, project managers, development managers, and executives.

Generalist developers or testers will generally not be constraints—rather, in circumstances where they are in short supply, they would be classified as insufficiently buffered resources.

If the schedule is to be protected from delays, the additional resource constraints must be scheduled. The schedule must be designed to allow the resource constraint, for example, the user interface designer, to move freely from one task to the next without delaying the start of any specific large grained component. The feeding chains were planned with feeding buffers based on the notion that the start date is the latest possible date that the feeding chain components can be started without endangering the Critical Path. If a feeding chain was delayed because a resource was unavailable, the project would be in jeopardy.

Hence, the specialist resources must be scheduled across the PERT chart. Uncertainty surrounding the availability of a specialist resource must be anticipated in the planning. In the user interface designer example, it must be recognized that some sections of the project may require more design or be more difficult to design than others. Uncertainty generated by the complexity of the design challenge for certain elements of the project must be buffered appropriately. The schedule must reflect this.

The PERT chart must be recast to show the resource constraints. Buffer sizes may need to increase. As a result, start dates of feeding chains may need to be modified. The ordering of parallel activities may need to be rearranged or the number of parallel paths reduced in order to accommodate the resource constraints.

This section should raise awareness that it is not a good thing to have too many specialist resources. Specialists are potential bottlenecks and must be scheduled on the PERT chart as CCRs. They must be buffered and protected. Too many of them would produce a scheduling nightmare, and all the protecting buffers introduced would result in increased Lead Time (LT), increased Operating Expense (OE), and reduced Throughput (T).

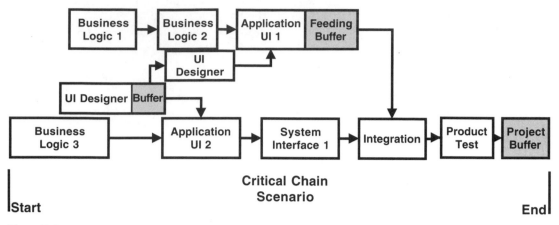

Figure 7–5
Critical chain modified project plan.

It should not be a surprise, therefore, that many Agile methods prefer generalist developers to specialists. This has been the trend in Lean Production, too. The specialist, single-skill workers preferred by Taylor [1911] and applied in Mass Production have given way to generalist, multiskilled workers in Lean Production factories.

Critical Chain Versus Critical Path

Eli Goldratt has called the resource constraint revised Critical Path the "Critical Chain." It shows the chain of construction activities and constrained resources that must be protected in order to ensure a smooth project delivery.

Figure 7–5 shows the project plan reworked to show the allocation of the UI Designer resource and the introduction of a Feeding Buffer to protect the feeding chain and a Resource Buffer to protect the UI Designer resource. The UI Designer is needed to design the Application UI modules for the complete system.

The start date for the feeding chain is backed out from the start date for the Integration effort. The Lead Time for the feeding chain is the time for Business Logic 1 & 2, Application UI 1, and the feeding chain buffer.

The start date for Application UI 1 is backed out from the availability of the UI Designer plus a protecting buffer to cover uncertainty in the design associated with Application UI 2. Note the position of UI 2 has been changed in the plan to accommodate the availability of the UI Designer resource.

The delivery of the whole project is protected by a project buffer. The project schedule is determined by the time to complete the Critical Path of Business Logic 3 + Application UI 2 + System Interface 1 + Integration + Product Test + Project Buffer.

Agile project planning should take advantage of the result that the aggregate uncertainty of a project is smaller than the sum of individual uncertainties. Planning should be done at the project level and within that using large grained aggregate components or subsystems.

The project delivery date should be protected by a project buffer determined by the aggregate uncertainty for the project.

A small series of sequential chains that can be executed in parallel should be planned. Each individual chain should be treated as a miniproject, and a feeding buffer should be calculated for that chain.

The significant and relevant issue with project tracking is whether or not the delivery date has been or is likely to be impacted by any uncertainties. Hence, Agile project tracking should involve the monitoring of the buffers designed to absorb uncertainty.

Buffers are consumed when the flow of inventory through transformation steps is halted because of problems. Problems should be recorded in an issue log and issues should be cross-referenced to the inventory they affect. The number of open issues and the trend in open issues should be monitored and reported to executives. The number of units of inventory blocked (not flowing) and the trend in blocked inventory should be monitored and reported to the executives.

Agile project planning can be achieved by creating a PERT or Gantt chart at the large grained delivery level and resource leveling it for the constrained resources. It is not necessary to completely resource level the Gantt chart— only constraints need to be resource leveled. Specialist resources should be treated as additional constraints and scheduled into the plan and buffered to protect them from uncertainty. A modified PERT chart that schedules resources should be created. The constrained-resource-buffered plan is known as the Critical Chain.

chapter 8

The Agile Manager's New Work

Switching a software development organization to techniques from Lean Production and TOC truly creates a paradigm shift. The Agile system of software production needs managers with new skills and new focus. Much of what they have learned needs to be forgotten. The truly Agile manager has new work to do.

New Roles for Agile Managers

There are four management roles to define for this new paradigm of Agile software development: the development manager (DM), the program or release manager, the project manager (PM), and the product manager.

The development manager runs the system of software production. The development manager is the equivalent of the plant manager. The DM is responsible for the continuous flow of working code production. She must understand the process of code creation and provide the developers and testers with the tools and environment required to build high-quality software. The engineers doing the real work must be happy and motivated.

Development Manager Role

It is the role of DM to ensure the motivation of the team. However, it may not be a DM role to create the motivators or motivations. That may be a role for more senior management. Hence, the DM has a responsibility to up-manage the executives in order to ensure the correct environment and motivation for highly effective code production. She understands that software developers are human and that, as De Luca's First Law says, the job of managing them is 80% psychology and only 20% technology [De Luca 2000].

The development manager must also look to increase productivity and create a learning organization focused on continuous improvement. The DM will work with the team to identify constraints, then negotiate protection of the constraints with the program (or release) and product managers. The DM is responsible for ensuring full exploitation of a constraint and implementing schemes to subordinate other resources and processes to the full exploitation of the constraint. The DM will also propose schemes to the executive management for elevation of a constraint and prepare a business case showing the improved ROI, using the equations from Chapter 3.

The development manager also takes responsibility for the overall Production Rate (R) and Lead Time (LT) of the system. R and LT are the two metrics by which the effectiveness of a development manager should be measured. R directly reflects the manager's ability to motivate the engineering team and to identify and eliminate constraints restricting productivity. LT shows the effectiveness of the flow. It is the measure of Value Efficiency from Chapter 2—the software equivalent of "the number of hours to build a car."[1]

The Program or Release Manager Role

A program manager has responsibility for controlling and coordinating a set of projects with mutual dependencies that are occurring in parallel. This can be aligned with McGrath's definition of marketing strategy for platforms [McGrath 1995]. A platform strategy leads to development of a product platform and a set of product developments that depend on the platform. The dependent products are usually developed in parallel. A platform strategy requires program management.

A release manager has responsibility for controlling and coordinating a series of sequential projects that build on one another. This is aligned with McGrath's definition of product line strategy. A product line is a series of releases of a product designed to target different market segments, gradually broadening the market for a product over time. A product line requires release management. In the following discussion, program manager also means release manager.

The primary role of the program manager is to control the release of the inventory into the system of software production. The program manager is at the end of the rope in the Drum-Buffer-Rope system. He must monitor the Throughput on the constraint and the queues that buffer system steps and feed the inventory into the system at a rate that can be consumed by the system whilst maintaining the protective buffers.

The program manager must also coordinate the delivery of working code—the output from the system—with all other activities required to realize the Throughput, for example, manuals, training, marketing material, PR, deployment, and logistics.

The program manager takes overall responsibility for Throughput (T) and Inventory-in-process (V). The effectiveness of the program manager should be measured by the metrics T and V.

Product Manager Role

The product manager is responsible for determining the release or product mix—the specific set of ideas that are requested as product features for the engineering cycle. The product manager is, therefore responsible for defining the input to the system—the product requirements—while the program manager is responsible for releasing those requirements into the system of software production at the appropriate time to maintain optimal flow.

[1]The number of hours to build a car is a standard metric of Lean Production in the auto industry. It shows how quickly the manufacturer can turn the inventory.

The product manager must estimate the Throughput (T) from a potential release and choose an appropriate feature set based on input from the development manager. The lead time and production rate of the software production system will determine the delivery date for the product or release. The delivery date is directly relevant to the appropriate mix of features. The product manager must strike this balance.

The product manager takes overall responsibility for NP and ROI and is responsible for the sum of money invested in inventory. The product manager has responsibility to determine the potential Throughput, select the delivery date, and control the investment. The delivery date controls the operating expense, (OE). Hence it is reasonable to make the product manager responsible for I, NP, and ROI. The better the product manager, the more NP he will be able to achieve with less I, which produces greater ROI.

The product manager must seek methods for improving idea generation and requirements capture. He must seek to reduce the average investment per function (AIPF). The marketing group should seek to become a learning organization. It must understand how its processes work and how to improve them. Marketing must be seen, in its own way, as a system—a system of idea generation.

Project Manager Role

The project manager is responsible for shepherding the inventory for a specific product or release through the system of code production. The PM may also, from time-to-time, have to expedite requests. The new PM role will look more like a manufacturer's expeditor role.

The project manager's new work is described in Chapter 7. The PM should maintain the Issue Log for the release and monitor the trend in open issues.

The PM determines the Critical Chain and creates the CCR-leveled PERT chart for a specific release. She also controls the internal release of batches of inventory through the system. However, the PM does not need to track individual line items. The tracking should be done at a coarse grained level to avoid creating too much work and too many unnecessary dependencies.

The PM will negotiate the project and feeding buffers with the development manager and then monitor the buffer consumption and report any significant events to executive management. Significant events are those that impact the Critical Path or delivery date of the project.

Buffers are consumed because inventory is blocked and an issue is raised. Hence, the PM must focus primarily on keeping the Issue Log empty and preventing issues from impacting the buffers and eventually the Critical Path.

The metrics a PM should monitor and be measured by are the number of open issues, their trend and age, the number of units of inventory blocked, their trend and age of the blockages, and the project and feeding buffer consumption and current status. All of these should be grouped into a single project dashboard. The entire health of a project can be described with these simple metrics.

Roles Versus Positions

The descriptions of development manager, program manager, product manager, and project manager, have been described as roles rather than positions or job titles. In an Agile organization, it may not be necessary to have individuals for each role. One talented manager could wear several hats and perform several of these roles. However, it is important to break the roles out because they perform different functions and have differing responsibilities for the metrics that contribute to the overall success of the business. Each role has a part to play in achieving the goal.

Chapter 7 looked at the role of the project manager in determining the Critical Chain and Critical Path. The remainder of Section 1 will look in detail at the new work for the development manager, program manager, and product manager.

chapter 9

Agile Development Management

The Role of the Development Manager

In Chapter 8, the role of the development manager was defined as responsibility for the system of software production. The development manager must ensure the flow of value through the transformation processes in the system. He is responsible for the rate of production output from the system and the time it takes to process a single idea through the system. To understand how to improve the rate of production and reduce the lead time, the development manager needs to understand how the system works, be able to identify the constraints, and make appropriate decisions to protect, exploit, subordinate, and elevate the system processes.

The Role of the Development Manager

Flow means that there is a steady movement of value through the system. Client-valued functionality is moving regularly through the stages of transformation—and the steady arrival of Throughput—with working code being delivered.

Identifying Flow

Figure 9–1 shows two cumulative flow diagrams. The first has a smooth flow. It is the perfect case where value is flowing through the system steadily. The second shows a ragged picture where there is no flow for several weeks and then a big jump as a large batch transfer of inventory moves through the system. It is no accident that the total inventory processed in the second diagram is lower. Because there is a less smooth flow, different elements in the system will be busy and then idle as the batch of inventory moves through the system. Smooth flow keeps the whole system busier. In cost accounting terms, smooth flow is more efficient—everyone in the system is occupied at a constant rate, though not necessarily at full capacity.

The development manager must try to achieve a smooth flow through the software production system. Producing a regular weekly cumulative flow diagram, including each of the stages in the system—analysis, design, coding, and testing—will show whether the client-valued functionality is flowing through the system smoothly.

Smooth flow can be interrupted by three causes: a bottleneck, poor quality, and an overly large batch size. Each of these will be examined in turn, bottlenecks and quality in this chapter and large batch sizes in Chapter 10.

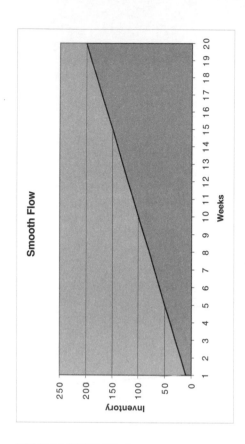

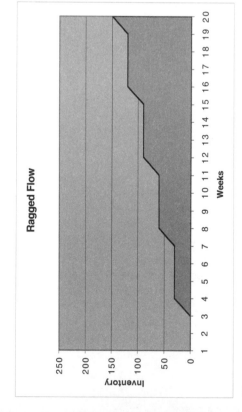

Figure 9–1
Visualizing flow.

Figure 9–2 shows the software production system with an overlay of the inventory queues in each step of the system. The system Production Rate (R) is limited by the local production rate of System Test, which is 30 units per month. Other parts of the system have higher Production Rates, but, efforts elsewhere are wasted. If the development manager runs other parts at maximum capacity, inventory will stockpile in front of System Test.

A bottleneck is the process step with the lowest Production Rate (R) in the system. In this case, the production rate of System Test ($R_{\text{System Test}}$) is less than Integration Test ($R_{\text{Integration Test}}$). The result is that inventory accumulates in the System Test step. Growing inventory levels suggest a bottleneck. Hence, the system constraint can be identified by tracking inventory levels at each step in the process and monitoring the trend in the level.

Using Cumulative Flow Diagrams to Identify the Bottleneck

In Figure 9–3, a very Agile software production system processes inventory quickly through each step in the process. However, System and Product Test (shown as a single bar) are blocked and inventory begins to grow. By week 7 there is obviously a stockpile of inventory in Test.

This should immediately focus management attention on the problem. Why is inventory stockpiling in Test? It could be that quality coming out of Coding is lousy, that Test is a bottleneck, or both.

Monitoring inventory allows management to see problems as they occur. In week 6 it would have been possible to predict that a problem was occurring and that inventory in Test was likely to continue to grow.

This highlights why Inventory (V) is a leading indicator and why it is a better indicator than Lead Time (LT). LT would not report a problem until Inventory had passed through the system completely. It is likely to be week 10 before a trend in LT can be observed in the example of Figure 9–3, at least three weeks later than was possible by monitoring V.

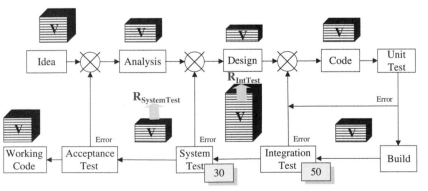

Figure 9–2
Production rate and queue growth.

Figure 9–3
Cumulative flow
showing Test as a
bottleneck.

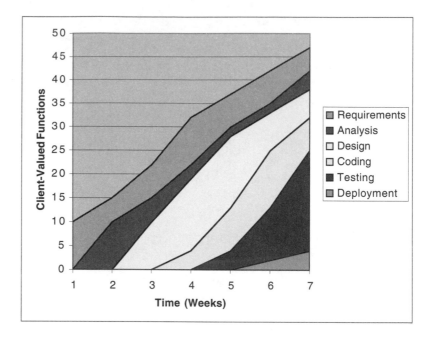

The True Cost of a Bottleneck

What happens to Q when capacity on the bottleneck is lost? For example, if the System Test department is a bottleneck and the test environment is lost for 2 days due to a server failure, the whole System Test team is idle for 2 days. What is the cost of that outage?

Did the business lose the cost of running the System Test department for 2 days? Assume an internal charge rate of $100/hour and five testers. Did the outage cost $8,000? Cost accounting would suggest that it might. Did it delay the delivery by 2 days? Yes, probably! What was the cost of that?[1]

However, Throughput Accounting suggests that the loss is calculated as the value of the lost Throughput. Assuming a 20-working-day month, the loss of 2 days is 10% of the capacity of System Test. If System Test can process 30 units of V per month, then 3 units of V were lost. Hence, 3 units of Q are lost for the month's production figure. If we assume that the capacity of System Test is constrained, then the shortfall of 3 units cannot be recovered. By losing 2 days of production on the bottleneck, 2 days of production for the whole system were lost. The business lost the cost of sending 3 units of inventory through the whole system, that is, the OE involved in producing 3 units plus any cost of delay, which is loss of Throughput due to the delay. If the average cost per unit is $10,000, the minimum cost of the loss would be $30,000—to which any loss of Throughput due to delay would need to be added. This is a lot more than $8,000!

[1]Calculating the cost of delay to a project is nontrivial. Donald Reinertsen provides basic coverage of this topic in *Managing the Design Factory*, pp. 23–30.

The loss of capacity on a bottleneck requires immediate management attention because it is reducing the overall effectiveness of the whole system and directly affecting the financial metrics and achievement of the overall system goal—to make more profit now and in the future.

Hence, it should be obvious that management must know and understand the bottleneck (or constraint) in its system. To know this requires measurement, as the true bottleneck may not be obvious.

Recovering and Stretching Software Production Constraints

In the software business, the effect of bottlenecks has tended not to worry executive management—particularly in younger startup companies. Management falls back on salaried staff. They are required to work free overtime to make up the lost production. Hence, management in the IT and software product business has never needed to be very good. Bad management can always be compensated for through copious use of free overtime. The bottom line is that a bad manager can be compensated for by abusing the engineering staff. It is industry legend that the capacity of the typical software engineer as a resource can always be stretched.

Larger businesses need to face reality—overtime cannot be used indefinitely to cover up for poor quality management. If staff work an extra 3 hours per day, there is a theoretical 35% increase in production capacity. However, the growing effect of tiredness and its effect on quality must be considered. Does excessive overtime really pay off?

The effectiveness of overtime can be measured by tracking the Production Rate (R) of the whole system and the local steps within the system. Through time, this will produce the proof. If R isn't rising when overtime is being worked, maybe there is a quality problem. To understand why R might not increase, it is necessary to understand the true cost of poor quality.

The True Cost of Poor Quality

The true cost of poor quality and the resultant rework is affected by the system constraint and the capacity of each element of the system. Poor quality reduces local production. Poor quality combined with a bottleneck reduces the production rate of the whole system. To understand how, it is necessary to consider each possible point of failure and each possible choice of constraint.

Failure at Unit Test

When a piece of software does not work, it is said to "have a bug". A bug is a failure. What is the cost of a failure? If a programmer unit tests a piece of code (a single unit of inventory) and it fails, the programmer modifies the code and retests it. This failure causes a small reduction in R for the development team. The cost of a failure in Unit Test is low. It is in the order of a fraction of a single unit of inventory through development.

If the cost of fixing a failed unit test was 20% of the coding effort, then 5 failed tests would reduce the local production rate by 1 unit. In the example of Figure 9–4, the Throughput of the whole system would be unaffected. It

Figure 9–4
Failure at unit test.

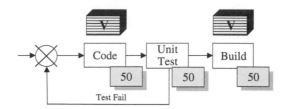

would remain at 30 units per month, providing total code production remained above 30 units.

$$\text{Code Production} = 50 - (\text{Failed Tests} / 5)$$

If there were more than 100 failed tests for 50 units of production, that is, 2 fails per unit, production would fall below 30 units, and the total production of the system would be reduced.

Failed Unit Tests When Coding Is the Bottleneck

If the development manager has already invested in System Test as suggested in Chapter 3 and elevated its capacity to 50 units per month, Coding is already a constraint. When Coding is a constraint, the effect of failed unit tests is more pronounced, as Figure 9–5 indicates.

Now the effect of test failures results immediately in a growing stock of inventory in Coding. If Design feeds Coding at 50 units per month and Coding has suffered a reduction in capacity due to bug fixes, the total Throughput of the system is reduced.

Failure at Integration Test

If a piece of code fails in Integration test, as shown in Figure 9–6, it has to be diagnosed and passed to the original developer(s) to fix. This can hold up a batch of code from proceeding to the next stage in the system. There is a consequent reduction in R, which is more pronounced as the delay affected the whole batch of code. If the batch has 12 units of inventory (1 build per week with a monthly production of 50) and fixing the cause of the delay takes 10% of the 4 manday Lead Time to program a single unit, the effective reduction on the Production Rate was one unit of inventory in coding.

In this case, a failure at Integration Test would reduce the local production rate of Coding by one unit per failure. In the example of Figure 9–2, where System Test is the constraint at 30 units per month, only 20 bugs per month in the integration of a weekly build are required to impact the total Throughput of the system.

Failed Integration Test When Coding Is the Bottleneck

Again, if Coding was already the constraint, failed integration tests become very costly. As soon as a test fails, the inventory at Coding begins to rise and the capacity of the whole system is reduced fairly quickly. This is shown in Figure 9–7.

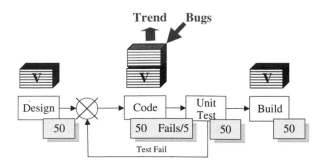

Figure 9–5
Failure at Unit Test
when Coding is a
bottleneck.

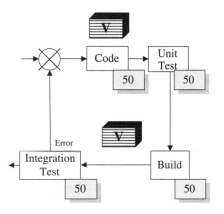

Figure 9–6
Failure at
Integration Test.

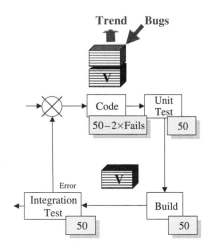

Figure 9–7
Failure at
Integration Test.

Failure at System Test

If a piece of code fails in System Test, as shown in Figure 9–8, it has not
performed as designed. It has to go back to Design. As such, Design will see
this bug arrive for rework, just as new requirements arrive. Bugs are inventory

Figure 9–8
Failure at
System Test.

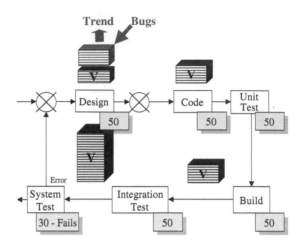

just like new requirements. If we assume that each bug found in System Test will typically take as long to fix as a new requirement takes to develop, the cost of a bug found in System Test will be 1 unit of R through Design, Coding and System Test.

In the example from Figure 9–2, System Test is already the constraint. Hence, every failure at System Test results in a reduction of Throughput for the whole system. Inventory will stockpile in front of System Test because it is the constraint. A significant number of failures will begin to erode the capacity of the other parts of the system.

Failure at Product Test

If a piece of code fails in Product Test, as shown in Figure 9–9, the code has failed to meet the requirements. The code must be sent back to analysis for rework. Each bug found in Product Test is a unit of inventory that must pass through Analysis, Design, and Coding again. The cost is one unit of V through Analysis, Design, Coding, System Test, and Product Test. At this point, the cost of a bug fix is the same as the cost of a new unit of inventory. It can be assumed that a whole unit of Production (Q) was lost. A failure at Product Test reduces the capacity of the system.

Failure at User Acceptance Test

If a piece of code fails in User Acceptance Testing, as shown in Figure 9–10, the requirement has failed to meet the user's expectation. The requirement has failed. The code must be sent back to properly capture the intended idea. The cost of such a bug is one unit of Throughput through Ideation, Analysis, Design, Coding, System Test, and Product Test. The cost is a whole unit of system capacity. In addition, the Investment (I) must be written off for the failed requirement and cost transferred to OE.

Figure 9–9
Failure at
Product Test.

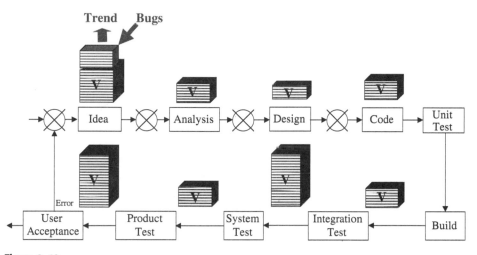

Figure 9–10
Failure at User Acceptance Test.

Throughout this analysis, the regression effect has not been considered. It was assumed that bugs stand in isolation. If some code fails regression testing, there may be multiple units of production lost through multiple stages of the system. If code fails stress testing, the architecture may be wrong. This may invalidate all of the currently processed inventory, that is, all the production achieved on the project may need to be reworked. Hence, poor quality architecture that fails and causes a major reworking of the system can be incredibly costly and significantly impact the system Throughput.

Regression Effects

Agile Development
Management

85

Quality can be improved in software through unit testing and peer review. It should be obvious that catching faults early has a direct impact on the production rate of the system. Capers Jones and more recently Karl Wiegers studied the effect of code inspections on software quality [Wiegers 2002]. From these studies it is fair to assume that if 10% of coding effort is invested into the act of peer review between developers, the bug count can be reduced by about 45%—or about 65% if unit tests are included. Furthermore, if 15% of coding effort is invested into formal inspections of developed code in addition to thorough unit tests, then 80% of errors may be eliminated before Integration or System Test.

Quality Before the Constraint

The cost benefit of quality is best shown by example. In the first example, the system from Figure 9–2 will be considered. The constraint is System Test with a capacity of 30 units per month. A defect rate of 2 failures per unit at System Test and 0.5 failures per unit at Integration Test will be assumed. Wiegers' results suggest that with peer review and unit test this can be cut to 0.4 defects per unit at System Test. Review and unit test will be assumed to eliminate failures at Integration Test.

Figure 9–6 shows the effect of failures at Integration Test when Coding is not the constraint. A failure rate of 6 bugs per build of 12 client-valued functions would result in halving the overall productivity of Coding to a mere 25 units per month. Immediately, the Throughput of the system is impacted.

Table 9–1 shows the impact of failures on System Test. The result of 2 failures per unit would normally reduce the Throughput to one third, that is, 10 units per month. However, if Coding is only producing 25 units per month, there will be slack in the System Test capacity. However, two thirds of capacity is still wasted. The resultant Throughput is 8 units per month.

Introducing a quality improvement will reduce the capacity of Coding. If reviews are performed, perhaps 10% of coding capacity will be lost. Hence, Coding will produce 45 units per month. After the quality improvements are instituted, the Throughput of Integration Testing will immediately jump to 45 units per month. As System Test can only process 30 units per month, the number of defects will be only 12, the resultant Throughput will be 21.5 units per month.

Table 9–1
Effect of failure at Integration Test.

	Before Quality	**After Quality**
System Test Defects	2 per unit	0.4 per unit
Integration Test Defects	6 per weekly build	0 per weekly build
Throughput	8 units per month	21.5 units per month

Spending 10% of coding effort and reducing the capacity of Coding to only 45 units per month, more than doubled the productivity of the whole system. When Coding is not the bottleneck, there is absolutely no reason not to spend time on quality. Putting quality before the System Test bottleneck more than doubles the capacity of the system.

Again, in this example, the lead time would be halved and the production rate doubled. The simple addition of basic quality procedures in Coding produce a doubling of productivity. Earlier delivery of more functionality has a potentially huge impact on overall system Throughput.

When Coding Is the Constraint

In the second example, Figure 9–7, Coding is already the constraint. As suggested in Chapter 3, System Test has been elevated, and the constraining Throughput is 50 units per month, which affects Design, Coding, and Testing.

The effect on Coding, from bugs at integration time, is unchanged from the previous example. A failure rate of 6 bugs per build of 12 client valued functions would result in halving the overall productivity of Coding to a mere 25 units per month. Immediately, the Throughput of the system is halved.

There are 25 units making it through to System Test, and there are 50 bugs associated with them. The capacity of System Test is now 50 units per month. So there is no problem processing 25 units. Table 9–2, however, shows a defect rate of 2 units being passed back to Coding, which will result in reducing it to one third—from 25 to a mere 8 units per month. Because there is no slack in Coding, every bug directly reduces the Throughput.

Again, introducing a quality improvement will reduce the capacity of Coding to 45 units, which makes it the system bottleneck. However, no failures at Integration Testing will keep the Throughput at 45, and there should be 18 bugs per month found in System Test. The overall system Throughput should be no worse than 32 units per month. So, when Coding is the bottleneck, spending 10% of effort on quality actually improves the productivity of the whole system four times.

Quality is essential for highly productive software development. Software quality is a main tenet of Agile software development. More working code delivered more often is achieved through high quality.

Table 9–2
Effect of failure at System Test.

	Before Quality	**After Quality**
System Test Defects	2 per unit	0.4 per unit
Integration Test Defects	6 per weekly build	0 per weekly build
Throughput	8 units per month	32 units per month

The development manager must focus on quality before and in the system constraint. Client-valued functionality must not pass through the constraint more than once, if at all possible.

How Batch Sizes Affect Flow

As Figure 9–11 shows, there are four steps involved in processing a unit of inventory through a transformation.

The **queue time** is the time a unit of inventory spends waiting to be processed by the current process step. It has passed from the previous step but is not yet work-in-process at the current step. For example, a design that has passed Design Inspection but has not yet begun Coding would be queuing for Coding.

Setup time is the time spent setting up equipment or resources in order to perform a process step. It is desirable to batch together inventory that requires the same setup. Minimizing setup time maximizes the use of a resource. If the resource is capacity constrained, that is, the system bottleneck, then minimizing setup time is essential to fully exploit the resource and maximize the system's production rate.

Process time is simply the time required for the task. For example, the time taken to code a given requirement, that is, literally, the time required to type in the code and get it to successfully compile, would be the coding process time for a coding task.

Paul Szego[2] has referred to the setup and maintenance overhead for a batch of client-valued functionality as the "administrivia." It is defined as the percentage of total working effort that software engineers perform on nonintellectual tasks, such as project planning meetings or setup of a development environment. It might more accurately be called Intellectual Efficiency, and be more formally defined as the percentage of process time against total setup, maintenance time, and process time.

$$\text{Intellectual Efficiency} = \frac{\text{Process Time}}{\text{Setup Time} + \text{Maintenance Time} + \text{Process Time}}$$

There is a natural tendency for engineers to want to optimize intellectual efficiency by creating large batch sizes of work to be processed through a single step. No one wants to spend time on trivial housekeeping tasks when there is an intellectual challenge and exciting code to be written.

Figure 9–11
Elements of process lead time.

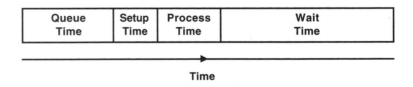

Queue Time	Setup Time	Process Time	Wait Time

Time

[2]Paul Szego was a member of the original FDD team. The concept of "administrivia" was discussed at the FDD community website, http://www.featuredrivendevelopment.com/ in February 2003.

However, larger batch sizes do not flow as well as smaller ones. Figure 9–1 showed two cumulative flow graphs. The smooth flow was almost certainly achieved with small batch sizes, where client-valued functionality is being transformed through a single process step every week. The ragged flow graph is almost certainly the result of larger batch sizes in which the lead time through a single step is greater than 1 week and more likely 4 weeks.

Small batch sizes are essential for flow!

Small batch sizes are also essential for quality. In software development human nature creates a tendency for engineers to be less exacting and pay less attention to detail when considering larger batches. For example, when code reviews are performed on small batches, the code review takes only a short time to prepare and a short time to conduct. Because there is only a small amount of code to review, the reviewers tend to pay it greater attention and spot a greater number of errors than they would on a larger batch of code. It is therefore better to spend 4 hours per week doing code reviews than 2 days at the end of each month or, even worse, one week at the end of each quarter. A large batch makes code reviewing a chore. Small batches keep it light. The result is higher quality. Higher quality leads directly to more production.

It is not essential to minimize setup time on a nonbottleneck, that is, if a process step does not use a capacity constrained resource, it is unnecessary to worry so much about the cost of setups. In Figure 3–1, where System Test is the bottleneck at 30 units per month, it would be acceptable to use smaller batch sizes in Coding as it has a capacity of 50 units per month. Efficiency might fall, but the net effect would be improved flow and reduced inventory-in-process. Hence, small batch sizes are a good idea on nonbottlenecks or in a system where the capacity is well balanced and every step is effectively a constraint.

Reducing batch sizes achieves flow and reduces total inventory in the system. Reducing batch sizes improves ROI!

Wait time is the time spent after the task is complete, but before it can be moved on to the next process step. Wait time is often a factor of the batching or release mechanism in the system of software production. If a single requirement has completed coding but must wait for five others before it can be passed to the next stage, then wait time will be involved.

Wait time is an inevitable side effect of batching to minimize setup time. Queue and wait time are waste because they incur operating expense. Wait time is reduced by the use of small batches. Equally, queue time for the next stage is reduced by the use of small batches.

Counterintuitively, small batch sizes reduce lead time and inventory in the system. Throughput is increased by maximizing the effective use of resources in the system.

However, the batch size must not get too small because the setup time would become problematic as it begins to outweigh the process time. In this event, Throughput would be reduced. It is essential to achieve the correct balance, to maximize the resource utilization whilst minimizing inventory and lead time. Section 2 will explore how flow is achieved in different software development methods.

A development manager monitoring the cumulative flow of code complete will observe an S-Curve trend in the chart. This is normal. Methods that measure Production Quantity (Q) tend to exhibit an S-Curve for percentage complete.

In Figure 9–12, an example project is shown. The three lines represent the three inventory (V) levels shown in Figure 5–1: client-valued ideas approved and awaiting development, client-valued functions in process of development, and client-valued functions as delivered working code.

The S-Curve Explained

This S-Curve is particularly useful. It helps illuminate a number of aspects of the project and provides the development manager with areas for improvement. Over time, the manager can focus on bringing the team up to optimal speed as quickly as possible and holding that optimal speed for as long as possible. The less pronounced the S-Curve, the more effective the team and the greater the Production Rate (R) will be. The flatness at the bottom and top of the curve can be explained. With this understanding, a development manager and the developers themselves can take the appropriate actions to improve the performance of the software production system. Figure 9–13 illuminates the elements of the S-Curve.

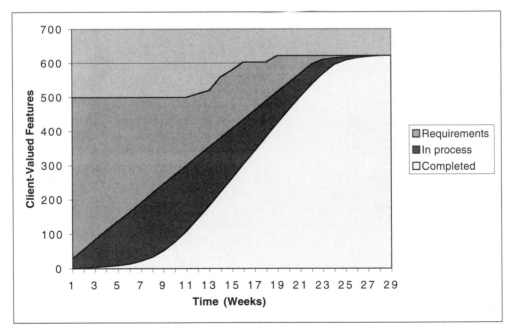

Figure 9–12
The S-Curve.

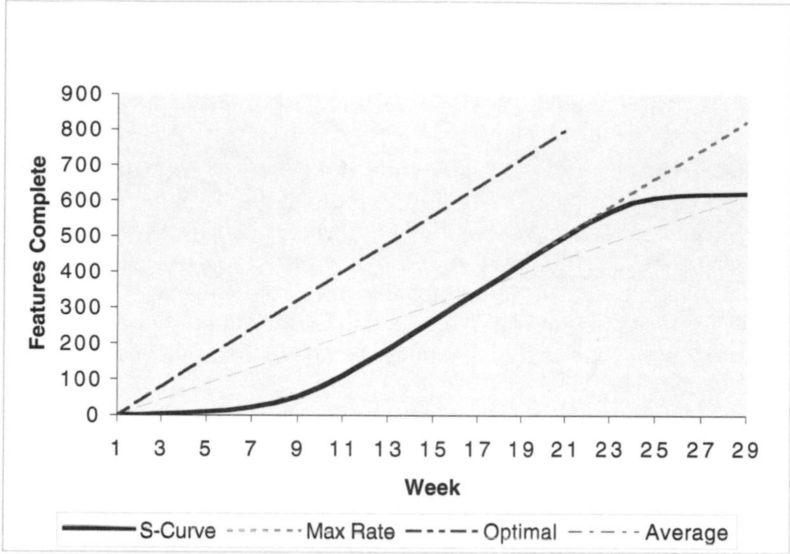

Figure 9–13
The S-Curve
explained.

Bottom of the S-Curve

It is very difficult to sprint right out of the gate. It is probably impossible to achieve optimum Throughput in the software production system at the start of a project. There are several reasons why this should be: inventory blocked due to ambiguous requirements, training of personnel, lack of understanding of the project domain, poor teamwork, changing designs, availability of tools, availability of environments, facilities, lack of technical infrastructure, minimal domain specific tools, and staffing levels. Some can be eliminated through better planning, others appear to be endemic. They represent the nature of the beast—software development.

When a new team is formed for a project, there will be an impact on R. This is endemic to the business. The team must work through its "forming" and "storming" [Weaver 1997] phases before settling into its new normal habits. As the team gets to know each other's strengths and weaknesses, there will be some friction. This friction will reduce the production rate of the team.

Occasionally, a team is dysfunctional. This will manifest itself as a low production rate and a flat curve. Dysfunction may result in poorly executed design or peer reviews or in petty arguments that block development. Monitoring the cumulative flow diagram arms the manager with information that can indicate a dysfunctional team, but only the manager can actually investigate and discover dysfunctional behavior. It is important to understand that a dysfunctional dispute between two individuals hurts the performance of the whole team.

Knowledge sharing is important to performance. A team that works well together will share knowledge. A team that is dysfunctional and poor at sharing will underperform. Encouraging openness and knowledge sharing and creating a means for communicating knowledge, for example, a news server or intranet knowledge base, will improve team performance.

Design changes will hurt at any time in a project. When someone discovers a requirement that necessitates the modification of a widely used interface, the regression effect across the system causes R to drop dramatically. This problem is endemic. There will always be a little unforeseen uncertainty related to analysis and design.

The production rate will suffer badly if a development team is ready to start a project but doesn't have all the tools and environments needed to make progress. Capacity constrained development resources must be exploited to the full. They must not be idle because tools or environments are not available. Hence, it is important that the project manager ensure tools and environments are in place early. A flat line at the start of a project may be a strong indication that the team doesn't have the tools or environments that it needs.

Top of the S-Curve

There are four reasons why the production rate tends to drop off in a project, regardless of software development method employed: increased integration effort, bug fixes, inventory blocked due to unresolved issues, and refactoring.

Increased integration effort is almost unavoidable. As a project becomes large, code from a new iteration must be integrated with the large existing code base. The number of problems found during build-integration and integration testing is likely to increase. The only way to avoid this is never to work on a large project or system. Hence, large projects, even those built in smaller iterations, should anticipate this effect and allow for it when planning the project buffer.

The effect of increased problems due to build-integration can be measured by measuring the time from the start of the build until the build is declared successful. This is the local lead time through Integration Test. The manager can then assess what the overall downtime for the development team might be. In extreme cases, all development stops until the build is declared successful. The effect on the production rate can be calculated. The trend in the build-integration time can be used to predict the future impact of build-integration on R. Hence, the contribution of build-integration to the cumulative flow diagram can be predicted.

As a project matures and more code is available for system and product test, the number of bugs reported rises. As the bug database rises, there is a tendency to increase the mix of bugs to new client-valued functions being coded. The result is that the overall speed of the team is maintained but an increasing percentage of the effort is devoted toward fixing bugs. Bug fixes are related to inventory that is already shown as code complete.

To minimize the effect of bugs on the code complete slope and to maintain R, it is vital to maintain high quality standards. Fewer bugs have a direct, positive affect on the production rate of the system.

As a project nears completion, inventory that has been blocked due to unresolved issues raised during analysis or design re-enter the Critical Path.

Eventually all client-valued functionality must be coded, or the client must agree to remove them from the scope. If they remain in the scope, the issues must be resolved. Issues that remain open near the end of a project reduce the number of client-valued functions that can be progressed to completion. The result is that the speed of the team slows. Some developers may become idle or more and more effort is concentrated on bug fixes because other inventory is blocked.

To avoid a tail off in R, it is vital to resolve issues before the client-valued functions re-enter the Critical Path. Hence, the project manager should be focused on fast and effective issue resolution. This maintains the overall Throughput of the system. A flattening in the curve is a good visual indicator that the project manager needs to work harder to resolve open issues.

Refactoring will also impact R. When working code already completed is being reworked, it is not being shown as new productivity. For every client-valued function being reworked, the system is losing the possibility of a unit of new production.

Refactoring is an important aspect of many Agile methods. However, it is important to understand that refactoring interrupts flow unless it is done as an almost continual process of small refactorings. It may be better to get the architecture right the first time, through use of prototyping off the Critical Path.

If refactoring is unavoidable due to a change in market conditions that force new architectural requirements upon the system, it is vital to convey to senior management the true cost of the refactoring. The true cost can be calculated from the reduction in production rate, the increase in lead time, the increase in inventory, and the lost opportunity for Throughput during the refactoring process. If the benefit from refactoring financially outweighs the cost, then the refactoring should happen.

Visual Control[3]

The cumulative flow diagram is just one aspect of visual control. Visual control is a technique used in Lean Thinking to facilitate self-organization. Visual control helps individual workers see what is happening in their work group— who is working on what, how much has been completed, and how much remains to be done. The Agile development manager should determine the visual controls that will help his team self-organize and then provide the means for those tools. FDD uses a web-based Knowledge Management System (KMS) for this purpose. Views from the KMS are also printed out and displayed prominently on the walls of the office.

A visual control might be as simple as displaying a list of client-valued functionality to be coded in a project iteration on a wall. Developers would be able to walk up to it, select an item, and date and initial the entry. This

[3]There is a very nice explanation of visual control in Womack and Jones' *Lean Thinking* that demonstrates its use in the Toyota Product Distribution Center in Chicago where stock pickers use a control board to self-organize their work [1996, p. 78].

lets all of their colleagues know that they have "claimed" that unit of inventory and it is being worked. It also lets everyone see when the item was started. Other visual controls include the Issue Log, the Task List, or the Bug Report Log.

Visual control is a vital mechanism for self-organization.

Summary

The development manager must monitor the flow of value through the software production system. This is best achieved with a cumulative flow diagram. Smooth flow results in a steadily climbing line for each step in the system.

Bottlenecks in the system can be identified by widening bars in the cumulative flow diagram. So monitoring inventory levels provides early warning of problems compared with monitoring lead times for completion of client-valued functions, because inventory is a leading metric whilst lead time is a lagging metric.

Bottlenecks are best exploited through improved quality. Investing in quality through the use of reviews and automated tests can improve system Throughput by several hundred percent.

Batch size is important to achieving flow. The development manager must work with the program manager to ensure that appropriate batch sizes are chosen and system resources are exploited as fully as possible.

There is a natural tendency amongst developers to create large batch sizes because they minimize annoying project management and administrative overhead. The development manager must monitor this closely and create an environment where there is an appreciation that achieving flow is more important than achieving intellectual efficiency.

Monitoring the inventory trend in the cumulative flow diagram provides visual clues about many aspects of a project's health. The code complete line on a cumulative flow diagram will tend toward an S-Curve. The development manager should understand this and seek to minimize the flattening of the S at the beginning and end of the project. Keeping the development team producing at the optimal rate maximizes the Throughput of the system.

The Agile development manager can achieve hands-off control and delegation through the use of visual control techniques. These allow developers to self-organize and communicate among themselves using a visual tool. The visual mechanism allows the manager to see what is happening so there is no need to ask. Visual control avoids the need for aggravating micromanagement.

chapter 10

Software Resource Planning

Manufacturing Resource Planning (MRP)

The concept of MRP is well understood in manufacturing and in other business areas, where it is called ERP (Enterprise Resource Planning). Succinctly, MRP is a planning mechanism that ensures the right things are in the right place at the right time to ensure the smooth flow of production. Although the concepts of MRP have been transferred to other areas of business, such as supply chain management, the method hasn't been used in software development. However, with an Agile software development model that seeks to track the flow of value through a series of transforming steps, the use of MRP methods becomes both useful and practical.

MRP systems use the concept of a Bill of Materials (BOM), which contains the inventory or raw materials required to perform a value adding transformation. A work order to start such a transformation (or manufacturing process) is not given until everything in the BOM is available. By ensuring that the BOM is on-hand to complete the job, the process time is minimized and potential waste due to delay is eliminated from the system. MRP helps to reduce inventory, lead time, and waste in a manufacturing system.

Software resource planning seeks to control the release of inventory in the software production system in order to reduce the work-in-process inventory, reduce lead time, and minimize operating expense and waste caused by excessive queue and wait times.

Drum Beat

In *Necessary But Not Sufficient*, Goldratt and his colleagues explain how to improve basic MRP systems with the Theory of Constraints [Goldratt, 2000]. Specifically, the MRP system is subordinated to the CCR in the system. The production rate of the CCR becomes the pacemaker or drum beat for the whole system. In the Drum-Buffer-Rope system for production subordination, the CCR is the drum, its production rate the beat. The buffer is the inventory buffer in front of the CCR protecting it from starvation. The rope is the inventory between the system input and the CCR.

In order to minimize the inventory in a system and maximize the production rate, it is necessary to plan the release of the material into the system such that it will be consumed at the rate it is released. Releasing too much material into the software production system will cause inventory to rise, lead times to rise, and production rates to fall.

The program manager must work with the development manager to plan the release of requirements into the software production system. The plan should follow the Agile project plan constructed using the Critical Chain method described in Chapter 7. However, the release of requirements into the system is controlled in real time. The program manager and the development manager must use the cumulative flow diagram to monitor the production rate and inventory levels in the system. They must monitor the project buffer and the feeding buffers and release an appropriate amount of material into the system at the appropriate time. If reality is straying from the original project plan, the program manager will be reporting that to the executives and refactoring the plan according to their feedback.

It is important that material be released into the software production system at the correct pace. The effect of swamping the system with raw material or starving it is severe and in the worst case can result in the complete elimination of Throughput. Equally, if the actual results are veering away from the original plan, there may be a need to expedite material through the system. This too will have an adverse effect. Finally, processing the wrong material or material that goes stale before it is delivered has an adverse effect on production. Each of these problems is considered in turn.

The Effect of Swamping a Process

Have you ever felt that you had just too much to do? Have you ever worked on a team where it was obvious to everyone that there was too much work to do? Have you worked for a business with an annual budget approval process? Suddenly, one day in the year, all the new work for the coming 12 months gets released into an eager organization. What happens next?

Swamping a process, such as Analysis, with too many requirements can result in several outcomes: The process is not completed properly or with sufficient quality; the time to complete the process is overly long, due to the large quantity to be processed; the time to process must be shortened so more resources are needed, which results in hiring temporary staff; the process breaks entirely under the strain of the workload.

The effect of swamping a stage in the process with too much work is to turn it into a temporary bottleneck. Now the organization must do everything it can to reduce the effect of the bottleneck.

Consider the case where the analysis process gets swamped by requirements, as shown in Figure 10–1, and the analysts (or management) are keen to show that they can keep projects moving. They may decide to short-circuit best practices and push through poor quality. This may be a simple act of time-boxing or guillotining the analysis process. What happens next?

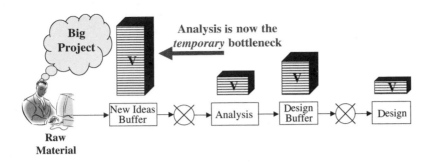

Figure 10–1
Swamping Analysis
creates a temporary
bottleneck.

As discussed in Chapter 9, poor quality analysis can lead to problems discovered late in the process. Failures late in the process can result in rework or waste. In both cases the system production rate is reduced.

Hence, it is undesirable to sacrifice quality for timely delivery. However, if a longer delivery time to process requirements is acceptable in order to maintain quality, by implication the system lead time increases. A long lead time increases operating expense, as investment must be financed for longer periods. Operating expense for any given project is increased because everyone must be paid for a longer period of time.

Longer LT increases project risk—the risk that the requirements will become stale and no longer suitable for the market. Longer LT may lead to increased waste, due to shifts in the market. Hence, longer LT reduces R and increases OE.

Alternatively, the temporary analysis constraint could be elevated with the addition of more headcount. This would keep LT short. Adding headcount very obviously adds OE. It may also cause additional effects. It may, for example, slow down the existing staff while they train the new staff and bring them up to speed with company processes and the subject matter of the project. Hence, adding headcount will increase OE and may impact R from existing resources.

The doomsday scenario is that the process simply grinds to a halt and the production rate shrinks to almost zero. This is the true state of "analysis paralysis." In this case, the flood of requirements raises so many issues that the whole organization is turned over to issue resolution. Nothing moves forward. People spend all of their time on conference calls talking about issues, reading the minutes of those calls and planning for the next call, reading the agenda, and preparing documents. All of it waste. There is no progress towards delivery of client-valued functionality.

The Effect of Starving a Process

For comparison, consider a maturing organization where there is a go-ahead development manager who successfully implements one of the Agile software development processes described in Section 2. The processes of Design and Coding become highly effective and efficient. The result is that

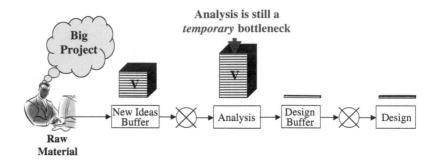

Figure 10–2
Starving Design implies Analysis is a temporary bottleneck.

software development consumes its raw material—analysis documents—very quickly. The upstream functions of Marketing and Business Analysis cannot create requirements fast enough for the development group. Development gets periodically starved of material, and developers are idle.

When a stage of the process is starved of raw material, as shown in Figure 10–2, the earlier stage of the process looks like a bottleneck. From the perspective of the development team, there is no upstream supply, hence there must be a bottleneck. Consequently, the organization must once again focus on relieving the bottleneck.

If a development team is sitting idle for a few days or weeks, they will not be laid off. So they will still cost money. OE is unaffected. It remains constant, but R is reduced. LT is clearly longer than it needs to be.

If supply is to be increased to the starved process, R must be increased at earlier steps in the system. In this case, more raw material must be pushed through the analysis step. Somewhat counterintuitively, this reveals that the effect of starving a process is very similar to the effect of flooding a process. Both create temporary bottlenecks.

Buffers

Figures 10–1 and 10–2 introduce new steps in the process diagrams from those used so far in the book. Each process step in the system is protected by a buffer of inventory. The buffer is there to prevent the process from starving.

The software resource planning mechanism must strike a fine balance between maintaining enough inventory in the buffer to keep the system busy whilst not overstocking buffers and causing the system lead time and overall system inventory to rise above optimal levels. The buffer size should be based on the expected or common cause, variance in the preceding process step.

Software requirements should be released into the system with the agreement of the program and development managers at just the right pace to maintain the buffer levels within acceptable tolerances. Buffers throughout the system should be monitored daily.

Buffers are filled by batch transfers of material from a previous step in the process. For the purposes of this chapter, a buffer of material is synonymous with a queue of material waiting to be processed. In order that processes are never swamped, it is important that batch transfers are kept small. In order that processes are never starved, it is important that batch transfers happen before a buffer (or queue) is emptied.

The Effect of Expediting Requirements

Expediting means rushing something through at the expense of anything else that may be in process. This means that everything in process will be subordinated to the delivery of the requested expedite functionality. The program manager will subordinate the current projects, release dates, prioritized requirements, batch setups, and agreed schedules to the requested functionality. In short, the system will drop whatever work is in process and expedite the request.

Expedited requests in software tend to take two basic flavors: the market driven feature request and the severity 1, "showstopper," (or sometimes severity 2, "major,") bug fix request. With the first, the marketing or sales team has detected that the product is insufficient to meet the requirements for a large client or that the competition has just released a new "killer" feature that is winning business for them and impacting sales for everyone else. Hence, the product must have the new feature immediately, or sales (Throughput) will be lost.

The second scenario is worse because it is often undeniable. If the software in production is broken, then it simply must be fixed. Angry customers may be on the phone. There may even be penalty clauses. Perhaps the customer is refusing to pay (affects Throughput). In the case where the software business runs a service, then that service may have been shutdown. Hence, Throughput is being lost every day until the fix is delivered.

Expediting reduces the production rate. Why?

When a decision was made to expedite a request, as shown in Figure 10–3, engineers in the software production system are asked to stop what they are doing. There is a setup time incurred to accommodate the expedited requirements. Engineers may be asked to work on a smaller batch size than normal. They may be asked to make radical environment setup changes. Everyone in the chain has to change to deal with the expedited request. While the whole chain focuses on the expedited request, other work may not get started or finished. Just the process of interruption, switching to a different task, and later switching back is costly [DeMarco 1999, p. 63]. Task switching either at a fine grained level or at a larger project granularity costs valuable time and reduces the total exploitation of capacity constrained resources such as developers and testers. If the system is set up to monitor the Production Rate (R), then the development manager will see a drop-off during a period of expediting.

Palmer and Felsing have a good example of this in A *Practical Guide to Feature Driven Development* [Palmer 2002]. The graph in Figure 10–4 is from an actual project. The highlighted flat spots represent reduced production rate. In both cases, the reduction was caused by the senior executives in the organization asking for a full presentation of the code built to date. The project had to slow down in order to expedite a request to put together a functional, visually pretty, slick, and professional demonstration. The code base had to be stabilized. The project director could not risk the introduction of new bugs as the presentation approached. Hence, capacity constrained resources, such as developers, were asked to stop work.

Figure 10-3
Expediting increases system inventory.

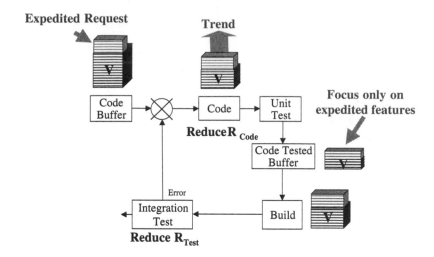

CLS - PD Completed Features on a Weekly basis

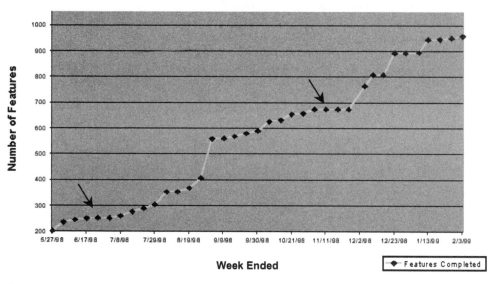

Figure 10-4
Periods of expediting cause reduced productivity.

Using the techniques presented here, it is possible to calculate the cost of these two presentations to the executives. We can use the value of operating expense for the days of lost production. With a project of 50 people, loss of 1 week of production for each demo, and an internal charge rate of $100 per hour for OE, each demo cost the business $200,000. Would the CIO have been so keen to solicit a formal presentation to his peers, if he had realized that it would suck $400,000 from his annual budget? What was the cost of the lost days of production? What effect did later delivery of the project have on Throughput?

The ability to cope with expedite requests for different software development methods is examined in greater depth in Chapter 34. Some Agile methods, particularly Extreme Programming, are more adept at coping with expediting. In some respects, Extreme Programming can be thought of as "serial expediting." As everything is an expedite request, the process does not incur additional cost for short order requests.

The True Cost of Waste

Waste is raw material that gets thrown away rather than delivered as finished product. In software terms, waste is requirements that get abandoned. These represent ideas that were no longer desirable. Waste usually manifests itself as a change request. Change requests take two basic forms: disregard a current requirement and replace it with a new one or modify an existing requirement in a way that requires abandoning part of the existing requirement.

Change requests can have an impact on the analysis, design, and coding of a software project. A change can have impact beyond the immediate requirement that was changed. Dependent code can be wasted because it too has to change. In manufacturing terms, this is like changing the specification of a part. Then the parts designed to plug into it must also be scrapped.

The cost of waste takes two forms. Firstly, investment in the previous requirement must be written off. This investment is lost. It must be treated as operating expense. Secondly, the operating expense incurred in the requirement being changed or scrapped should be considered. The further through the lifecycle, the more transformations have taken place and so the greater the cost of accepting the change. If a change was isolated and didn't incur a regression effect across the rest of the project, the maximum cost of a change is the cost of taking the unit of inventory through to finished product. This cost of change could be estimated as a fraction of the ACPF. If there was an equal distribution of changes across the lifecycle, it would be half the ACPF for a typical unit of Q written off as waste. The key point is that late changes cost almost as much as a delivered unit of Q. Hence, later changes will have a high impact on the production rate.

In order to maximize the Production Rate (R), waste from changes must be minimized.

Causes of Waste

There are three typical reasons for a change: The customer changed their mind; the market shifted and the idea is no longer valid or the requirement is no longer justified; or the requirement document did not accurately capture the essence of the originator's idea. A close cousin to the third reason is that the analysis was faulty and a proper shared understanding of the requirement was not achieved.

The customer is less likely to change its mind if it is given less time to change its mind. Hence, shorter lead time, and faster release of finished product, is likely to lead to less change and less waste from a change of mind.

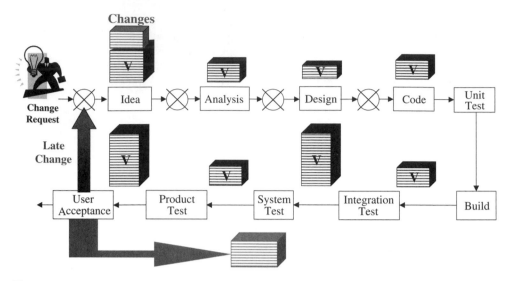

Figure 10-5
Cost of a late change.

In order to minimize waste from a customer changing its mind, inventory and lead time from idea creation to working code delivery must be minimized.

We live in volatile and unpredictable times. Globalization and low friction communication such as the Internet mean that markets emerge, develop, mature, and evaporate in only a few short years. Shifts in the marketplace are inevitable. Once again, the longer it takes to deliver a software project, the more likely the market is to shift and the more likely requirements will become obsolete. Obsolete requirements cause change requests and lead to waste in the system. In order to minimize waste from shifts in the market, inventory and lead time must be minimized. With fewer requirements, delivered more quickly, there is less chance the market will move before the system is delivered.

Failure to capture the requirement or failure to properly analyze the requirement are the main causes of quality-driven waste as shown in Figure 10-5. The cost of such waste is higher the further the fault progresses before being spotted and corrected. The most costly is failing to correct the fault until customer acceptance testing. In this case, the cost of waste is equivalent to losing a full unit of production.

The failure to capture the requirement or failure to properly analyze the requirement must be viewed as a quality issue. It can be addressed by using higher quality staff to capture and analyze the requirements. Hence, the cost of reduced production rate due to quality-driven waste can be offset against the cost of better paid, higher quality business analysts and system analysts or training for developers or testers in the art and science of analysis.

If a customer genuinely doesn't know what it wants then specific ambiguous requirements should not be added to a critical deliverable. If exploration or research is required to gain clarification, a separate research project or prototype should be undertaken. Research projects and prototype development, as explained earlier, do not represent software production for the purposes of this text. Such tasks should be taken off the Critical Path.

Often the HR department undervalues the skills of business analysts, and in some companies analysts are paid less than software engineers. This can result in the wrong people being hired for the job. The problem comes from a lack of systems thinking and a failure to understand that poor quality analysis leads to big problems later.

The result could be very costly to Throughput. If the cost of an average unit of Production (Q), is $15,000 and the small team from the example in Figure 3–1 can produce 90 units of Q per quarter—perhaps 10% of them lost due to quality-driven waste—the decision to hire a poor quality analyst at a low salary may cost $135,000 per quarter.

I worked on a very large IT project in which it was later noted that more than 90% of the requirements had suffered change—for all three reasons stated above. This project had around 50 people for 18 months. If a typical American internal charge rate of $100/hour is assumed, the OE for this project was $15.6 million. Assuming an equal distribution of waste detection throughout the project lifecycle, it is possible to state that 45% of production quantity was lost due to waste, that is, to change requests. This equates to $4.85 million, assuming that none of the shortfall was recovered by other means, such as unpaid overtime.

By reducing inventory levels through reduced project scope and delivering smaller, more frequent releases, coupled with a plan to improve the quality of analysis with better people and a larger budget for the analysis, it might have been possible to save several millions of dollars and deliver the project up to 6 months earlier.

The moral of this story is that big, expensive IT projects that will take more than 9 months to deliver carry huge risks. Inventory waste—software change requests—is inevitable on such projects. The cost of this waste can be measured and must be used to predict waste on future projects.

Summary

Flooding a stage in the software production system will result in increased OE and will very likely result in reduced R. Failing to feed raw material into the system at an appropriate rate may result in process steps being starved. The effect of starving a process is, counterintuitively, the same as flooding a process—OE is increased and R decreases. Expediting requirements through the system should be avoided. Expediting increases OE and reduces R.

Waste must be minimized. Requirements that get scrapped before delivery reduce R and increase OE. Waste will increase if lead times are long. Waste can be reduced by reducing LT. Hence, reducing LT also has a positive derivative affect on R and OE.

chapter 11

An Agile Maturity Model

Based on the theory presented in Section 1 and the analysis presented later in Section 2, Agile methods are founded in techniques that have been used successfully in other industries. This suggests that the software development industry requires a new model for organizational maturity. The existing SEI Software Capability Maturity Model is failing the industry because it is based on the wrong model for project management and conformance to quality. It also lacks the extra dimension introduced by Agile methods—the human element—because it has an unacceptably high barrier to entry and, most importantly, because it introduces requirements on organizations that do not point in the direction of the goal—to make more profit. Chapter 19 demonstrates that the SEI SW-CMM and traditional development methods lead companies to adopt practices that increase lead time, increase inventory levels, increase investment, and reduce production rate.

A new maturity model is required: a model that has meaning for all types of software development businesses and a model that is synchronized with the overall goal—to make more profit.

I would like to propose just such a model. I call it "The Learning Organization Maturity Model."

This new model, shown in Table 11–1, seeks to focus a software development organization on continuous improvement and learning. It seeks to examine whether the business is under control and whether it is focused on making a profit. This is a model that is compatible with any Agile method and with any RSM.[1] It has five stages—ironically, just like the CMM.

Stage 0—Analysis Ability

Stage 0 represents the basic barrier to entry. For example, if an Extreme Programming team does not know how to write a story on an index card, they cannot get started with that method. It is, therefore, vital that the development organization gain a basic proficiency in the conceptual model of the chosen method. An FDD team, for example, would need a basic grounding in UML class modeling with Archetypes and the Domain Neutral Component and an ability at Feature analysis and creating a Feature List and Plan.

---

[1]RSM refers to rigorous software methodology as defined by Highsmith [2002].

Table 11–1
Learning organization maturity model.

Stage 0	**Analysis Ability**	
	Decompose system input into basic units of measurement.	
Stage 1	**End-to-End Traceability**	
	Implement system for capturing & monitoring measurements.	
Stage 2	**Stabilize System Metrics**	
	Inventory; lead time; production rate	
	Demonstrate basic statistical process control—show that system is stable against a target and within a tolerance.	
Stage 3	**System Thinking and a Learning Organization**	
	Focus on continuous improvement. New targets: lower inventory, shorter lead time, higher production rate. Identify constraints; exploit constraints; subordinate to decision; elevate constraint.	
Stage 4	**Anticipated ROI and the Failure Tolerant Organization**	
	Encourage risk taking. Focus on Throughput ($), not production quantity. Focus on market research/feedback (i.e., external constraints).	

Stage 1—End-to-End Traceability

Stage 1 represents the first true steps on the road to an organization that shows ability to continuously improve and produce better and better financial results. In order to show those results, it is necessary to measure. As Tom DeMarco correctly observed, "You cannot control, what you cannot measure" [Wiegers 1996].

Stage 2—Stabilize System Metrics

Stabilizing system metrics is a demonstration that software development can be brought under control. It is demonstrating that it can deliver conformant quality. It is showing that it can meet its customer expectations within some acceptable tolerance.

Achieving stage 2 is a significant challenge. Many software organizations never get there. Stage 2 provides a basic grounding for running a proper business. With a development team showing this level of maturity, it becomes possible to make serious financial plans based on future development work.

Stage 3—System Thinking and a Learning Organization

Stage 3 asks the team to demonstrate that it can learn and use the learning to produce improvements. Stage 3 could last for years. Stage 3 involves gradually tightening the screws on the achieved metrics. Ask for just a little more productivity. Ask for just a little more quality. Ask for just a little shorter lead time. Stage 3 forces management to look for the constraints, to determine how best to exploit them, to subordinate the rest of the process to that decision, and then to consider investment in order to elevate the constraint. When the organization has achieved this, go around again and ask for even more. When the metrics begin to level out or even reverse, perhaps the team is becoming risk averse.

Stage 4—Anticipated ROI and the Failure Tolerant Organization

In his book on systems thinking, Peter Senge asks, "Is there a sixth discipline?" [Senge 1990]. Having spent 300 pages explaining the five disciplines of a learning organization—personal mastery, mental models, shared vision, team learning, and systems thinking—Senge goes on to ask whether there is more to come. I believe that there is. The logical next step after achieving a learning organization is to achieve a failure tolerant organization [Farson 2002]. Failure tolerance is the sixth discipline!

If software development organizations that are not afraid to push the boundaries and never afraid to take on projects with high risk are to be built, there must be an environment in which line managers are unafraid to take risks. This can be achieved, as explained in Chapter 12, by rewarding them based on anticipated ROI. Naturally, in order to do this properly, the organization must be completely mature along its entire value stream. The software production system does not work in isolation.

Summary

Producing the best financial results doesn't happen overnight. Even being able to calculate the financial metrics in this book takes considerable maturity in an organization. However, a software engineering organization can benefit greatly and realize some of the financial benefits even before it is capable of measuring the success. Ironically, if the goal is financial, getting there requires a process that reveals itself inside out.

First, an organization must learn to identify and measure what is important. Then, it must demonstrate that ability throughout its value chain. Next, it must stabilize its operation and show that management has control of the numbers. Next, it should seek to continuously improve those numbers. Finally, it must become failure tolerant in order to push the boundaries to the limits of competitiveness.

chapter 12

Setting the Governing Rules

Section 1 argues that traditional project management that defines tasks at a fine grained level and track and report those tasks is outdated. Supporters of Agile software development methods say such fine grained planning and tracking is unnecessary, inaccurate, and wasteful. The uncertain and nonlinear nature of software development means that both fine grained plans and effort-based estimates are likely to be wrong.

The essence of Agile software development is that it is highly delegated. Many Agilists prefer the term, "self-organizing." The point is that plans should be made at a high level and the desired adaptive behavior should be left alone to emerge from the system.

Allow Adaptive Behavior to Emerge

The role for the executive is, therefore, to establish the simple rules governing the system of software production. The executive must determine the rules, then leave the system alone to adapt accordingly. If the desired adaptive behavior does not emerge, then the rules must be tweaked. Executives must resist the opportunity to interfere, control, or micromanage the process. Each layer of management must delegate responsibility for the activities beneath them to the staff doing the work.

The Role of the Agile Executive

Donald Reinertsen defined three layers of control with systems of design [1997, p. 201].

Table 12–1 clearly defines the role of the executives as having responsibility for selection of the software development lifecycle method to be used. Selecting an established method such as RUP or XP effectively defines the governing rules. Alternatively, a business may decide to follow the general principles of Agile software development, but define its own set of rules—rules that can be measured using the metrics presented in this text. The executives are creating an environment for operational excellence and continuous improvement.

The role of the manager in Reinertsen's model becomes one of responsibility for continuous improvement. The manager must seek to gradually change the parameters to encourage the organization to improve. The manager has

Reinertsen's Three Tiers of Control

Table 12–1
Reinertsen's three levels of system control.

Executives	Select the system (or method) of production. Define the governing rules.
Managers	Set/adjust process tolerances. Adjust attributes of variable rules.
Staff	Adjust performance by responding to feedback from system metrics.

responsibility for generating more profits now and in the future by increasing production, reducing inventory, and reducing lead time, leading to lower operating expense.

The role of the staff in this model is to enjoy the empowerment that comes with a highly delegated system of control and to respond appropriately to the feedback that is created from the rules introduced by the executives and configured by the development manager.

The Process Improvement Problem

DeMarco and Lister noted that there is a problem with process improvement initiatives [DeMarco 1999, p. 186]. Such initiatives are primarily focused on quality and estimation improvement, that is, better control over scope, time, and resources, whilst maximizing the production rate through use of quality improvement techniques such as peer code reviews.

Using the SEI SW-CMM[1] scale as a basis for their observations, they believe that inertia builds as the organization grows in maturity and climbs the CMM scale. This could be thought of as a balancing loop that limits growth of process maturity. In theory, an organization with a high CMM level should have a high production rate, due to good planning and high quality. However, organizations that rise on the scale become risk averse and fail to undertake the truly valuable projects. In effect, they pass up the most profitable opportunities. So they may achieve high levels of production rate, but the value is low. The suggested effect is that Throughput (value delivered to the business from sales) falls in organizations with a high CMM rating because the organization is unwilling to undertake higher risk projects that might have a greater ROI.

The Theory of Constraints and the financial metrics from Chapter 2 provide the tools to resolve this conflict. DeMarco and Lister assume that the managers are governed by rules based on an increased production rate. A high production rate is achieved through high quality and low amounts of rework. Hence, the manager strives to improve quality and general organizational maturity because it leads to an increased production and they receive bonuses or promotion based on achieved production rates or quality metrics.

[1]The Software Engineering Institute of Carnegie Mellon University defined the Software Capability Maturity Model, http://www.sei.cmu.edu/.

On the face of it, setting the governing rules for the system based on production rate appears to make sense. However, it is obvious that it will lead to a risk-averse development organization. Faced with a choice of building a system that looks like a clone of one he just finished, or building another that uses new, untested technology and attacks a business problem that his team hasn't seen before, a manager will naturally feel better with the former choice. A project that looks like a previous one can be accurately planned and the production rate can be guessed within a few percentage points error. The manager can bank his bonus. The riskier project with new technology and new business problems will definitely impact the production rate and quality while his team learns new skills and understands new business issues. A manager incentivized by production rate or quality assurance will never choose a risky project, if given a choice.

Govern the System with Anticipated ROI

The answer to this is provided by the ROI metric. It is known that system rules must not encourage local efficiency or local production rate. Line managers must understand their place in the value chain and be focused on overall system production. However, managers must be remunerated based on ROI. Only ROI shows a more positive value for riskier projects—assuming the riskier project has a higher intrinsic value.

What is more, the incentive must be based on expected ROI, rather than actual ROI. If managers are measured based on actual ROI, they would be carrying all of the risk. This would make them risk averse. The desired result would not be achieved. The manager would still prefer the less risky project with the higher production rate. By using expected (or anticipated) ROI as the measure of incentive, it is possible to encourage managers to take the risks that the business needs to take. The business as a whole will carry the risk.

Therefore, in a mature software development organization the managers must be measured based on delivery of software with the highest available ROI at the time when the product or project was introduced into the system. In other words, a manager's bonus should be paid on delivery, but the value of the bonus should be evaluated at the initiation of the project.

Setting governing rules based on potential Throughput necessitates the ability to measure and track the value of Throughput throughout the system. The Agile manager must be capable of measuring the functional requirements at ideation and tracking them through to delivery. Measuring functional requirements allows the inventory of ideas captured within the software production system to be quantified. If Inventory (V) can be measured, the rate of transformation of inventory—the Production Rate (R)—can also be measured. If the inventory can be quantified at ideation, it is possible to measure how long it takes for a single functional requirement to pass through the system, that is, Lead Time (LT).

In an immature organization, process that allows tracking requirements through the lifecycle must be introduced first. It must be possible to track ideas through Analysis, Design, Coding, and Testing. This is a fundamental stepping stone towards manageability and profitability. Introducing end-to-end traceability in the software development lifecycle is a nontrivial first step. This first barrier to entry defeats many organizations. However, the Agile manager simply must achieve this first basic step.

Chapter 11 examined in depth the concept of a maturity model for a learning organization. The five stages of such a maturity model are: stage 0—improve analysis skills; stage 1—end-to-end traceability; stage 2—measure inventory, lead time, and production rate; stage 3—value chain alignment of line management as a team, overall system thinking, and constraint theory to focus improvements in inventory, lead time, and production rate; stage 4—focus on overall anticipated ROI. Each stage in this maturity model requires a different set of governing rules and appropriate metrics to push the organization towards the subsequent level.

Governing Rules for Managers

Managers in an immature organization must be measured initially by their ability to implement end-to-end traceability. Managers must set the goal of implementing requirements tracking systems for the purpose of tracking the flow of value through the system. In order to do this, there is a base level of analysis required. Depending on the skill set and maturity of the organization, the manager may first need to implement a skills gap training program on analysis techniques. The team must be able to identify what they are measuring.

Once it is possible to measure inventory, production rate, and lead time, the focus must change to improving the production rate and reducing the lead time and inventory by setting ever more difficult targets. This will focus the managers' thinking and require them to identify constraints and then exploit and elevate each in turn. The governing rules for managers must be based on the production rate of the whole system, not just the local part of the value chain for which a single manager is responsible. The effect of focusing the managers on the overall system production is to force all the managers in the value chain to work together as a team. If they are measured based on local production rate (local optima), the organization is likely to become dysfunctional. This resolves one of the fundamental problems in organizational hierarchies, that there is no such thing as a management team![2]

Finally, when the system is working close to maximum capacity, the governing rules must change to measure the manager based on ROI. The manager must be allowed to let the production rate fall, if it produces a potentially greater ROI.

[2]In *Peopleware*, DeMarco and Lister observe that a group of line managers with a similar rank in an organization chart are not a team unless their goals and values are commonly aligned [DeMarco 1999, p. 213].

Skills Gap Education

If analysis and requirements engineering are skills that are lacking in the organization, the manager should set goals based on addressing these deficiencies. Measure the manager by the improvement in the skill set of the developers on the team. Hence, it is necessary to determine the current maturity level of the organization in order to adequately determine the goals for the manager.

As demonstrated in Chapter 2, education can be treated just like any other system problem and the value added can be measured. The Throughput is measured as the skill set improvement of the employees undertaking training. The skill at the end of a period of measurement less the skill level at the beginning of the period is the Throughput achieved. So it is possible to set a specific measurable tangible goal for the manager based on skill level improvement across her team.

End-to-End Traceability

The next goal for the Agile manager involves achieving end-to-end traceability with the goal of demonstrating ability to measure Inventory (V), Production Rate (R), and Lead Time (LT). The goal should be measurable based on the coverage of projects in the software production system and the compliance with data input for metrics tracking. It will be necessary to audit the figures in order to assess the manager's achievement. The long-term target is full traceability for all inventory in the software production system.

Production Metrics

Once traceability is achieved, goals must be switched to targets based on the truly valuable system variables: inventory, lead time, and production rate. The manager should set targets for these. The initial goal should be to stabilize the numbers and demonstrate control of the software production system. Stabilizing means bringing the fluctuation in levels of measurement within an agreed tolerance, that is, 10 to 15 Use Cases per week might be a production target for a UDP system or 18 to 22 Story Points per week for an Extreme Programming system.

Continuous Improvement—The Learning Organization

When the basic system metrics have been stabilized, it is time to turn up the profitability heat by setting ever improving targets for production rate, inventory levels, and lead time. The manager should be asked to make improvements in the metrics. This will cause her to focus on identifying the system constraints and deciding how best to exploit each in turn, then on mechanisms for subordinating everything else to the decision, and later on making a business case for investment to elevate the constraint.

Every time a constraint is elevated, the metrics should improve until a new constraint is encountered. Senge calls this "limits to growth archetype," in which a resisting force or slowing action prevents further growth from a previous improvement [Senge 1990]. When a growth-limiting balancing loop is encountered, the intuitive reaction is to push harder. However, Senge advises seeing the limiting factor as the new constraint. Action should be taken to remove the new limiting factor, that is, elevate the new constraint. "This may require actions you have not yet considered, . . . or choices in rewards and norms."

The Failure Tolerant Organization

As was discussed earlier, managers can become risk averse when they are measured purely by production metrics. They cannot risk missing their production targets by taking on a risky project that involves retraining staff, using new technology, or employing more people who may not be versed in the methods of their highly efficient system of software production.

It is, therefore, necessary to set governing rules that accept that taking risks may result in reduced performance. Farson calls an organization that is adaptable and motivated to take risks "failure tolerant" [2002].

By setting a production target based on production of risky projects with a potentially higher ROI, the manager should be rewarded for delivery of those riskier, higher ROI projects. It is important to use anticipated ROI and provide the reward on delivery. It is important to provide positive feedback as quickly as possible when trying to encourage appropriate behavior. The manager is a system, too. If the organization waits to see whether the project is successful in the marketplace and rewards the manager based on the actual ROI, two things happen. Firstly, the reward is too far in the future and too intangible to the manager—there is no obvious cause-effect due to the time delay. Secondly, the business is asking the line managers to carry the risk that should normally be born by the investors in the business. Managers should not be asked to carry unnecessary risk. They must be rewarded for delivering on what they can control. That reward must be based on anticipated ROI.

Calculating ROI requires the organization to be capable of accurately valuing I, the investment in inventory, that is, the cost of acquiring the requirements, and of accurately valuing the finished product in order to determine T. This requires a very mature marketing department capable of measuring the product marketing costs of acquiring the requirements and capable of accurately predicting the size of the market and the market price the finished product will fetch.

This example is an occasion in which the constraint moves outside the control of the Vice President of Engineering. The constraint on overall system improvement is no longer an engineering one. The constraint is now a marketing department capability. Without the capability to accurately value investment in requirements or estimate the acceptable sales price, the organization will not be able to implement the governing rules required to continue the process of improvement. Hence, growth is limited by marketing department maturity.

Engineers must be encouraged to focus on exploiting themselves as a capacity constrained resource. This is referred to as "self organization" by many Agile methodologists. The concept is that the team members themselves organize to optimize their work.

The business must set goals designed to create behavior that is in the best interests of the overall system. It may be unfair to expect every engineer to see and understand the big picture. It may not be necessary to ask engineers to use system thinking. They need not understand the Theory of Constraints. Instead, they must be told how management intends to measure them. Expect their behavior to modify accordingly.

The correct metrics to exploit the engineer as a resource are lead time and quality. Engineers should be asked to minimize their local lead time rather than maximize their production rate. If they are rewarded for production rate and that rate begins to greatly exceed the rate of others in the value chain, they will create a downstream stockpile of inventory and may erode upstream buffers. Minimizing lead time—the time to perform their stage of transformation of the client-valued functionality—shows that engineers can be responsive and Agile without building inventory downstream or depleting it upstream.

Engineers should be encouraged to do high-quality work. Quality should not be sacrificed by reducing lead time. It is desirable to minimize the quantity of inventory returning through the system. It is understood that rework reduces the overall system production. Poor quality will affect production rate, inventory levels, and lead time.

By asking the engineer to minimize lead time and maximize quality, for example, to minimize bugs per client-valued function whilst also minimizing the time to create that client-valued function, the business is setting objectives for engineers that are aligned with the management objectives of improved production rate, minimized inventory, and short overall lead times. In turn, these objectives are aligned with the overall executive metrics for T, I, and OE. These, in turn, are aligned with the stockholder and board objectives for NP and ROI.

Engineers can be afraid of measurement schemes. They may rebel against them from fear of misuse. The result is that they do not cooperate with the gathering of metrics and inhibit or prevent the necessary end-to-end traceability.

In order to get participation and cooperation from the engineering team, it is necessary to practice fair process [Kim 1997] and insure that team members understand what is being measured and why. They are all highly educated knowledge workers. They can handle the detail. In addition, management should set the engineering measurements against teams of engineers rather than individuals. This reflects the teamworking nature of Lean and Agile methods. Team measurement shares the benefits and risks by aggregating them across a set of individuals.

In addition to local lead time and local quality, the teams of engineers can have a portion of their incentive or bonus based on overall system, rather than local, production rate. This helps to awaken them to system thinking and to gain an understanding of their actions as part of a larger whole.

Team Measurements

chapter 13

Staffing Decisions

B ad management causes staff turnover. As discussed in the Introduction, it isn't the only reason why software engineers look elsewhere for an employer, but it is perhaps the most common reason.

Software development organizations have a tendency to take staff turnover in their stride. They often state that it is just "industry standard" or "normal." There is cognitive dissonance about the fact that the problem is management induced and preventable. There is also a complete failure to understand the true costs associated with staff turnover and the consequent effect that bad management has on the financial health of a software development business.

Conventional View of Turnover Costs

The conventional approach to calculating the cost of staff turnover is based on cost accounting. It focuses on the additional expenditure required to replace a member of staff with a new recruit. The cost of recruitment is normally seen as a combination of the following characteristics: advertising the position (recently this has become almost negligible with web-based recruitment), the relocation package for the new employee, the recruitment agent fee, and the opportunity cost of having existing staff interview the candidates (recall the time sheets for engineers in which interviewing is declared as an overhead). There is a vague notion that there is an opportunity cost while the new employee is brought up to speed and receives training. However, this measure, which is really a Throughput measure, is seldom elaborated and is poorly understood because the organization is not measuring it.

Throughput Accounting View of Turnover Costs

Throughput Accounting does not focus on cost but rather on the effect on production and Inventory. The cost-based elements of advertising, the agent's fee, and relocation would all be assigned to Operating Expense. OE does increase with higher staff turnover. However, it is much more important to understand the effect on system Throughput and Inventory. What really matters is whether the staff work in the system constraint.

Using the example from Figure 3–1, System Test is the CCR. It has a capacity of 30 units per month. If System Test employs 10 people and one of them leaves the business, then the capacity will be reduced by 10%. For the purposes of simple math, assume that the new capacity is 27 units per month. The result is that the Throughput of the whole system is reduced to 27 units per month. By losing 1 member of staff from a software production system which employs perhaps 50 people, there is a 10% reduction in overall productivity.

If the employee had worked in Coding rather than System Test, the net effect on the system would have been negligible providing quality was high and there was slack in the system. But, the result of losing a single member of staff in System Test will increase LT by approximately 10%.

Cost of Replacing a Full-Time Engineer

Assume that it takes, on average, 60 days to replace a permanent staff member, with a best case of 30 days and a worst case of 120 days. Further, assume a new hire will take 3 months to become totally productive. If this is averaged out, it is fair to say that a further 6 weeks of productivity is lost after a new hire starts. Hence, the best case, average, and worst case scenarios are 75 days, 105 days, and 165 days of productivity lost.

In the example of System Test, Throughput is reduced by 10% when a single tester leaves. Lead time is increased by 10%. The cost of operating the system of software production is $15,000 per day. Hence, the additional OE incurred by the loss of single tester is $112,500 at best, $157,500 on average, and $247,500 in the worst case as shown in Table 13–1. This additional cost must be added to the traditional costs for advertising, the agent's fee, and relocation. Not included in this calculation is the possible loss of Throughput from Sales due to any slippage in the delivery date of the product.

Cost of Replacing a Temporary Engineer

The use of contract labor is widespread in the software development business. It is widely assumed that contractors are easy to hire and fire and that they can be treated like commodities. This assumption can be examined by analyzing the effect on production of losing a contractor, when the contractor works in the system bottleneck.

Table 13–1
OE incurred due to loss of a permanent hire.

Permanent Hire	Best	Average	Worst
Days to hire	30	60	120
Days to full productivity	90	90	90
Total days lost	75	105	165
Impact on lead time (days)	7.5	10.5	16.5
OE incurred ($)	112,500	157,500	247,500

Table 13-2

OE incurred due to loss of a contract hire.

Temporary Hire	Best	Average	Worst
Days to hire	15	30	45
Days to full productivity	90	90	90
Total days lost	60	75	90
Impact on lead time (days)	6.0	7.5	9.0
OE incurred ($)	90,000	112,500	135,000

Assume that it takes on average 30 days to replace a temporary member of staff, with a best case of 15 days and a worst case of 45 days. It is unlikely that a contractor will become productive much faster than a regular hire. Hence, it will take her 3 months to become totally productive. So the impact of learning the project may still be equivalent to 45 days of lost production.

Using the same example of System Test, Throughput is reduced by 10% when a single tester leaves. Lead time is increased by 10%. As the cost of operating the system of software production is $15,000 per day, the additional OE incurred by the loss of single tester is $90,000 at best, $112,500 on average, and $135,000 in the worst case, as shown in Table 13-2.

Impact on Project Buffer

Assume that a 6-month project has a 20-day project buffer (15%). In the example given, the loss of 1 tester for an average period of time will cause 50% of the project buffer to be lost. Any sales tied to the promised delivery date are put at risk.

Missing the delivery date will undermine the customer confidence in the business and its management. It also will lead to longer term system effects such as a lack of willingness to negotiate over the uncertainties in future systems because of the loss of trust.

The executives responsible for a software production system must understand the system constraint in order to make appropriate management decisions. To understand the impact of staff turnover on the system as a whole, it is vital to know where the constraints are. This can only be achieved by measuring the flow of inventory through the system and monitoring it regularly.

Understanding the System Constraint Is Essential

Adding Staff to a Bottleneck

When additional staff is hired, there is a rise in OE. In the example of a 50-person software production system, the effect is to increase the OE by about 2%. However, in the example, adding someone to System Test will increase productivity by 10%. The payback is obvious.

However, it must be understood that new staff does not become productive immediately and the production rate will not rise immediately. In fact, it may initially fall as other staff is distracted to help the new hire.

It is very tempting for senior executives to suggest that engineering productivity can be increased or costs can be cut by outsourcing. In fact, doing so is becoming more common. Offshore development in India claims to provide labor rates at 25% of U.S. levels. In Russia or China it can be as low as 10%. Executives used to making cost-based decisions in a cost accounting world see these labor rates as very attractive.

However, it should be obvious by now to any reader of this book that there is more to the decision than the operating expense involved in paying software developers.

Outsource to Elevate a Constraint

First, the motivation for outsourcing should be understood. If it is simply to move development offshore to save costs and all development is going to move, then there are some process maturity issues to consider. How good is the organization at managing a vendor relationship? How good at writing requirements? What will be the lead time from the vendor? And how agile is the offshore development vendor? What is the process for handling change requests, and how much does it cost?

Another reason for outsourcing is that the existing engineering department is resource constrained. Marketing has asked for a long list of features in the next release, and the engineering director has responded with a request to cut the list significantly. The cry then goes up, "Can we get more developers and put more features in the release?" In other words, outsourcing is being used as staff augmentation.

For example, the business could add 20 software engineers in a remote office in India to the existing workforce. Will production quantity increase, and will Marketing get the features they want any sooner? On the face of it, the answer ought to be "yes." However, the answer is much more likely to be "no." Why?

The simple explanation is that the software engineers may not be the system constraint. By adding outsourced resources, the capacity of one element of the system is being increased or elevated. However, if a nonconstraint is elevated, no increase in Throughput will be achieved.

If the constraints in the software production system are the UI designer and the System Test department and 20 software engineers are added in a remote office on another continent, will the UI be designed any faster or the system test scripts executed any quicker? The answer is "no!"

Put simply, management must focus on elevating the constraints. If the UI designer is the constraint, management should seek to outsource UI design or elevate it by some other means, such as staff augmentation by hiring a contractor.

Offshore Development and Process Maturity

If a decision is made to move software development offshore, will it really lead to greater profits now and in the future? Quality is essential to maintaining the production rate of the software production system. Hence, if a high-quality local team is traded for a poor-quality offshore team, it may cost less per hour, but there will be many more hours while bugs are fixed.

However, the offshore company understands this, and several of them have high CMM ratings—Level 4 or Level 5. This is probably significantly higher than the business seeking to outsource development. So quality isn't an issue, right? No, probably wrong! By outsourcing one piece of the system, the business is merely moving the constraint somewhere else.

How good is the business at writing requirements? How often are the requirements right the first time? How long are the lead times for requirements, and how long will it take to turn them into finished code? How many of the requirements are likely to have changed due to changing market conditions before the software is ready? And why is all of this relevant?

If there is no process maturity elsewhere in the organization, for example, in gathering and writing requirements, then the business risks the worst quality problem of all—the outsource team delivers exactly what was asked for! But what was asked for wasn't what was really needed!

Agile software development methods advocate the use of on-site customers and fast feedback loops—feedback on the design and development on a daily basis. They do this precisely because they assume poor process maturity in the front-end of the system, and they acknowledge that today's business environment is fastpaced and ever changing. Agile software development methods are designed to cope with change quickly and with minimum cost. When an organization chooses to outsource a piece of the system such as software development, they still need the requirements, analysis, UI design, usability engineering, and product test in-house. However, they create a situation where there is a large batch transfer to and from an outsource organization in the middle of the system. This will increase the inventory in the system, the lead time, and the risk that ideas for client-valued functionality become stale.

The trend in Lean Production is to source components locally. Japanese automobile manufacturers operating in the United States are forcing their Asian suppliers to open factories in the United States, generally within a 200-mile radius of their car assembly plants. The reason is simple. In Lean Production, lead time is king! The metric by which everyone is measured is "number of hours to build a car." This is a Throughput Accounting metric.

The Agile software development equivalent of a local supplier is an on-site customer who can validate and feed back on the true meaning of the requirements. The on-site customer prevents poor quality from working its way through the system to the point where it is most costly, as discussed in Chapter 9.

Before executives rush to outsource the work of software developers, they might like to reconsider. Perhaps the answer is to improve the quality of software development management and to change the working practices to enable software developers to be as productive as they can be.

An offshore development organization may audit as SEI SW-CMM Level 5. They may have quality assurance to deliver exactly what was asked for, but when it arrives, it may not be what the business needed. This could mean that the original investment in requirements must be written off along with a large percentage of the operating expense involved in creating software. The project is then started again. It's the same old problems of software engineering in a world of a PMI/ISO quality and management model—it just costs a little less money.

It is possible that something done to save operating expense may result in significant cost increases and reduced Throughput because of delayed product. This highlights why Throughput Accounting produces superior management information. It focuses the business on profits and investment and subordinates cost to the achievement of more profit now and in the future through greater Throughput and reduced inventory.

It is important to properly analyze the Throughput Accounting implications of a decision to outsource and to understand its true contribution to Net Profit and ROI before any decision is made. Using the metrics presented in this text, it would be possible for a large organization to compare the ROI of projects run locally using Agile methods against that of an alternative project out-sourced to a low-cost offshore vendor.

chapter 14

Operations Review

The purpose of a monthly operations review is to create a culture of openness and trust, to share a common understanding of the issues confronting management and staff, and to debate the opportunity for improvements. It is a learning opportunity, vital to the health of a learning organization. An operations review is designed to surface issues so that management and executives can do their jobs and help to remove obstacles before they impact the financial performance of the business. An operations review is not simply a forum for delivering good news. Issues should be surfaced not concealed, disguised, or shrouded in a sea of meaningless data.

Purpose

The operations review is not intended as a control mechanism. Daily feedback based on production metrics should be used for control. Operations review is about learning, building trust with value-chain partners, and teaching senior executives about the business.

Everyone in the business who holds the position of line manager or above should attend the operations review. It should not be a cloistered gathering of a few directors and a single VP. Besides including all individual contributors holding the rank of manager or above, it should involve immediate management succession planning candidates, that is, team leads slated for full management jobs within the next 12 months.

Attendees

The business unit's boss and some of his or her colleagues should be present. Senior vice presidents should take an interest in the running of the software business. Even if they don't attend every month, it is important for the lower ranking managers to see that the senior bosses not only take an interest but also understand the operational issues facing the business every day.

In addition, all business owners upstream and downstream in the same value chain should be invited. When a business needs to work and negotiate with partners in a value chain, those partners need to understand the issues and learn to trust each other. Unilateral openness is required to kick start the process of system improvement. The trust built through openness is an emergent property of lean systems.

An operations review should be held monthly—not quarterly! In the fast pace of the business world in the 21st century, a quarterly review is not agile enough to respond to rapid changes in the market. Healthy monitoring of a business by its management needs to be monthly. The review should be 2 to 3 weeks after the end of the month to which it refers. The data analysis team working for the finance or operations director should be asked to focus on its own lead time. They should try to prepare the review material as quickly as possible after the end of the month. Ideally, most of the data should be self-generating from the day-to-day metrics used by the line management.

The review itself should be no more than 2 hours. A Friday afternoon at 2 P.M. is a good time. Everyone can leave for the weekend directly afterwards with a clear picture of their business in mind.

An operations review will visually present the information that the business needs to operate successfully.

The difference between data and information is, says Eli Goldratt, the difference between the inputs needed to derive an answer versus the actual answer [Goldratt 1990, p. 6]. Information is the answer to a question. Management information is the answer to a question about the health and running of a business. Management information answers questions executives need answered in order to make informed decisions about investment in and operation of a business that must be run for profits now and in the future.

Lead with Financial Information

The goal of a business is to make money and to return a reasonable amount to the stockholders for their initial investment. Managers should never be allowed to forget that. All operations reviews should lead with the financial data. The presentation of this slide and its supporting slides should be made by the director of operations, the director of finance, or the responsible vice president or business owner with the fiduciary duty to the shareholders.

Chapter 2 defined the important financial metrics, that is, the financial information needed to make executive decisions. An operations review should report: the Throughput (T) for the month, the total Throughput for the year to date, the trend, the variance from plan, and a year-on-year comparison to the same month from the previous year; the on-going level of Investment (I), for the month, the trend, the variance from plan, and a year-on-year comparison; the Operating Expense (OE), for the month, the total for the year-to-date, trend, variance from plan, and a year-on-year comparison; Net Profit (Loss) [NP] for the month, year-to-date, variance from plan, and year-on-year comparison and annualized ROI for the month, variance from plan, and year-on-year comparison.

In a single slide, such as that shown in Figure 14–1, using a single spreadsheet and three graphs, management can see at a glance whether its business is healthy or not. Any issues to be revealed later will already be visible in the financial information presented on the first slide.

2003	Actual	Jan	Feb	Mar	Apr	May	Jun	YTD
Gross Sales		3.00	3.10	4.10	4.20	5.00	5.50	24.90
Direct Costs		0.40	0.40	0.60	0.60	0.70	0.80	3.50
Throughput		2.60	2.70	3.50	3.60	4.30	4.70	21.40
OE		1.50	1.50	1.50	1.60	1.50	1.60	9.20
NP (Loss)		1.10	1.20	2.00	2.00	2.80	3.10	12.20
Deployed Investment		35.0	37.0	39.0	43.0	47.0	32.0	38.8
Annualized ROI		37.71%	38.92%	61.54%	55.81%	71.49%	116.25%	31.42%

2003	Plan	Jan	Feb	Mar	Apr	May	Jun	YTD
Gross Sales		3.00	3.35	3.70	4.40	5.10	5.80	25.35
Direct Costs		0.50	0.60	0.70	0.90	1.10	1.30	5.10
Throughput		2.50	2.75	3.00	3.50	4.00	4.50	20.25
OE		1.50	1.50	1.50	1.50	1.50	1.50	9.00
NP (Loss)		1.00	1.25	1.50	2.00	2.50	3.00	11.25
Deployed Investment		37	37	37	37	37	37	37

Figure 14–1
Ops review financial information.

The financial data could be supported with separate slides for each of the three main metrics—T, I, and OE. The Throughput slide would break out what was delivered and list specific sales. The Investment slide would break out the sunk capital in tangible assets and the working capital in the intangible asset of ideas for client-valued functionality. The Operating Expense slide would break out specific areas of cost with a primary focus on head count and salaries, including the mix of permanent to contract staff.

The specifics of how to account for Throughput in three different types of software business are discussed in Chapters 15 through 17.

Production Metrics

The second major slide in the presentation should be presented by the director (or VP) of engineering. The manager responsible for running the system of software production should be the one presenting the slides on production metrics. The production metrics should echo the financial metrics. As described in Chapter 5, the production quantity for the month (Q), echoes Throughput (T). The Inventory (V) echoes Investment (I), and the average cost per function (ACPF) provides a normalized view of OE.

The cumulative flow diagram for the whole system is the main visual tool for the production metrics—both inventory and production levels can be read from it.

The example in Figure 14–2 shows a business with a very ragged flow, poor inventory control, a typical inventory turn of around 4 months, and a poor delivery rate. There is a great opportunity for improving this business. By month 6, there appears to be a steadying of the graph, but there has been no software delivered for 2 months. Everyone in the business should be made to understand the issues relating to flow and regular smooth delivery of working code.

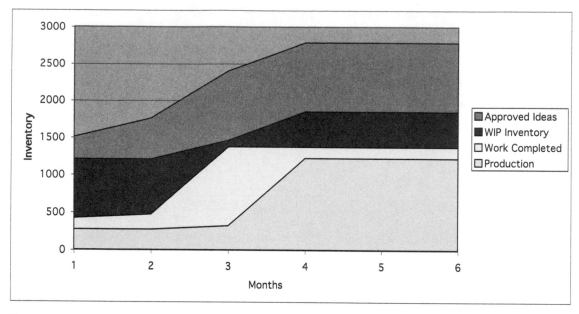

Figure 14–2
Ops review production information.

Figure 14–3
CCR information.

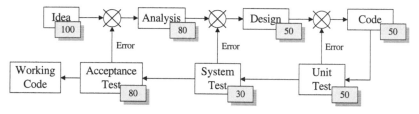

- Current CCR is System Test
- Testers relieved of all non-essential tasks, extra PMs assigned to complete administrative tasks, Analysts assigned to future Test Plans
- Requirements release restricted to 100 per quarter
- Plan to recruit five temporary staff immediately

The second important production slide should list the production rate at each step in the process and should name the current system constraint, the CCR, as shown in Figure 14–3. The trend in production through the CCR should be shown. Action being taken to protect and exploit the constraint should be listed, so that everyone in the business understands the actions of the development manager or director of engineering. Proposed actions to elevate the constraint should be presented, if appropriate. A single additional slide showing the business case for the elevation in ROI terms, as described in Chapter 3, should be presented.

Program Management Metrics

The program manager should be asked to present a parking lot summary of all the projects in the system, similar to that in Figure 14–4. A single parking space should be allocated for each project. The color in each space reflects the overall health of the project, which is monitored through the usage of the project buffer, described in Chapter 7. The color indicates the likelihood that the project delivery date will be met. Overlaid onto each parking space are the delivery date and the percentage complete for the project.

Project Management Metrics

Each project in production should then present in turn. The project manager responsible should lead the presentation. There is no right or wrong way to order the presentations. However, senior executive time can be at a premium, so the more important projects should generally be presented earlier in the meeting. More important may mean of higher value, greater strategic value, or having the closest delivery date. There is no prescription for determining the most important. The business owner needs to figure that out by herself.

Each project should report the cumulative flow diagram for the specific project. Any questions regarding the flow of inventory in the project should be fielded by the development line manager responsible.

The project tracking metrics from Chapter 7—the project buffer usage, the usage of each feeding buffer, the quantity of inventory blocked and the trend, and the number of open issues, the trend, and the average age—should be presented on single slide with the cumulative flow diagram.

The entire health of a project is presented visually on one slide, as in Figure 14–5.

Issues requiring executive attention, that is, issues that are blocking the flow of inventory and impacting the Critical Path of the project should be listed on a slide as in Figure 14–6. Specific issues should state the tracking number, title, summary, date opened, number of days open, number of units of inventory affected, proposed action required or action being undertaken, and the executive accountable.

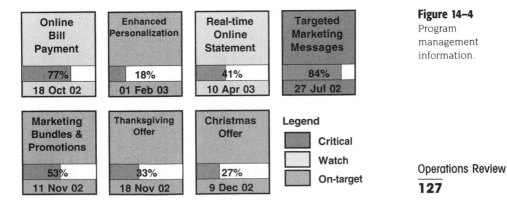

Figure 14–4
Program management information.

Figure 14–5
Project management
information.

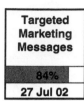

Targeted Marketing Messages		Percentage Used	Days Remaining
	Project Buffer	90%	2
84%	**Feeding Buffer 1**	150%	0
27 Jul 02	**Feeding Buffer 2**	3%	17

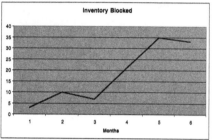
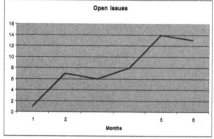

Figure 14–6
Issues requiring
executive attention.

Project "Targeted Marketing Messages" – Critical Path Issues

Title	Opened	Days open	Affects	Action	Owner
Privacy Protection	4/10/02	80	4	FTC Query	Legal (regulatory)
Market Segmentation Rules	5/17/02	43	3	Analysis doc being prepared	Dir of Consumer Marketing
...	...	...	...	...	...

Minute Taking

The director of operations for the business unit should have recorded the minutes of the meeting. All issues raised should be assigned to an executive for resolution. All decisions or commitments made by senior executives should be recorded.

Each meeting should open with a brief review of the open actions for executives from the previous meeting and the status, that is, closed, in-process, or blocked.

Summary

The operations review is a monthly event for the entire management team of the software business and all its value-chain partners. It should take no longer than 2 hours and should lead with the financial information.

By presenting just a few simple metrics—T, I, OE, NP, ROI, Q, V, and ACPF—the health of the business can be judged at a glance. By detailing only a few more metrics for each project—buffer usage, open issues, and blocked inventory—the health of individual projects can be judged at a glance. Every one of these metrics is self-generating from the day-to-day management information needed to run an Agile software production system.

By surfacing only the significant issues that impact the system constraint and the Critical Path of projects in trouble, executive attention is focused on what is truly important to the operational success of the business.

Operations review[1] truly is the essence of Agile management!

---

[1] The monthly operations review became an integral part of life at Sprintpcs.com, the Internet business unit of Sprint PCS, an American mobile phone company, from January 2001. The business unit employed 350 people with an annual budget around $70 million. The event was regularly attended by at least one executive vice president and often several. It was generally held on the third Friday of each month at 2P.M. The process described here represents a refinement and improvement. The metrics are simpler, and the visualizations better. The focus is the same—lead with the financial information, follow with the production information, and alert executive attention to the important constraining issues holding back progress. Allow those with direct accountability to do the presenting.

chapter 15

Agile Management in the IT Department

To show the effectiveness of a corporate IT department, it is necessary to show that it can add value to the business, that IT is a source for profit in the overall value chain. This completely reverses the traditional view, based on cost accounting, that IT departments are cost centers. IT has been seen as a pure operational expense, not a source for value generation.

Corporate IT's Value-Added Contribution

What information is necessary to know whether or not the IT department adds value to the organization? To determine this, it is necessary to examine what represents Throughput (T).

When an IT system is deployed in the corporation, the IT department has essentially delivered and sold that system to another part of the business. The value of this system was determined by the budget for the system. Hence, the sales price is the system budget. Throughput can be defined as the system budget less any direct costs, including the cost of components such as relational database licenses or middleware products such as an application server. It is safe to assume that the corporation would not have approved the project were there not a demonstrable ROI. Therefore, it follows that if the IT department can deliver within the budget, it has shown added value and matched its ROI expectation.

Henceforth, the assumption that T equals the system budget less direct costs will be referred to as the "Budget Basis" for financial metrics.

$$\text{Throughput}_{\text{Budget basis}} = \text{System Budget} - \text{Direct Deployment Costs}$$

However, the Budget Basis for measuring the IT organization makes a huge assumption. It assumes that the business case made for the system being deployed accurately calculated the expected benefits. A budget for the system was allocated based on such a plan. The Budget Basis is not very agile. It depends on an accurate estimate of the level of effort, leading to an estimate of the costs before the project was undertaken. It probably relies on the scope being locked down in order to estimate the effort and to assess the benefit.

The Budget Basis shows whether the CIO is capable of living within his budget, but it does not prove whether or not there was a true return for the stockholders and whether or not the IT system deployed actually delivered value. Hence, the Budget Basis can only be used to evaluate the performance of the CIO and the IT department against the plan and to calculate the inaccuracy of the original estimate. It cannot be used to determine true stockholder value.

To determine whether or not an IT system made real sense for the business, it is necessary to assess the value of the improvement after the system was deployed. This can only be done historically, once real numbers are available. This will be referred to as the "True Basis" for financial metrics. With the True Basis, Throughput is determined by the value added to the business by the newly deployed IT system, less any direct costs involved in operating it. For example, a system that allows bank lending officers to make loans to customers would generate Throughput if the number of loans made was greater than before the system was deployed or the cost of sale for each loan was decreased.

Possible Definitions for Valued-Added by a Bank Lending System

$$\text{Value Added}_{Loans} = \#\text{Loans}_{Post\text{-}deployment} - \#\text{Loans}_{Pre\text{-}deployment}$$

$$\text{Value Added}_{LoanAmount} = \$\text{Lent}_{Post\text{-}deployment} - \$\text{Lent}_{Pre\text{-}deployment}$$

$$\text{Value Added}_{Income} = \$\text{Income(from Loans)}_{Post\text{-}deployment} - \$\text{Income}_{Pre\text{-}deployment}$$

The new IT system added value if it helped to generate additional business, directly contributed to reducing the variable costs associated with a sale, or reduced the overall operating expenses for the business. The costs of operating the IT system and maintaining it would need to be deducted from the value added. The result would be the genuine Throughput contribution of the IT system:

$$\text{Throughput}_{IT} = \text{Income}_{Post\text{-}deployment} - \text{OE}_{Business\ (downstream\ from\ IT)}$$

The Throughput figure from the perspective of the IT department is the sales figure less the operating expense incurred downstream from IT in the value chain. OE downstream can be treated as direct costs against sales for a given time period:

$$\text{New Throughput} = \text{Throughput}_{Post\text{-}deployment} - \text{Throughput}_{Pre\text{-}deployment}$$

The value added by the deployment of the system is the increase in T after deployment (New Throughput). To calculate $T_{true\ basis}$, direct costs such as system operation and deployment must be deducted from the new T:

$$T_{True\ basis} = \text{New Throughput} - (\text{System Operation} + \text{Deployment})$$

If there has been a true contribution from the new system, then T will be positive after the costs of operating the system and deploying it are subtracted out of the value-added figure.

If the objective sought from management information is assessment of the IT department and assessment of the CIOs ability to perform against plan, the Budget Basis for financial metrics should be used. For the CIO and managers within the IT department, this makes most sense. These numbers represent the part of the business under their direct control. However, the Budget Basis carries a risk—the risk of local optimization and a loss of focus on the goal of the whole business.

The True Basis, on the other hand, reflects the value added to the rest of the business when operating the delivered system. The True Basis evaluates the capability of the whole company, not the IT department or the CIO.

Calculating the Budget Basis for IT Assessment

For the purposes of the IT contribution assessment, all activities upstream of software development, for example idea creation, requirements gathering, and business analysis, are treated as investments—investments in potential business improvement. The net profit of the IT department, determined on a Budget Basis, can be shown:

$$\text{Net Profit}_{\text{Budget basis}} = T_{\text{Budget basis}} - OE_{\text{IT department}}$$

Using Throughput Accounting, the Return on Investment would be

$$\text{ROI} = \frac{T_{\text{Budget basis}} - OE_{\text{IT department}}}{I_{\text{Requirements}}}$$

The Budget Basis for NP and ROI provides a normalized method for assessing one CIO against another or one IT group against another within a large organization. Primarily, it shows whether they can work to plan and whether the plans were accurate. An accurate plan would lead to a Net Profit of approximately zero. With the Budget Basis, there is little value in calculating the ROI figure.

Calculating the True Basis for IT Assessment

The net profit of the IT department, determined using the True Basis, would look very similar:

$$\text{Net Profit}_{\text{True basis}} = T_{\text{True basis}} - OE_{\text{IT department}}$$

Using Throughput Accounting, the Return on Investment would be

$$\text{ROI} = \frac{T_{\text{True basis}} - OE_{\text{IT department}}}{I_{\text{Requirements}}}$$

The True Basis provides a normalized method for evaluating the value added in the value stream of a business by its IT organization and the resultant effectiveness of the IT development efforts. The normalized nature of such a metric means that one IT organization can be fairly compared against another from a different company.

A better IT department will add more value to the business. As a result, the True Basis Net Profit and ROI equations will show improving positive results. To improve these numbers a CIO must increase T and decrease I and OE.

Improving Throughput

To increase T, the IT department must look to help the business identify technology opportunities that can best generate additional Throughput for the whole business. Those opportunities should then be turned into IT projects.

An IT department will not start to look for ways to improve T unless they are measured using the True Basis. The Budget Basis must be dropped if a CIO is to be focused on the most important metric—Throughput. The behavior of organizations often starts at the top with how the big boss is measured. To get the desired behavior from an IT staff doing real work, it is necessary to measure the CIO using the True Basis.

Reducing Investment

To decrease I, the CIO must encourage and motivate his analysts to find better ways of capturing requirements. The focus should be in capturing what represents "just enough" to deliver the desired Throughput and understanding the Pareto Principle (the 80–20 rule) that perhaps 20% of the functionality will produce 80% of the Throughput. ROI can be maximized by learning to understand the law of diminishing returns and to stop gathering requirements when there are enough to generate the significant amount of new Throughput.

It would also be advantageous to spend less money acquiring the requirements. A strict monitoring of the dollars invested to acquire a feature (function) should be maintained. The IT department should look for ways to reduce this. Penny pinching might be an option. Ask staff to web conference rather than travel, for example. That would have a positive effect. However, it would be better to find a leaner method for capturing requirements.

A leaner approach to capturing requirements would involve writing fewer documents and producing fewer interim deliverables during the requirements process. The Agile approach here is to encourage face-to-face meetings between subject matter experts and IT developers and to provide an on-site requirements expert during the lifetime of the project. Doing this reduces the paperwork and reduces delays while paper documents are reviewed, debated, and approved. Reducing the time to produce, read, review, and approve such documents directly reduces the waste in the system. Such documents are by-products of the software development system. It may be necessary to have a specification document for audit and traceability, but any other paperwork that could be replaced by a face-to-face meeting introduces waste. Waste increases the amount of investment required and directly affects the operating expense.

Reducing Lead Time

There is working capital sunk in the inventory of ideas for IT projects. This must be financed, and financing it costs money. Hence, the shorter the finance period, the lower the finance charges, which means less OE will be incurred. The faster requirements can be turned into finished code and delivered to a customer, the quicker investment in inventory is released.

Shorter lead times provide higher Throughput. An Agile IT department can choose to deliver greater value to the business more often using existing resources or to deliver the same amount of value per year using fewer people. Reducing lead time reduces the carrying cost of inventory, but more importantly it reduces OE through lower staffing levels or increases Throughput, if staffing remains the same. Shorter lead times increase the profitability of the IT department.

Reducing Operating Expense

To decrease OE, the CIO must do more with less. This will include finding an appropriate Agile working method and encouraging the management chain to create an environment for software engineers to do good quality work, leading to higher productivity. The organization must be highly delegated, and staff must be properly motivated. Somewhat counterintuitively, reducing OE requires more money for educating the management on how to motivate people and avoid micromanagement.

OE is made up of several components. It contains the cost of amortizing the capital investment in the IT department and the cost of financing that investment, that is, the interest paid to the bank on any loans. It also contains the cost of financing the inventory, that is, the interest paid on any loans used to fund the working capital to pay the staff to generate the requirements. It may also be desirable to depreciate the investment in requirements to account for their perishable nature and tendency to become obsolete. OE also includes salaries for all of the staff, cost of office space, telephones, computer networks, Internet access, consumables, and many things provided for the comfort of the staff while they are working, such as ping-pong and foosball tables.

OE can be reduced by needing fewer people. The most effective way of needing fewer people is to reduce the amount of work-in-progress, that is, reduce the inventory level in the IT department. Inventory levels can be reduced in two ways: The size of the systems being built in any single release can be capped, and the relevance of the requirements in a release can be improved.

Limiting the inventory caps the amount invested in inventory and the amount of work-in-progress at any given time. New inventory can be added to the system only when some current inventory is delivered as working code.

The CIO can limit inventory by adopting the techniques described in Chapters 9 and 10.

Summary

An Agile IT department is one focused on high-quality business analysis, selecting only the most valuable feature requests for development whilst capping the total release size using strict inventory control. The result will be shorter development cycles, requiring fewer people at significantly reduced cost.

The effect of these measures will significantly reduce OE, which has a direct positive affect on profitability. With Net Profit increased and investment decreased, there will be a significant improvement in ROI.

Monitoring the flow of inventory is the most important action a CIO can take to improve the performance of the IT business unit. The key metrics for a CIO are the level of inventory of ideas in the system (V), the total sum of money invested in IT (I), and the cycle time to deliver inventory into production (LT). These metrics will indicate whether operating expense is falling or rising and whether the Production Rate (R), and the rate of delivered value, Throughput (T), are improving. Together, higher Production Rate (R), and reduced OE can only mean one thing—an IT department that is adding more value to the whole business.

chapter 16

Agile Product Management

This chapter explains to those who make software for a living and sell that software as a product how to apply Throughput Accounting to their business. The software development organization within the business will be referred to as the "engineering" organization. Because Agile Product Management is a huge topic on which an entire book could be dedicated, the scope of this chapter is restricted to identifying how product management can help engineering be more effective and to devising metrics that show the effectiveness (value added) of engineering in a software product company. In the examples shown, assume a very Agile software organization that releases a new version every quarter. For the sake of brevity, only a limited number of software licensing and business models will be considered. Other models may require adjustment to the suggested financial equations.

Sales and Throughput

In order to run a software product business effectively, like other businesses where fact-based decisions can be made, it is necessary to understand the unpredictable variable in the finance equations—Throughput. T is revenue generated from sales less the direct costs of making the sale. Sales is the only variable completely out of the control of software development professionals. The Marketing department is responsible for forecasting the value of sales, and the Sales department for actually making sales. There are, therefore, two values for sales—predicted sales and actual (historical) sales. Actual sales are useful for an operations review that reflects on "where we've been," but predicted sales are needed in order to plan the development work for the software production system.

Calculating Throughput (T) from predicted sales is relatively straightforward. Direct costs related to product sales are fairly predictable, although costs for professional services related to deployment and integration with existing legacy systems can be somewhat harder to predict. T is, therefore, derived from a forecast figure and may have an uncertain amount of direct costs estimated into it:

$$T_{Sales} = Sales_{Forecast} - Direct\ Costs_{Estimated}$$

Marketing forecasts are as big a black art as typical software engineering level-of-effort estimates. Hence, the data for predicted sales could be wildly wrong. It is important for the business to implement operational metrics so that the absolute effect can be measured postdelivery. Data can be difficult to gather. It requires discipline and operational excellence in other areas of the business. Thus, being capable of measuring the effectiveness of engineering is more than just a localized engineering issue.

Learning Is Not Restricted to Engineering

Any CEO, COO, CFO, or GM reading this book should immediately be alerted to the implications—process improvement in engineering will necessarily drive process improvement throughout the whole business. The implications are not to be underestimated. Failure to improve the maturity of a product marketing group will produce poor quality data and poor quality input to the engineering organization. That data is used to make hard decisions about investment in engineering and the product being produced. Agile Product Management is, therefore, the next big challenge for the high technology industry. One of the best ways to be Agile is to build only what the customer needs, wants, and values and to not waste energy creating features the customer ignores.

What this should also be telling CTOs, VPs of Engineering, and line managers within the engineering organization is that their success relies on the success and competency of their colleagues elsewhere in the business. They will need the support of senior executives who understand value chains and the necessity of having several departments cooperate and work as a team. Crossfunctional teamworking is essential to the success of an Agile business.

Management Accounting for Product Development

There are two different management accounting approaches available for controlling the software product business—cost accounting-based and Throughput Accounting-based. Readers will be familiar with the former and probably find it most intuitive. The business attempts to assign costs and attribute value to the activities that incurred the costs. Software developers know only too well the burden of completing a time sheet every week. The chore involves trying to remember how many half-hour units (or hours, quarter-hours, or even tenths of hours) were spent on different projects or tasks and which of them can be assigned to billable projects and which are general overhead activity such as "reading email."

The traditional cost accounting approach is hard to achieve because the data is hard to collect and often grossly inaccurate. Most developers cannot accurately remember how they spend their time and their time sheets are often fantasy documents. A simpler alternative based in Throughput Accounting is proposed. In this alternative, the potential residual values of older products are ignored and the business as a whole is treated as an ongoing process. One upshot of this system is no more time sheets for software developers.

This chapter specifically addresses the business model of perpetual software license rather than a leased or web service—Application Service Provider (ASP)—model. Leased and ASP models are addressed in Chapter 17.

Taking the on-going process approach, T is simply the value of Sales made in a given time period, for example, Sales Revenue per quarter, less the cost of sale, such as salesman's commission. The engineering Throughput ($T_{Engineering}$), is the residual value after the operating expense for the downstream business activity is deducted. Upstream activities in the value stream are treated as investment for the purpose of assessing the value added by engineering as part of the overall value stream of the business.

$$T_{Engineering} = T_{Sales} - OE_{Downstream}$$

The net contribution of product engineering is $T_{Engineering}$ less the operating expense ($OE_{Engineering}$) for the Engineering department:

$$\text{Net Profit}_{\text{True basis}} = T_{Engineering} - OE_{Engineering}$$

This is a very simple model. Perhaps too simple! Is it really effective? This requires examination.

Were any engineering personnel laid off when the previous version of a product was completed, or were they assigned to another product or a new version of the same product? The answer is usually that staff are retained. Using a short time window of 1 month, 1 quarter, or even 1 year, the staffing level remains more or less constant. Staffing is a fixed cost.

Is the old version of the product still available after the new version is released? This is not the common practice of the software industry. It is usual to try to sell the new version—the "upgrade"—to the existing customer base at a discount because they are credited for investment already made in earlier versions. New customers receive the new product. This pricing structure tends to affect thinking about how value should be attributed. It is seductive to think that value should be assigned to the content of the new product that was available in older versions. However, this is a phantom. The reality is the revenue was realized in the current time period for the current version.

In a future time period, will this situation be different? No! The latest version, whatever it is called, will be for sale and the previous version will have been discontinued. It might be a newer version than for sale now, because the development team will have completed another upgrade, but the sales model is unchanged. The new version replaced the older one.

So there is a repeating situation where the latest version is for sale and the business is spending money creating the next version. Cost accountants may be twitching with this simple notion that costs from this quarter being spent on the next version are deducted from sales this quarter of the previous version.

Therefore, a minor adjustment to the simple model is required to take into account this time-related difference. If the period for review is quarterly and the Agile development organization is releasing a new version every quarter, then the $OE_{Engineering}$ figure from the previous quarter should be used against the sales from the current quarter. This aligns the revenue generation from the product with the money spent creating the product.

$$\text{Net Profit}_{\text{True basis}} = T[t]_{\text{Eng}} - OE[t\text{-}1]_{\text{Eng}}$$

where t is the current quarter and t-1 denotes the current quarter less 1 quarter, that is, the previous quarter.

The ROI equation can be calculated by taking the Net Profit and dividing by the Investment made in requirements for the current version of the product, which was incurred in the previous time period:

$$\text{ROI}_{\text{True basis}} = \frac{T[t]_{\text{Eng}} - OE[t\text{-}1]_{\text{Eng}}}{I[t\text{-}1]_{\text{Requirements}}}$$

Appropriate-ness of the Time-Based Throughput Model

With this simple method, a glaring choice has been made to write off the current product as soon as it is replaced. This suggests that it is treated as zero value, as soon as the next version comes along. The entire investment in requirements made for the previous versions, [t-2] and beyond, will be written off entirely. This seems very radical. It needs deeper examination.

Firstly, the old version is no longer for sale. The value of its sales is precisely zero. It seems appropriate to value the old version as worthless because it will never generate any more sales. If it is worthless, then surely any investment made in it must be written off.

Secondly, historical sales are not considered in the sales figures. Only the current time period is under review. Hence, there is no contribution from the old product in the calculations. Again, as it adds no value into the calculations, surely it is OK to treat investment in the old versions at zero value.

As a management accounting tool, these figures indicate whether the product development organization continues to add value. If the equations become negative and the business is convinced that the problem cannot be corrected within the next time period, then it should be considering ceasing investment in the product.

As soon as a decision is made to "end-of-life" the product, the mode changes because the notion that the product does have a residual value has been introduced. The product will live beyond the current time period. To calculate the total ROI in the product, the full historical data must be used, that is, the total investment and total sales for the entire life of the product. There should be no on-going OE contribution from engineering because they will have been laid off. Hence, OE is frozen at the end of the engineering lifetime of the product—assuming that no further maintenance is conducted and bug fixes or patch releases are not made. There should be no further contribution to investment because no more requirements gathering activity is required. Investment is also frozen at the end of the engineering lifetime of the product. The contribution of the product across its entire life can be calculated with these equations:

$$\text{Net Profit}_{\text{Product Lifetime}} = T_{\text{Product Lifetime}} - OE_{\text{Engineering Lifetime}}$$

$$ROI_{Product\ Lifetime} = \frac{T_{Product\ Lifetime} - OE_{Engineering\ Lifetime}}{I_{Engineering\ Lifetime}}$$

Cost accounting seeks to attribute value from parts of the product sold against activities involved in creating it. The product must be divided into piece parts and an attempt made to value the contribution of those piece parts to total revenue. The value generated from the piece parts is then assigned against activities that may have contributed to the creation of the piece parts, and some derivation is made as to whether or not those activities added value or not.

Imagine that the new version is ready. It took 1 quarter to produce and will sell for 1 quarter before it is replaced with the next version. The sales forecast must try to predict how many of the sales are attributable to the features in the new version It is necessary to predict how many sales would have been lost to the competition if the features in the new version were not made available. That is to say, new features have both a positive additional effect and a prevention of potential negative effect.

The sales mix of new sales against upgrades must be considered. Upgrades can be apportioned directly to the features in the new version, whilst new sales must be cost assigned across the new version and each of the previous versions. When an upgrade is sold, it is safe to assume that the purchaser is buying the new features in the current version. However, when a sale is made to a new customer, this customer may be buying the product for all sorts of reasons. Some of the older features may be attractive, but so might some of the newer ones. Trying to determine an attribution for this gets ugly very quickly. Calculating all of it is possible, but error prone and problematic.

Is there an alternative? A system that takes a continually cumulative view of the product? In this scenario, sales and operating expense for the entire life of the product to date would be accumulated. This would certainly tell us whether the product has added value or not, but it would not tell us whether the business is currently adding value or not. It is effectively using the end-of-life equations above for the total return from the product in an on-going fashion. Such metrics would tell us whether the product produced a return on investment or not, but it would not indicate whether the latest version produced a return on investment. The problem is that the contribution of individual versions is lost in a calculation aggregated over the entire life of the product.

To decide which method is best, it is necessary to recap why management accounting information is calculated at all. Management wants information with which to run the business and make investment decisions. They want to know where to invest the shareholders' funds in order to produce an acceptable ROI. They also want to be able to evaluate one investment opportunity against another to determine the best possible ROI achievable with the available funds. The officers of the company have a fiduciary duty to make such considerations.

Looking at the simple Throughput-based model first, it reports the current NP and ROI. It allows management to assess whether engineering is currently adding value or not and whether the ROI is above the acceptable limit or not.[1]

Considering the more complex and problematic cost attribution method, it too can tell us whether we are adding value or not. However, as new sales data becomes available, there will be a requirement to make NP adjustments for each of the previous quarters as new sales contribute profits to previous periods in the lifetime of the product. Most accountants would find this unacceptable. The cost method is not ideal as a management accounting tool because management may discover later, after numbers have been restated, that they made a wrong decision.

The aggregate method does not tell the management whether or not the business is currently adding value. Large value-add in the past could mask losses in the current or recent quarters. It also does not indicate the current ROI because ROI is unknown without a current figure for NP. The aggregate method is not suitable for use as a management accounting tool. Because it doesn't report what is happening currently, it cannot be used as a control mechanism. It cannot be used in the system of software production as a feedback loop.

Hence, only the simple Throughput method really delivers clean management information to help run the business in an on-going fashion. As shown in Chapter 2, Throughput Accounting produces management accounting information that can be used as feedback to control a business system.

Making On-Going Investment

The Throughout Accounting method fails in one respect. It cannot indicate whether it would be a better strategy to cease investment in future versions and turn the product into an end-of-life cash cow. However, it can provide an ROI trend graph. An accelerating declining trend in ROI could be used to indicate that ceasing further investment and declaring end-of-life would be the best option.

Product Mix

It is possible to determine whether the whole product adds value in an on-going basis or whether there is a continued ROI. However, it would be good to be able to determine the product mix for each release or version and to determine whether or not the product mix is the most effective for maximizing the on-going NP and ROI. When the product marketing manager shows up with a laundry list of features for the next version, how should they be prioritized? Which features contribute most to Throughput? Should those that contribute less be left for a future version?

[1]The assessment is a Throughput Accounting version of NP and ROI and not suitable for GAAP-based external reporting, that is, the business must still maintain a cost accounting model for external reporting.

It is important not fall into the trap of trying to attribute costs and sales values to individual features. The intuitive approach is seductive, not least because the mental model of cost accounting is so pervasive. Trying to assign costs and sales values to individual features gets messy very quickly, and the calculations will be time consuming, inaccurate, and ultimately worthless.

Asking, "Which feature should be in or out of a release?" or "What feature is most profitable?" is the wrong approach. In the Throughput Accounting world the system of software development and product release must be treated holistically. It does not break down into product cost or product profit [Goldratt 1990, p. 98].

The correct approach is to ask "Which release composition will generate the most Throughput, incur least Operating Expense, and require the smallest Investment in Inventory?" Marketing must ask, "Which features are required to close which sales?" and "What are those sales worth?" After deduction of direct costs, there will be a predicted value of T based on a specific feature mix. The mild assumption being made here is that the features required to close a given sale are the "killer" features without which the sale would not be made. This allows attribution of all T for a specific sale to a small feature bundle. Value is not being assigned to specific features but aggregated into the total proposed feature mix for the next release.

Determining the Correct Mix

Marketing now has a means to evaluate the product mix based on grouping of features that enable sales or new markets. To determine the correct mix and how to prioritize the list, marketing must first look at its goal (or target) for the next release. The goal may be a revenue (Throughput) target. At other times, it might be a market share target or a market segmentation or differentiation target. It may be a brand enhancement target through a technical approach to communicating brand essence and values. Once the goal is known, groupings of features can be prioritized based on their contribution to that goal.

The product manager, in negotiation with the program and development managers, is responsible for managing the scope constraint for any given project release. The development manager can communicate the current and planned capacity of the software production system. The program manager can communicate the rate at which she can feed requirements into the system. The product manager must communicate the desired delivery date in order to meet the marketing goals for the next version. Together, they will determine the capacity of the release—the number of units of inventory that can approximately be included. In order to protect against uncertainty in complexity, size, and risk of individual requirements, the scope must be buffered. The product manager must be prepared to let some requirements slip. Hence, the marketing goals for the next release must be defined at three levels: the minimum acceptable level (must have), the desired level (preferred in order to meet the business goals), and an optional level (additional growth beyond plan).

Managing the Scope Constraint

Table 16-1

Prioritized product mix list.

Requirement/Release	Group	Rating
List the Features for the Project/Release	1	Essential
Set the Milestones for a Feature	1	Essential
Set the CPW for the Feature	1	Essential
Set the Subject Area for the Feature Set	1	Essential
List the Feature Completion Dates for the CPW	1	Essential
List the Virtual Team Members for the CPW	1	Essential
Set the Feature Set for the Feature	1	Essential
List the Feature Completion Dates for the Release	2	Essential
Total the Features for a Product	2	Essential
List all Feature Sets for the Subject Area	3	Desired
List the Subject Areas for the Product	3	Desired
List Change Requests for the Release	4	Optional
Total the number of open issues in the Issue Log for a given Release	4	Optional

The minimum acceptable level may be set as breakeven. Figures for NP and ROI should not be negative. The desired level might be the preferred minimum ROI figure for the business, for example, 13%. Anything beyond that would be optional. Alternatively these numbers might be cast as market share numbers, for example, minimum is hold-market-share, desired is grow-market-share by 2 points, and optional is grow-market-share by more than 2 points. The product manager is responsible for guessing the feature selections that will achieve the minimum, desired, and optional goals. If the product mix can be ranked according to groups of features assigned as essential, desired, or optional, a buffer can be determined for the scope of a given release.

Table 16-1 shows a sample of features for an FDD Knowledge Base tool for tracking FDD projects. The features are sorted by grouping and impact on the marketing goal for the next release.

Product Mix When Revenue Is the Goal

Marketing must decide how many new sales are required and how many upgrades to the existing customer base are necessary to meet the revenue target. New sales probably require a broadening of the product—features that extend the scope of the existing product. Repeat sales (upgrades) probably require deepening of the product—features that make existing features more detailed or elaborate on existing functionality.

The types of features that appeal to the existing customer base are probably different from the features that appeal to the potential new customer. A broadening of the product extends the market segments to which the product is targeted and enables sales to a new customer base. Deepening the product increases the functionality in an existing segment and strengthens the product against attack in that niche. Hence, the mix of features is important. Sales intelligence and market research is very important in order to quantify the likelihood that a feature or group of features will enable a sale and produce Throughput.

It will also be necessary to know the maturity of the market in a given segment and how much growth is possible, that is, if there are new customers in an existing segment without the need to broaden the product into a new segment.

Groupings of requested features should be categorized against the market segments which they enable.

Table 16–2 segments the market for our example FDD Knowledge Base product in two dimensions—by user role and price. Some features deepen the versatility of the product for an existing target audience while other features broaden the product to appeal to other user roles.

The potential revenue generation from each segment as shown in Table 16–3 should then be used to determine the product mix.

This technique provides a means to evaluate the Throughput generated by the proposed release. However, determining the true value of the release requires an understanding of the OE and I involved.

Table 16–2
Features required by (user) segment enabled.

Free $0–$500	Feature Group 4			
$500–$1,000 >$1,000		Feature Group 2 Group 1	Feature Group 3 Group 2	
Price Per Seat/ User Role	**Project Manager**	**Development Manager**	**Program Manager**	**Product Manager**

Table 16–3
Anticipated revenue by segment.

Free $0–$500 $500–$1,000 >$1,000	$10,000	$70,000 $30,000	$30,000 $20,000	
Price Per Seat/ User Role	**Project Manager**	**Development Manager**	**Program Manager**	**Product Manager**

Product Mix and the Effect on Investment

Investment is easily calculated based on historical data for capturing requirements. A figure for average investment per function (AIPF) is probably available. If no historical data is available, it is easy to set a cap and limit the total exposure for requirements definition. With an AIPF figure available, I will be a linear projection of the number of features in the release. More features may generate more Throughput (T), but more features will also require greater investment and force engineering to carry a larger inventory. A larger Inventory (V) will increase the Operating Expense (OE).

Product Mix, Risk, and Delay and the Effect on Operating Expense

OE can be affected by other factors in the product mix. For example, the business may want to broaden the product into a new field of specialization. In order to do so, it will need to hire an expert in the field to help create the product. This will increase the Operating Expense. Perhaps it wants to include something that is known to have algorithmic complexity or requires some invention (or extreme innovation). It may decide to hire some expertise to help alleviate the risk involved.

Risk could impact the schedule and delay the release. Delaying the release will delay the generation of Throughput from repeat sales and some new sales. However, alleviation of risk increases the Operating Expense. Hence, there is now a financial mechanism for evaluating risk mitigation. The potential Throughput value from a feature inclusion can be compared against the increased Operating Expense for risk mitigation. Alternatively, the cost of risk mitigation can be compared with the potential lost Throughput due to eventual delay in availability of the release. The business can use this information to decide whether or not it makes sense to include that feature in the product mix.

How Constraints Affect Product Mix

Throughput Accounting uses a technique to determine product mix that looks specifically at the NP against the system constraint. Note the singular on "constraint." Throughput Accounting is cleaner when there is only one, and it is generally assumed that no two potential constraints affect the business at the same time. At any given time, there is only one constraint affecting the overall Throughput. Thomas Corbett [1997] has argued that there are very good reasons for constructing business processes and operating structure so that there is only one constraint that is known and can be managed.[2]

Throughput Accounting uses a metric of dollars per period on the capacity constrained resource (CCR) to determine product mix. Hence, if System Test is the system constraint, the System Test effort required to test a feature must be determined. Then divide the sales value of the aggregated feature mix by the total System Test man hours for the proposed release feature mix. Several scenarios can be run, with features included or excluded. Different mixes of features for the release can then be ranked according to the

[2]Corbett, in *Throughput Accounting*, provides a proof that perfectly balanced capacity is suboptimal and a system with a single identifiable CCR is preferred [1998, p. 172].

Table 16–4
Prioritized feature list by $ per hour on CCR.

Requirement/Release	Group	# Man Hours to Test	Group Total Testing	Throughput	$/hour of CCR
List the Feature Completion Dates for the Release	2	32			
Total the Features for a Product	2	32	64	$60,000	$937.50
List the Features for the Project/Release	1	8			
Set the Milestones for a Feature	1	8			
Set the CPW for the Feature	1	16			
Set the Subject Area for the Feature Set	1	20			
List the Feature Completion Dates for the CPW	1	16			
List the Virtual Team Members for the CPW	1	8			
Set the Feature Set for the Feature	1	8	100	$70,000	$700
List all Feature Sets for the Subject Area	3	16			
List the Subject Areas for the Product	3	20	36	$20,000	$555.56
List Change Requests for the Release	4	64			
Total the number of open issues in the Issue Log for a given Release	4	64	128	$10,000	$78.13

number of dollars of Throughput per hour on the CCR, that is, the number of dollars of T per hour of System Test.

In order to consider how the product mix of features will affect the constraints, the proposed feature mix must be examined and it must be determined how they will place demand on the CCR. Hence, the LOE on the constraint, such as the UI Designer or System Test, must be determined for a given feature mix, then, divide the potential Throughput for that feature mix by the LOE on the CCR, as shown in Table 16–4:

$$\text{Rank}_{\$pmccr}* = \frac{T_{\text{Potential for Release}}}{\text{time}_{\text{CCR for Release}}}$$

---

*$pmccr = dollars per minute of the capacity constrained resource.

The results from this equation can then be ranked for the proposed feature mix. Other feature mixes can be considered, and a ranking table produced showing the ideal feature mix that maximizes Throughput for the period of the next release cycle.

For our example FDD Knowledge Base System from Table 16–1, and the market segmentation in Table 16–2 taken together with the revenue generating potential shown in Table 16–3, it is shown in Table 16–4 that Feature Group 4 only produces $78.13 per hour on the CCR. Hence, Feature Group 4 should probably be dropped from the release plan and effectively the product manager is deciding not to enter the "project manager" market segment with the next release of the product.

Summary

Throughput Accounting requires data that is easier to collect and more accurate than cost accounting data for the purposes of determining the value-added effectiveness of a product engineering organization.

Throughput Accounting produces more effective information for control of a product company. It can be used to determine the product mix for a given release based on the anticipated revenue generated by groupings of "killer" features that enable sales in given market segments.

The product mix must be prioritized in order to protect the scope constraint in the system. This can be achieved by calculating the dollars per hour of time on the system CCR and ranking from highest to lowest.

chapter 17

Financial Metrics for Software Services

Determining the value added from software services is a little different and presents a different problem from that presented in Chapter 16 for software products. First, it is necessary to define a software service in this context.

A service is something paid for on a renewing basis. The user does not gain perpetual rights—there is an implied annuity. The telephone system is a service. There is a monthly recurring charge plus additional charges for usage. Yahoo! email is a service. The online edition of the *New York Times* is a service. Software sold on a leased basis or Internet web service/application service provider basis is a service.

High technology services, such as telephone systems, tend to have one common characteristic—high fixed costs and low marginal costs. Traditional services such as pizza delivery, which are labor intensive, tend to be the opposite—low fixed costs and high marginal costs. There are some exceptions that live in the middle ground, for example, the *New York Times* has high marginal costs for production of content, but low marginal costs for delivery— particularly if delivery is via a website on the Internet. This chapter considers high technology services with low marginal costs and high fixed costs, for example, telecommunications systems.

Fixed costs mean sunk cost invested in infrastructure to provide the service. Hence, service businesses treat their investments in software engineering development and deployment equipment as a fixed cost investment.

This is a double-edged sword for the engineering group. There is a simple degenerate management accounting possibility—a transfer cost to the rest of the business is agreed. This agreed transfer price represents the sales revenue for engineering and the sunk cost investment for the rest of the business. The Throughput for engineering, ($T_{Engineering}$), is simply the agreed transfer price less any direct costs. If engineering can at least break even on the agreed transfer price, that is, $T_{Engineering}$ is equal to or greater than OE, then engineering is adding value to the business. This leads to precisely the same set of equations as presented in Chapter 15.

Defining a Software Service

This seems unsatisfactory because it delegates the responsibility for profitability to the rest of the business and potentially masks the true value of the software. With services, the product is sold a little bit at a time, rather than all at once as with traditional software products. So the equations in Chapter 16 can't be used.

Service Business Economics

Service businesses have some unique economics that contribute to their financial worth. There is the cost of acquisition of new subscribers. There is also the cost of churn—when a subscriber leaves the service for a rival. This cost is actually a lost future revenue cost. Services are valued by the number of subscribers, the subscriber growth rate, the cost of acquisition, the average revenue per user per month (ARPU), the cash cost per user per month (CCPU), and the churn rate. The churn rate is the percentage of subscribers who leave the service every month. Actually, the interesting figure is the length of time that a subscriber stays with the service. This is known as the lifetime of the subscriber. The most influential metric is the lifetime revenue per subscriber (LRPS), which is calculated by the average revenue per subscriber, less the cash cost per user, multiplied by the lifetime, less the cost of acquisition.

$$LRPS = (ARPU - CCPU) \times \text{Avg. Lifetime} - \text{Cost of Acquisition}$$

Determining Throughput for Software Services

In order to effectively compare software services with other software development activities, it is necessary to define the meaning of Throughput for a service. This requires that the business model for the service provider be recast in terms of Throughput Accounting rather than cost accounting. In order to understand this, it is first necessary to understand the existing cost accounting-focused model for service providers:

$$EBITDA = ARPU - CCPU$$

This equation states that earnings per subscriber before interest, tax, depreciation, and amortization is the average revenue per user per month, less the cash cost per user per month. Calculating EBITDA rather than a pure Net Profit allows the high cost of sunk capital to be ignored, which enables the service to be evaluated based on free cash flow of the on-going business. EBITDA is primarily a psychological number. It is used to project the long-term value of a service after the sunk cost is depreciated. EBITDA by highlighting free cash flow is supposed to help the stock price.

The EBITDA equation looks a little like our Net Profit equation. However, we should not mistake ARPU for T or CCPU for OE. Why not? ARPU represents the sales per subscriber to the service. The figure is averaged over the aggregated subscriber base. The sales figure for a given time period is ARPU multiplied by the number of subscribers. ARPU does not deduct out any direct costs. Hence, it is not an equivalent for T. Service industries assume that marginal costs are low. However, the direct costs are important. For example, if a customer spends $10 per month on Yahoo! email but pays by credit card, the cost of the credit card transaction is a direct cost. If this is 50 cents,

Throughput is at most $9.50. In traditional service industry cost accounting, this cost is assigned to CCPU.

What else gets assigned to CCPU? Cash Cost per User is an average of the total operating expense divided by the number of subscribers, where operating expense does not include any carrying costs for investment in capital equipment. Investment in inventory is assumed to be nil (or negligible) because there is no inventory in a service business. Hence, there is no figure for investment.

However, inventory is seldom negligible. Phone companies carry subscriber equipment, such as handsets, as inventory. Cable TV companies carry set top boxes as inventory. Even pure Internet operators such as Yahoo! are carrying ideas for their next version as inventory.

In theory, the CCPU figure can be multiplied by the number of subscribers to give us a figure for normal operating expense for the business, including any amount of direct cost associated with the generation of ARPU. How useful is this figure? Is CCPU really a variable cost? And does it vary directly?

If next month, 100,000 subscribers leave the service, will the operating expense decrease by 100,000 times the CCPU? Were some staff laid off? Were the overheads reduced? Were any computer systems switched off? Was the power consumption on the network reduced? Was the capacity of the service reduced? Of course not! The truth is that a reduction in the number of subscribers creates a jump in CCPU. Why? Because a large proportion of CCPU is fixed operating costs rather than variable costs associated directly with the subscriber.

Wait a minute! Am I proposing that the standard method used as a management tool for most service businesses, such as telecommunications, is wrong? Yes! Cost accounting was born of an era where direct costs were by far the largest contributor to operating expense. However, cost accounting is obsolete [Goldratt 1990]. In a world in which more than half (and probably most) of the operating expense is overhead, it is simply not useful to try to assign those costs. Hence, a new mental model and financial framework is needed to usefully evaluate the contribution of development of new services. A holistic systems thinking approach is required.

The Throughput Accounting approach to a service industry treats the whole service as a system. Throughput is the total sales for a time period less the direct costs of servicing those sales. Direct costs include the cost of sending a subscriber a bill through the mail and the cost of accepting the payment. No attempt is made to break out the Throughput figure per subscriber.

$$T_{service} = \text{Total Sales} - \text{Total Direct Costs}$$

The Operating Expense will not include direct costs, but will include all of the overhead. No attempt is made to assign overhead against individual sales. In order to better compare this new alternative with the existing cost accounting-inspired EBITDA model, the costs of sunk capital are not included in the Operating Expense figure. This new figure is known as Operating Expense before interest, depreciation, and amortization—OEBIDA:

$$OEBIDA_{service} = \text{Total Overheads}$$

Net Profit for Services

To get the Net Profit figure, the OEBIDA is subtracted from T. The result is a derivative figure for Net Profit that might be described as Net Profit before interest, tax, depreciation, and amortization—NPBITDA:

$$NPBITDA_{service} = T - OEBIDA$$

Return on Investment for Services

Having defined a figure for Net Profit, it is desirable to have a comparable figure for ROI. However, this particular ROI figure will want to ignore the sunk cost of capital. Specifically, this new ROI figure considers the return on investment of adding new software features to the service. For simplicity, assume that no new hardware is required to run the software or, upgrade the capacity of the service. In other words, the service is not hardware constrained. With a phone company, for example, there will be no need for any more switches. However, the software on the switch may be upgraded.

The constraint, in this example, is the market. The business wants to make more profit through increased sales. Hence, more subscribers must be attracted to the service. In order to recruit more subscribers, more features must be offered. New features also serve to keep the service offering current and attractive, which helps to retain existing subscribers. The ROI equation looks very familiar to those for other types of software business:

$$ROI_{True\ basis} = \frac{NPBITDA_{service}}{I_{Requirements}}$$

Attributing a Value to a Release

With services, attributing value for the sales generated is much more difficult than with software products. When an upgrade to a service is released, that is, new features are delivered, the old service is not discontinued. The subscribers that joined the service earlier, joined because of the features available at that time. Hence, they saw, and presumably still do see, the value in the older features. The upgrade is of potentially little or no value to them. So it is clear that the revenue from different subscribers must be split across the releases if the Throughput being generated by each release is to be evaluated properly. This goes against the trend adopted heretofore in this text in which assigning value or cost to specific features has been avoided.

Consider the example of an Agile software services business that makes a new release every 3 months. Revenue from all new subscribers joining the service—subscriber acquisitions—must be attributed to the latest release. Revenue from everyone else should be attributed to the release current when they joined the service, unless they would otherwise have left the service were it not for the features in the new release. In other words, when the new release keeps the service competitive, it introduces new differentiating features and plays catch-up with competitors' differentiators. When the new features act to retain an existing customer, that customer must be treated as a new subscriber who just joined the service. The only way to find this number is to conduct market research to determine the number of subscribers who would have churned to another service were it not for the new features.

Hence, when the lifetime figure for a subscriber is calculated, the number should be modified to account for the saved churn rate. For example, subscribers joining the service this quarter are expected to stay for 40 months. However, market research suggests that 50% of them would leave early, on average after 20 months, were it not for the continual introduction of new features. Hence, when considering releases individually, the average lifetime per subscriber is actually 30 months. This lower figure takes into account that a subsequent release will save the subscriber from churning. In effect, the subscriber churned to a subsequent release rather than to a rival service.

Having devised a mechanism to determine the true lifetime of a subscriber in the service, it is possible to calculate the revenue generated by a single release of a service as

$$\text{Total Sales}_{\text{release}} = (\# \text{ new subs} + \# \text{ saved subs}) \times \text{lifetime per sub}$$

This gives us a Throughput equation of

$$T_{\text{release}} = \text{Total Sales}_{\text{release}} - \text{Total Direct Costs}_{\text{release subs}}$$

The Operating Expense must be subtracted for the period when the release was current in order to get the Net Profit figure. It is only necessary to deduct Operating Expense for the period the release is current because future releases will account for future Operating Expenses. This is allowed because direct variable costs have been separated from overheads:

$$NPBITDA_{\text{release}} = T_{\text{release}} - OEBIDA_{\text{release current}}$$

Now that a figure for the Net Profit generated by the features in the current release of the software service has been determined, it is possible to calculate ROI. ROI is the Net Profit number divided by the cost of acquiring the requirements for the features in the new release—the investment in ideas for the release:

$$ROI_{\text{release}} = \frac{NPBITDA_{\text{release}}}{I_{\text{requirements in release}}}$$

In order to determine just how many features should be included in future releases, the product manager can examine the trend in ROI. If ROI is falling, that might suggest less be invested in future releases. This would maintain the ROI figure. However, if consumer confidence in the service is falling because it is perceived as uncompetitive, he might seek to invest more in requirements. The initial hit on ROI would be traded in the hope of stimulating much higher revenues later and consequently producing a higher return on investment at a later date.

Product Mix

The mix of features for a given release of a service can be evaluated in exactly the same fashion as those for the software product described in Chapter 16. The figure calculated for Throughput$_{release}$ from this chapter should be replaced into the equations, otherwise they remain unchanged.

Dealing with Uncertainty

It is also worth mentioning that the financial figures calculated from this chapter will have a degree of uncertainty attached to them. The market research will never be perfect. However, this entire text has been governed by an underlying assumption that management steers a business by approximations and learns to cope with uncertainty. Overall, it is better to have some numbers correctly aligned with a systems thinking approach to the business than no numbers or numbers aligned with the wrong model.

chapter 18

The Business Benefit of Agile Methods

I t is time to revisit the 12 principles of Agile methods and examine what they really mean from a business perspective.

Our highest priority is to satisfy the customer through early and continuous delivery of valuable software.

Agile methods believe in Throughput dollars. The highest priority is to deliver client-valued functionality and to do so in a systematic, process-oriented fashion of continuous production. Agile methods believe in a system of software production that delivers client-valued functionality at a steady pace. However, this principle might be better rewritten as *"Our highest priority is to satisfy the customer by maximizing delivery of valuable software.*[1]*"* This modification emphasizes Throughput rather than lead time and flow. Early delivery of partial releases may have no Throughput value because deployment of an incomplete system is impractical. Early delivery merely mitigates risk.

Welcome changing requirements, even late in development. Agile processes harness change for the customer's competitive advantage.

Agile methods accept that change is a fact of life. They also accept that delivering a stale requirement is valueless. There are no Throughput dollars associated with a useless and obviated requirement. Agile methods seek to eliminate these by coping with change, even late change. It is this attribute that gives Agile methods their name. The ability to cope with change shows genetic fitness. Fitness implies agility.

Deliver working software frequently, from a couple of weeks to a couple of months, with a preference to the shorter timescale.

Agile methods believe in short lead times and by implication, low inventory levels. As such, Agile methods are compatible with the production solution for the Theory of Constraints as described in *The Goal*

---

[1]Suggested by Philip Bradley on the FDD community website, http://www. featuredrivendevelopment.com/node.php?id=531.

[Goldratt 1984].[2] Through a preference for short lead times and lower inventory, Agile methods encourage smaller levels of Investment and reduce the Operating Expense of producing software. Agile methods deliver greater value added and more Net Profit through a focus on regular flow of Throughput dollars and through a reduction of Operating Expenses. Agile methods generate a greater ROI, through reduction of the Investment and increased Net Profit.

Business people and developers must work together daily throughout the project.

Agile methods recognize that waste is extremely costly and rework is undesirable. They advocate an on-site client who can catch misunderstandings and correct problems with analysis and design. This reduction of waste and consequent reduction in rework will increase Production, shorten Lead Times, and directly contribute to increased Throughput dollars, reduced Inventory, and reduced Operating Expense.

Build projects around motivated individuals. Give them the environment and support they need, and trust them to get the job done.

This principle hints at leadership and delegation. With respect to the Theory of Constraints, this principle is really saying that the management should focus on identifying constraints and removing them through exploitation and elevation. "The environment and support they need" implies an environment free from constraints, where optimal Throughput can be achieved.

The most efficient and effective method of conveying information to and within a development team is face-to-face conversation.

Face-to-face conversation is preferred because it minimizes setup time and eliminates by-products such as documentation. In Lean parlance, face-to-face communication minimizes waste and lead times. The focus isn't on zero documentation, but on an optimal set of minimal documentation, that is, just enough to keep the project moving forward and keep the idea transformation going, but not enough to represent needless by-product that is never read or referenced.

Face-to-face interactions are also thought to increase quality by improving communication. Writing and reading documents can lead to misunderstanding. Further, it is often true that the author of the document is a specialist document author who plays a role as interlocutor between the customer or client for the system and the developers. The translation effect from the interlocutor can lead to misunderstanding and errors. These errors cause rework.

[2]In *The Goal* Goldratt identifies the goal of all business as making a profit [1984]. Profits, not working code, are the most important method of judging a software business.

By minimizing lead time and maximizing quality through face-to-face interactions, Agile methods shorten lead times, which reduce Operating Expense, reduce Inventory levels and Investment, and maximize production—generating more Throughput dollars.

Working software is the primary measure of progress.

Agile methods advocate that the main metric is production quantity (Q), that is, working code that delivers client-valued function. It is possible to measure this as completed Inventory or as Throughput dollars. Regardless of which, Agile methods have identified and focused on the most important metric—T. Agile methods are directly compatible with Throughput Accounting. They measure delivered value.

Agile processes promote sustainable development. The sponsors, developers, and users should be able to maintain a constant pace indefinitely.

Agile methods recognize that cash flow is important and that lead time is important. By focusing on the development of sustainable systems of software development rather than the stop-go cycles of heavyweight alternatives, Agile methods turn Investment into Net Profit faster, generating a greater Return on Investment. In Lean terms, Agile methods encourage flow and believe in slack (below maximum efficiency). Slack allows for regeneration of staff and training to improve their skills.

Continuous attention to technical excellence and good design enhances agility.

Agile methods recognize that rework and waste are costly to production and profitability. Hence, they value high-quality craftsmanship. Agile methods recognize the personal mastery discipline [Senge 1990] as a vital element in maturing a learning organization.

Simplicity—the art of maximizing the amount of work not done—is essential.

Agile methods realize that simple designs can be built more quickly, can involve less testing, and are less likely to have faults. Through a focus on simplicity of design, Agile methods reduce lead times through faster coding, less testing, less likelihood of bugs, and overall higher quality. Once again, reduced lead times lead directly to lower Investment and reduced Operating Expense. Simpler designs that can be built faster potentially increase the overall production, leading to higher Throughput dollars.

The best architectures, requirements, and designs emerge from self-organizing teams.

This is perhaps the only principle of Agile methods that cannot be easily justified in business terms. The premise that self-organized teams, rather than teams commanded and controlled by a manager, produce better designs leading to shorter lead times could be tested using the metrics described in this book.

At regular intervals, the team reflects on how to become more effective, then tunes and adjusts its behavior accordingly.

Agile methods believe in the principle of a learning organization [Senge 1990]. By building a culture in which every team member is encouraged not only to do what they do, but also to think about how they do it and devise mechanisms for doing it better, Agile methods encourage a culture of continuous learning. This culture is compatible with the Theory of Constraints and with the new Agile maturity model for the learning organization presented in Chapter 11.

Perhaps the most important business benefit from Agile methods is the tendency toward a culture of continuous improvement. Even if Agile methods do not immediately lead to better profitability, the cultural change that will come from implementing them and the subsequent iterations of learning will lead naturally to a more profitable business.

More Than Agility

Agile methods suggest that these software development approaches designed to cope with change will deliver successful projects rather than failed projects. Success, in and of itself, would be a huge improvement for the software industry. This is still a world in which up to 30% of projects become extinct before they have ever delivered any business value for the client. By focusing on genetic fitness, agility delivers survivability.

However, Agile methods are actually about much more than simple agility. Perhaps they are misnamed. Other names are possible—"Lean Development" is a term being popularized by Mary and Tom Poppendieck and Bob Charette [Highsmith 2002; Poppendieck 2002]. Lean, as has been explained, is about just-in-time delivery with total quality. It doesn't take a huge mental leap to map this to lower Investment, lower Operating Expense, and increased production and realize that "Lean" means "Profit." So perhaps "Lean Development" would communicate a better message to the business community. Agile methods are really all about better profits. "Lean" certainly implies more than just survivability.

However, Lean Development is talked about as "an agile method." This is perhaps unfortunate. It would be a better term for the set of methods thought to be Agile. Let me, then, make a final suggestion. Perhaps these methods should be called "More Profitable Development Methods"!

Making Profitable Development Happen

Such a suggestion may provoke your CEO into replying, "What do you mean 'more profitable methods'? Can you prove it?" That is exactly the reply you were looking for. Ask for a sensible budget, and tell him that you'll be inviting him to your operations review within 3 months. You hope to show him through use of monthly operations reviews that Agile methods truly are more profitable within 6 to 9 months. The results will be presented to him in a single slide at the start of each review—the financial metrics for a system of software production. You will back this financial information with hard production metrics for Production Quantity, Production Rate, Lead Time, and Quality. You will demonstrate that Agile methods added more value and lead directly to improved Net Profit and ROI.

Go and choose the correct Agile method for your organization. Use the remainder of this book to help you select one. Or, devise your own Agile method from first principles. Adopt the Theory of Constraints and use Lean Development tools [Poppendieck 2002] to elevate the constraints and improve the agility of the software production process. Be an agent of change! Clearly communicate to the team why you are changing, what you are changing to, and the benefit you see from making the change. If applicable, use a greater fear to overcome the fear of change—the fear of outsourcing, then go and demonstrate the competitive advantage to be gained from successfully deploying Agile development.

A Survey of Methods

This section surveys various software development methods. First, it will examine two flavors of what Agile methodologists call "traditional" or "heavyweight" methods. The first is a general interpretation of the Software Development Lifecycle (SDLC), often referred to as the Waterfall method, incorporating structured analysis and design. This method is used to represent a very traditional software development process. Although such a process is seldom used today in the precise form described, it will serve as an example of how traditional methods got into trouble and why they are no longer favored.

Next, a traditional object-oriented software development method will be considered. Initiated by Ivar Jacobson, it has been known by several names: Object-Oriented Software Engineering (OOSE), Objectory, Rational Unified Process (RUP), and Unified Development Process (UDP).

For the purposes of this book, the precise definition of RUP/UDP used is that defined in *The Rational Unified Process: An Introduction* by Philippe Kruchten [2000]. It is reasonable to assume that most practitioners of UDP working in IT organizations around the globe are trying to implement the process as described by Kruchten or as described in the sister publication and thicker volume by Jacobson and colleagues [Jacobson 1998].

Three of the most popular Agile methods will then be considered— Feature Driven Development (FDD), Extreme Programming (XP), and Scrum. There is a slight bias of content towards FDD due to the experience I have had with this method in the last 5 years. The section concludes with a brief look at a generic Rapid Application Development (RAD) process.

Each method will be examined and explained using the management methods from Section 1. How to assign the variables I, OE, V, Q, and LT will be defined for each method.

chapter 19

Production Metrics for Traditional Methods[1]

SDLC

The software development lifecycle, or SDLC, is based on the theory of structured methods and is considered the traditional software methodology. It involves distinct phases and gates in which the entire inventory for a project is processed through each phase and then approved through a gate before being released into the next stage, as in Figure 19–1.

In order to evaluate traditional methods of software development using the management techniques from Section 1, it is necessary to determine how to assign the variables I, OE, V, LT, and Q.

Raw Material

The raw material in a traditional structured development project is captured as the ideas for the new software product, delivered as a functional specification. The functional specification should describe the client-valued functionality desired in the delivered product. Very approximately, a functional specification should describe an outcome derived from a number of inputs using a formula, or algorithm, or logical argument.

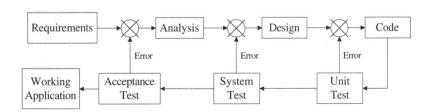

Figure 19–1
Systems representation of SDLC.

---

[1]A traditional method is defined by Highsmith [2002] as a Rigorous Software Methodology (RSM). This definition is used here.

Inventory

Inventory in structured methods is measured using the Function Point (FP) metric. Function Point analysis can be performed on the functional specification. The guidelines for such analysis are contained in a manual published by the International Function Point Users Group (IFPUG), which has around 100 pages of theory. Hence, Function Point analysis has a high barrier to entry and tends not to be widely used. The IFPUG reports that there are around 2,000 trained FP analysts in the world [Yourdon 2002]. While this number sounds small, it is almost certainly far higher than the number of analysts trained in Agile methods. The inventory (V) is, therefore, a formal list of Function Points derived from the functional specification.

The key advantage of FPs as a metric for inventory is their repeatability. FPs are standardized and controlled by an international body. As such, metrics across projects, teams, companies, and countries can be compared against the common yardstick—the Function Point. With Function Points variance is low and repeatability is high. This is a critical factor if traditional methods are to be successful, because they rely heavily on accuracy of estimates.

Investment

Investment in structured methods can be calculated as the cost of creating the functional specification and all costs related to performing the Function Point analysis. This may necessarily include user interface design as part of the functional specification. It is important that the costs measured relate directly to creation of the client-valued functionality as a specification.

The term "heavyweight" has been coined to describe traditional methods because they tend to be paperwork intensive. Hence, it is important to be critical about what represents a value-added description of the client-valued functionality and what represents additional elaboration and orthogonal views onto the same information. The costs associated with producing additional documents that duplicate the client-valued function for a different audience should be considered waste and accounted for as overhead, that is, OE.

Lead Time

Lead Time in structured methods can be defined as the time to take a single Function Point through the lifecycle of analysis, design, coding and testing until delivery. In practice this would be the average Lead Time for an average Function Point, where the average is obtained over a batch of FPs passing through a given phase of the development cycle together. It should also be possible to define Lead Time metrics for each lifecycle stage—analysis, design, coding, and testing.

Throughput

Throughput can be defined as the dollar value added from the delivered Function Points. It is also possible to report the average cost per Function

Point, which would be defined as the Operating Expense divided by the number of FPs delivered. The IFPUG already has a large body of data for this metric.

Production Rate

Production Rate is quite simply the number of Function Points in any given time period. It would be possible to report FPs per day, week, month, quarter, or year.

Inventory Cap

An Inventory Cap in structured methods would relate directly to a limit on the number of Function Points being held in Inventory throughout the entire software production system, that is FPs waiting development, FPs in-process, FPs complete but not yet delivered. While requirements are being gathered, it is necessary to be counting the FPs as the functional specification emerged. When the Inventory Cap is reached, no more requirements would be gathered.

Process Step Time

The process step time in structured waterfall methods can be broken down for each process—analysis, design, coding, and testing.

Analysis Process Time

Queue time would be the time an FP spends before being analyzed. The Setup time would involve any time required to start the analysis. It might, for example, involve time to read requirements documents. The Process time is the time spent doing the analysis and producing the output analysis documents. Finally, the Wait time would be the time spent after analysis before a complete set of FPs is ready for release into the design phase.

Design Process Time

The Queue time would be the time spent before an FP is designed. The Setup time would involve any preparation for designing a set of FPs, such as reading the analysis documentation. The Process time is the time spent doing the design, reviewing the design, and reworking it. The design to design review substages may introduce additional Wait time—the time spent while a designed FP waits to be reviewed. The Wait time for the whole step would be the time spent after a design review before an FP is released in the coding stage.

Coding Process Time

The Queue time would be the time spent after the FP is released into the coding stage but before coding begins. The Setup time would be time spent reviewing the design documentation and any additional development environment setup and tools configuration. The Process time is the time spent coding and code reviewing the FP. The code to code review substages may introduce additional Wait time while a coded FP waits for its review. Finally, the Wait time would be the time spent after code review before an FP is released into the testing stage.

Testing Process Time

The Queue time is the time spent after an FP is released into the testing stage before testing begins. The Setup time is the time spent establishing the testing environment and time spent reading the analysis, design, and coding documentation and any test plans that exist. If test plans do not exist, writing the test plans would also be considered Setup time.

The Process time is the time spent actually testing. Process time in the testing phase can include debugging and generally reworking the code. Hence, the Process time may involve several iterations through test scripts and debugging. Finally, Wait time is the time spent after testing is complete before the FP is released to the customer.

If several stages of testing were broken out, that is, System Test, Product Test, Regression Test, Stress Test, and so forth, each of these stages would look similar to the generic testing stage described here.

Inventory Issues with Structured Methods

The real issue with structured methods hasn't been their structural decomposition of the problem, the use of Function Points, or any of the software analysis and design techniques involved. The real issue is the high levels of inventory carried in traditional structured projects and the focus on documentation as the means of moving the inventory from one stage to the next. Documentation can be thought of as an emergent property from a traditional system of software development. Every time an idea is transformed, a document is produced. In fact, with traditional methods there may be documents created when no value was added, that is, no transformation took place. The additional document simply added another orthogonal view or perspective onto what was already known and understood.

The Waterfall Method is attributed to Royce[2] in the late 1960s. Perhaps it seemed like the intuitive thing to do. If a single functional requirement went through a series of transformations, why not force all requirements to go through the same transformation together? It seems the most efficient way to do it—only one setup for the entire system inventory. This concept gave rise to the model of phases of development—one phase for each transformation.

Waterfall appeals to the idea of intellectual efficiency. There is just one administrative overhead for the maximum batch size. The flipside of this is that it leads to a large work-in-process inventory.

---

[2]Dr. Winston Royce is credited with publishing the first paper on the Waterfall model [Royce 1970]. However, several others enhanced the work throughout the 1970s. Brooks is often credited with popularizing the model through his essays later published as a chapter in *The Mythical Man Month* [Brooks 1995].

Waterfall may also have been attractive to cost accountants. In a typical factory process, cost accounting and GAAP actually increase the value of inventory as value is added to it. Hence, as raw material is processed towards a finished product, it becomes more valuable. The figure for investment in inventory actually grows. Inventory is treated as an asset.

This was also true of software. GAAP allowed software to be capitalized based on the amount of hours of work that had been contributed to it. Hence, the Waterfall method of using strict phases for a whole project presented an easy method for accountants to account for the work-in-process on large scale projects. By pushing the project through strict phases, or gates, it was possible to accumulate the hours spent and the cost of those hours and declare them an asset on the balance sheet. This would have been difficult, if not impossible, to achieve with an iterative method simply because it would have been necessary to break the inventory down into small, measurable chunks and actually track those small pieces. Without a fine grained metric for inventory (that is, assuming immature organizations that don't count Function Points) and a suitable tracking system, cost accounting preferred to have projects move through strictly gated phases that showed progress in a fashion useful for typical cost management.

Hence, the Waterfall method specified that the inventory be pushed through each of the lifecycle stages in a single block. This leads directly to longer lead times than can be achieved through pipelined iterative methods. Additional wait time is introduced while the gates or stages are approved.

In addition, this financial mechanism also encouraged the production of greater amounts of paperwork. The more time spent creating paperwork, the more value had been added. This error was caused by accountants measuring effort expended rather than Throughput. In a system that is nonlinear, there is no direct correlation between input effort and output value. Cost accounting led to a local optimum that was neither desirable—due to the waste generated—nor globally optimal.

Waste and Long Lead Times

With a large batch of functional specifications to be processed through a single phase of the development lifecycle, a batch must be broken down into manageable chunks for any given phase of that lifecycle. Hence, many requirements spend a long time waiting to be processed or queuing to be passed to the next phase. Large batch sizes mean high inventory levels—inventory that spends most of its time waiting and not flowing. Lack of flow creates long lead times and waste.

Figure 19–2 shows a cumulative flow diagram for an idealized Waterfall project. It is idealized because nothing ever goes wrong. Each day's activity proceeds without hindrance. Each phase of the project is completed, and there is a 4-day wait until the approval to commence the next phase.

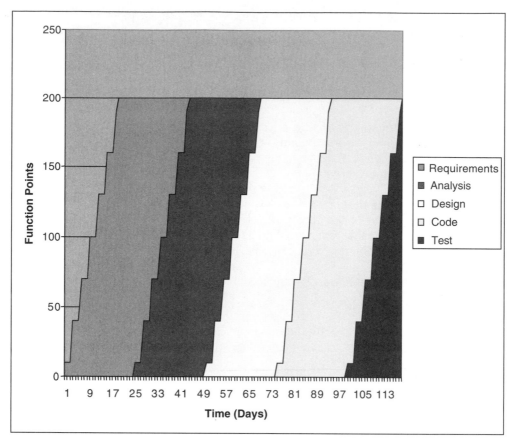

Figure 19–2
Cumulative flow for a Waterfall project.

Variance Reduction and Waste

Traditional structured methods follow the PMI/ISO model for project management. They require that the specification first be set out in a requirements document and agreed before work commences. Based on the specification, a budget of resources is allocated and a schedule is derived. The specification is fixed. In fact, the standard measure of quality is that the specification was delivered precisely as described.

The problem with this approach, and the reason it has been abandoned by Rapid (RAD) and Agile methods, is that the specification is the project element with the most uncertainty. The schedule is based in units of time. Time can be treated as an invariant, reliable, repeatable constant. The budget and resources for a given project have very little variance. Within a few percentage points, the project manager will know how many people and how much money he has to work with. However, the specification has a great deal of uncertainty attached to it. Often, exactly how to solve the issues and meet the demands they create are not known before commencing a project. In fact, if everything was understood, the project would be of little value. Someone would have done it before. Software projects tend to have an element of the unknown. Some projects have a lot of unknowns and some only a few. But regardless of the problem domain, the requirements or scope represent the element with the greatest variance.

The traditional specification-budget-schedule model has caused the software engineering community to seek better methods of reducing variance. The entire Function Point analysis method has been derived to standardize analysis and reduce variance. With traditional structured methods of functional decomposition and entity-relationship database design, the Function Point represents an accurate way of estimating a project—providing that the requirements don't change.

In order to better understand the product being built and improve the estimate, more and more methods of analysis emerged. In its quest for certainty and elimination of variance, the software engineering community created more and more paperwork—all of it waste!

Simply put, by deciding to value specification over delivery date and measuring the outcome accordingly, the industry started a vicious cycle that led to longer and longer lead times, more and more documentation by-product, and less and less chance of success.

Requirements change! They are more likely to change as the lead time gets longer. The more paperwork produced, the greater the chance of change, which leads to the need to produce yet more paperwork. In an attempt to control variance, the industry defeated itself.

The reality of software development is that the requirements are subject to change. Variance and uncertainty are inevitable. That is why the traditional SDLC methods and the PMI/ISO project management model are flawed for the controlled production of software products.

Specialists and High Inventory Levels

Traditional software development methods also modeled themselves on the mass production systems common in western industries in the 20th century. Mass production science is referred to as Taylorism after Frederick Winslow Taylor and his time and motion studies [Taylor 1911]. The economist Adam Smith had described the division of labor [Smith 1776]. Taylor applied that theory to mass production systems. His approach was implemented by Henry Ford in the assembly line—where each worker on the line had a single specialist skill. In the melting pot of America in the early part of the 20th century, with many foreign laborers who spoke little English, the assembly line was a huge improvement. Training a man on a single skill was much easier than trying to train him as a full craftsman. It was more than 30 years before the Japanese began to improve upon Taylor's mass production[3] and another 30 years before these improvements were adopted in the West.

---

[3]The origins of the Toyota Production System's just-in-time approach were laid in the late 1940s. The Quality Assurance methods of Edwards Deming were added in the 1950s. These techniques did not take hold in western manufacturing until the early 1980s.

Traditional methods in software development had individuals who were highly skilled in a single stage of the lifecycle, such as the analysis stage. These specialists were called analysts. Each stage of the lifecycle had its own specialists. There was an assumption that this method worked well for manufacturing industries, why shouldn't it also work for software? There was clearly a similar system process involved—or so it was believed!

By adopting a phased approach, with a specialist for each phase, it makes sense to maximize the batch size so that a large number of similar items can be processed by the same worker at the same time. In cost accounting, this is known as efficiency. It is the efficiency of the worker that is being measured, not the efficiency of the progress of the inventory (or the flow). This is a crucial point. Cost accounting was invented as the management accounting method for Taylor's mass production and its application to software encouraged the growth of batch sizes. Lean or Agile production methods focus management on the efficiency of the inventory in the system, not on the efficiency of the workers or machinery. Focusing on the efficiency of flow encourages small batch sizes.

Idleness, Efficiency, and Growing Inventory Levels

When the inventory is passed along to the next stage, the specialists in the current stage become idle! Idleness means that efficiency—as measured by cost accounting—has fallen, and this is considered a bad thing. Hence, idle workers are found more work to do.

What happens next is that idle workers start work on another project while the one they just finished moves to the next stage in the lifecycle. By starting a second project, the inventory level just doubled.

With four or five stages in the lifecycle, inventory could increase by four or five times without extending the lead time and without overloading the set of specialist workers. Thus in an SDLC system, inventory levels grow and grow, in order to keep the specialists from becoming idle.

Lack of Slack

What was not anticipated in SDLC was the quality problems with each of the large batches of inventory sent through the system! As the first batch approaches the final stages, much of it will be sent back to early stages for rework. Poorly defined requirements may go all the way back to the beginning. Suddenly, the teams of specialists are not simply processing inventory for a single project, but are reworking inventory from projects that were "thrown over the wall" some time before.

This results in overloaded specialist workers, and the lead time begins to grow. Software projects can rarely allow lead time to grow much beyond the plan, and hence, management starts to add additional labor to alleviate the growing lead times. Systematically, the budget and manpower required grows and grows.

The Vicious Cycle

Now, with more specialist workers who can from time to time become idle, management is tricked into loading the system of software production with even more inventory in the name of efficiency. A vicious cycle has begun. Before long there are 3,000 people in the IT department, excessively long lead times, huge sums sunk as investment in inventory, and very little overall Throughput to show for it.

What started as a good set of intentions and a desire to have acceptable management control over software development, like any other part of a typical manufacturing business, resulted in a highly ineffective, underperforming, overstaffed IT engineering group.

What Went Wrong?

SDLC adopted the wrong mental model—specification-budget-schedule. Then, it used cost accounting for management control. This led to a mass production-inspired use of specialists for each phase in the lifecycle. In the name of efficiency, batch sizes for processing by specialists became very large. This created a system that denied the basic uncertainty in the task of software development. By focusing on reduced variance and efficiency, a vicious cycle ensued. The result was failure. By adopting the wrong mental model, the software industry created the wrong system and measured it with the wrong metrics—metrics based on energy expended rather than output.

The solution comes from unwinding this systemic problem completely to find the correct leverage point—adopt the correct mental model, define the correct system, measure it in the right way, and be successful. That mental model puts the element with the greatest uncertainty in the position where it is subservient to the elements with greater certainty. A RAD mental model of schedule-budget-scope is the correct model. A system that measures delivered value rather than efficiency is the correct one. Such systems for software production are known as Agile methods.

Raw Material

UDP is an architecture-centric, Use Case driven method [Kruchten 2000]. It first captures requirements in a Vision Document. The Vision Document is said to contain the key stakeholder and user needs and a list of the main features of the system. UDP's Vision Document might be called a Marketing Requirement Document (MRD) in SDLC. It captures the ideas for the software project and represents the raw material for the system of software production.

Unified Development Process[4]

---

[4]There is continued debate about whether UDP can be classified as Agile. It would be defined as a Rigorous Software Methodology by Highsmith [2002].

Inventory

The Vision Document is translated into Use Cases. Use Cases can be used to describe the business activities, as well as the system behavior. What is consistent about Use Cases is that no two authors, of the many who have written on the subject, seem to agree on how they should be written. As a unit of measure, Use Cases are not ideally suited, due to the lack of agreement on format. However, a software development organization can agree on a format and the recommendations of a specific author,[5] so it can be assumed that a consistent unit of inventory for the system of software production is available.

Nevertheless, Use Cases cannot be considered an object-oriented equivalent of Function Points. Function Points have dependability and a proven track record of low variability (or high repeatability). The same could not be said of Use Cases. It is easy, then, to understand why traditional methods using object-oriented techniques have struggled, despite the use of objects. The input still has a high degree of uncertainty, and the method still uses a mental model of scope-budget-schedule. Hence, the UDP is still a method trying to eliminate variance rather than accommodate it.

In a UDP project, Use Cases describing the business, the stakeholder-valued functionality, are the base unit of inventory. Use Cases written later, in the Construction phase within UDP, specifically to elaborate system design, are not inventory. They represent a specific stage of transformation. To count them would be to double count. In UDP, a business Use Case can lead to several more Use Cases before the software is completed. In fact, if these additional system Use Cases are not specifically used to generate code, but are produced to try to reduce uncertainty, they might better be classified as documentation by-product—or waste!

Investment

The Inception phase in UDP must be considered as a period during which the requirements are acquired. The Inception phase leads to the creation of the Vision Document and related material. The cost of this must be treated as investment for the purposes of Throughput Accounting. The cost of the Inception phase may not, however, represent the total cost of acquisition of the requirements. The costs incurred by the stakeholders may also need to be included, not just the costs of the engineering organization. With UDP the operating expense incurred during the Inception phase must be measured and treated as a sunk cost—investment.

Requirements gathering may continue during the later phases of a UDP project. In which case, it would be necessary to have the engineering team fill out time sheets in order to determine the portion of overheads to be assigned to I, rather than OE.

[5]There are perhaps 100 books listed at Amazon.com with the words "Use Case" in their titles. Amongst the most famous authors in this field are Geri Schneider, Alistair Cockburn, Larry Constantine, and Ivar Jacobson. However, there are many more. Indeed, new books on Use Cases are still appearing. Almost every author offers a different basic template—there is no standard, no equivalent of the IFPUG for UDP and Use Cases.

Lead Time

Lead Time in UDP is the time it takes a Use Case to pass through the Elaboration, Construction, and Transition phases. Lead Time can be measured for a given iteration, which is defined as a batch of inventory passing through a given phase of UDP. The Lead Time for a phase of UDP will be the time for a single iteration. The total Lead Time for a UDP-based software engineering system will be the sum of the iteration times for Elaboration, Construction, and Transition.

Throughput

Throughput is realized at the end of the Transition phase. Throughput is the dollar value added of the software delivered into production at the end of the Transition phase.

Production Rate

Production Rate can be measured as the number of Use Cases passing from any one phase in UDP to another phase, in a given period of time. The Production Quantity (Q) for the whole system will be the number of Use Cases delivered out of the Transition Phase. R will be Q per time period, for example, 10 Use Cases per quarter.

An Iterative Incremental Process

The advocates of UDP claim that it is not a traditional Waterfall method, rather it is an iterative incremental method. In this instance, iterative means that the whole set of requirements is not processed through each of the four phases of UDP at once. Instead, smaller batches are processed, and the system can become pipelined. Some of the inventory may be in the Transition phase whilst other inventory is WIP in the Elaboration or Construction phases.

It should be easy to see from this how a UDP process can be tuned to deliver better results, faster, with less expense. A well run UDP project will produce added value from a software production system. Figure 19–3 shows the cumulative flow signature for a typical highly iterative UDP project. Note that the increased pipelining reduces the overall project lead time from the SDLC system shown in Figure 19–2.

Inventory Cap

UDP doesn't specify a minimum or maximum inventory level. Nor does it specify a period for iteration or the size of an increment. UDP claims to be flexible and iterations as short as 2 weeks are possible. Therefore, it is possible to use the techniques described in this book to minimize the inventory levels, minimize the lead times, and still be performing a coherent UDP process.

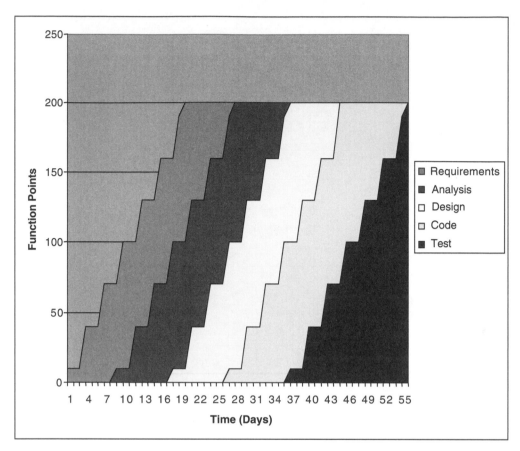

Figure 19–3
Cumulative flow for an iterative UDP project.

Artifacts

UDP is an artifact heavy process. UDP advocates five models for the system, plus Business Use Cases, a Vision Document, supplementary requirements documents, system Use Cases, a phase plan, an iteration plan, and the list goes on and on. It is important to realize that these documents may be necessary to build a good system using UDP, but they do not represent deliverables of interest for Throughput Accounting purposes. The only metrics that should concern management for control purposes are those that relate to the progress of a given unit of inventory—a Business Use Case.

With regard to documentation, UDP is a by-product heavy method. The cost of these by-products will surely manifest itself in a higher OE figure compared to Agile methods discussed in the later chapters.

Project Management

For project management purposes, UDP tracks delivered value by delivered Use Case. It is necessary to trace every artifact and every line of code back to a business requirement in a specific Use Case.

According to Kruchten, UDP projects must manage the Use Case as a single unit throughout the lifecycle. Use Cases are used to drive the business model and system context, creation and validation of design models, definition of test cases, planning of iterations, creation of manuals, and deployment. Hence, a good UDP IT shop should already have the tracking system necessary to implement the lessons learned in this book.

Process Step Time

The process steps in UDP have two granularities. There are iterations and phases. Technically, an iteration should be the lead time for a batch of inventory through a given phase. For each iteration, we should be able to measure Queue time, Setup time, Process time, and Wait time.

The Queue time will be the time between commencement of the iteration and the Use Case being accepted as work-in-process.

The Setup time will be time spent gathering artifacts, resources, tools, and system environments before an iteration can start. Setups may involve stakeholder participation. Hence, time spent working with stakeholders to gather information should be accounted for as Setup time.

Process time is the time spent on the phase transformations—the creation of a number of artifacts that belong to that phase of the system. For the Elaboration phase, the original ideas should be transformed into Use Cases, Supplementary Requirements, Software Architecture Description, Executable Architectural Prototype, Risk Assessment, Business Case, Development Plan for the Construction phase, and a Preliminary User Manual. When all of these are done, the Process time is complete.

The Wait time is specified as the time spent after the processing is complete but before the inventory is moved on to the next phase of the process.

The larger grained measure would be the phase step time for a deliverable or release of a product. This would involve several iterations.

At the largest granularity, a single release could be treated as a process step. In this case, the Inception phase should be treated as Setup time and the Elaboration, Construction, and Transition phases as Process time.

UDP's Lack of Agility

There are probably three reasons why UDP cannot be classified as an Agile method. Most fundamentally, UDP adopts the PMI/ISO mental model for project management, scope-budget-schedule. Most of the artifacts in

UDP—and there are many—are designed to try to eliminate variance and improve the overall ability to estimate. UDP is a heavyweight method because of all of these artifacts—artifacts that arguably would not be necessary were UDP to adopt an alternative mental model.

UDP does not recognize software development as an innately human activity. It does not recognize the engineer as a capacity constrained resource.

Finally, UDP offers us the Use Case as its basic unit of inventory. Use Cases are not very fine grained. In fact, a system that involves as many as 500 Function Points may only involve 25 to 50 Use Cases.

It is harder to be agile when you can only measure things in a clumsy, coarse grained manner. It may, indeed, be possible to reduce the lead time for iterations, reduce the inventory level, and reduce the operating expense in a UDP system. However, it is hard to do so quickly and efficiently when the raw unit of measure is large. Because Agile methods require fast and effective feedback, they rely on a fine grained measurement. It is debatable whether Use Cases provide this granularity.

The effectiveness of a control system has a lot to do with the sample rate and accuracy of the instrumentation. If a UDP project involves 10 developers for 3 months coding 35 Use Cases,[6] how well can a metric that tries to measure developer Throughput as Use Cases per day be trusted? The results being obtained will be in the range 0.05 through 0.15 Use Cases per day. For day-to-day project management, the poor granularity and high standard deviation in the size, scope, and definition of a Use Case make trusting such a metric for production rate difficult. The project is surely exposed to risk and uncertainty. The likely outcome is that the delivery date is missed because it was not possible to react early enough and quickly enough to compensate for variance in the system.

[6]A project of similar size measured in *Function Points* may well involve 350–500 FPs, that is, an order of magnitude more measurement points.

chapter 20

Financial Metrics in Traditional Methods

The unit of Inventory in structured methods is the Function Point. The functions in the functional specification could equally be used in businesses that do not count Function Points. However, the vast body of knowledge about Function Points makes them the best choice. They have low standard deviation and repeatability of analysis. The Inventory in the system of software production is the total number of Function Points at any stage in the process: FPs not yet started, FPs in process, and FPs completed but not yet delivered in a release—all count as Inventory (V).

Inventory

In Chapter 2, Investment (I) was defined as the money sunk in the total Inventory of raw material plus the Investment in the system itself—the PCs, the servers, and the software tools. In software terms, Investment is the cost of acquiring the ideas for the product to be developed in the form of a functional specification.

Investment

In structured methods, Investment is defined as all the costs associated with the requirements and analysis stages of the lifecycle. In order to obtain a proper Function Point analysis of the Inventory, it is necessary to generate the Functional Specification and analyze it sufficiently to get to a granularity where FP Analysis is possible.

The cost of generating and maintaining any documentation during requirements and Analysis must be considered part of the Investment figure.

$$\text{Investment}_{Release}\ (I_R) = OE_{Requirements} + OE_{Analysis}$$

If any of the activities were out-sourced and incurred direct costs, those would also be attributed to the Investment figure. For example, hiring a management consultancy to define the market and develop in-depth market research would be considered Investment. Hiring an experienced mentor to facilitate the Analysis should also be accounted for as Investment.

Investment Across Multiple Releases

In a sophisticated SDLC development organization, multiple projects will be happening concurrently. Different projects will be at different stages in the lifecycle, being worked by different specialists on the staff. Hence, it is necessary to account for the costs of the Inventory throughout the software production system, at each lifecycle stage.

The capability of determining the sunk cost of specific raw material being delivered into the system is required. This can be calculated by dividing the Investment for a given project (I_p), by the number of Function Points in that project (V_p). This cost then becomes the average Investment per Function Point for that project:

$$\text{Average Investment per Function Point (AIPFP)} = I_p / V_p$$

With Function Points from multiple projects being tracked through the process, they can be tagged individually with their original AIPFP. Hence, it will always be possible to sum the total Investment in Inventory throughout the software production system.

Because the system is a continuous process, it makes more sense to use a time-based metric for reporting, that is, the average Investment level for a given month or calendar quarter:

$$I_{Quarter} = AIPF_{Quarter} \times \text{Average Inventory}_{Quarter}$$

Operating Expense

All costs, including direct labor, for the design, coding, and various testing stages, must be treated as the total operating expenses for the SDLC process. For a single release, this can be directly attributed against the Inventory of Function Points. Hence, if a project is expected to take 16 months to complete through design, coding, testing, and deployment and the total costs involved in running the software production system for a single week are known, the total $OE_{Release}$ for that release is easily calculated:

$$OE_{Release} = \text{Estimated Delivery Time (Months)} \times OE \text{ (per Month)}$$

Operating Expense Across Multiple Projects

In a software production system processing multiple projects simultaneously through different stages of the lifecycle, it becomes slightly more complicated to calculate Operating Expense. There are Function Points that are carrying different levels of Investment as a sunk cost at different stages. It is tempting to try to track the input against Function Points of a given project and try to attribute costs to these. This sounds awfully similar to cost accounting, which, of course, would be natural in an SDLC project. It instantly creates the need for detailed, if often inaccurate, time sheets.

The Throughput Accounting approach would treat the system as a continuous process. Hence, OE for a given period of time, such as a month or calendar quarter, is reported for the whole system—not individual projects:

$$OE_{Quarter} = \text{Total Costs for FPs Design thru Deployment}_{Quarter}$$

Throughput

Throughput is defined as the value of the delivered Function Points less the direct costs involved in deploying that functionality into production. This is calculated as the sales price (or budget) less any direct costs such as middleware, Operating Expense involved in deployment, database licenses, and hardware.

For a single project release in an IT department, the budget figure should be used as the transfer price with direct costs deducted. This was referred to as the Budget Basis in Chapter 15.

Across multiple projects or multiple releases of a single project, it is always better to think of the system of software production as a continuous process. Therefore, the methods from Chapters 15 through 17 should be used to determine a suitable Throughput value for the Inventory of Function Points delivered in a given time period.

Net Profit in Structured Methods

The Net Profit equation looks exactly like those from Chapters 15 and 16. For a single project:

$$\text{Net Profit}_{Project} = T_{Project} - OE_{Project}$$

The whole system that produces more than one project as a continuous process of software development would produce this equation:

$$\text{Net Profit}_{Quarter} = T_{Quarter} - OE_{Quarter}$$

Return on Investment in Structured Methods

The Net Profit figures together with our earlier equations for Investment in structured methods can be used to calculate the ROI:

$$ROI_{Project} = \frac{T_{Project} - OE_{Project}}{I_{Project}}$$

$$ROI_{Quarter} = \frac{T_{Quarter} - OE_{Quarter}}{I_{Quarter}}$$

The ROI equation should be used as a normalized method for assessing the value added by the software development process where T is calculated using the True Basis from Chapter 15.

Accounting for Change

When a change request arrives in a SDLC project, the change must be understood and prioritized. Change requests involve additional requirements and analysis work. The cost of this must be added to our Investment (I).

Some change requests, rather than extend the scope, obviate some of the existing scope of a project. This will result in obviated Function Points from the earlier FP analysis. In Lean Thinking terminology, these obviated FPs are Inventory waste. They must immediately be written off from the Investment figure and shown as OE. Hence, the Investment figure must be reduced by the AIPFP multiplied by the number of FPs affected by the change.

$$I_{Postchange} = I_{Prechange} + I[_{change}]_{R\&A} - (AIPFP \times \#FPs \; obviated)$$

$$OE_{Postchange} = OE_{Prechange} + (AIPFP \times \#FPs \; obviated)$$

chapter 21

Production Metrics in FDD

Feature Driven Development was created between 1997 and 1999 at United Overseas Bank in Singapore by a team led by Jeff De Luca. The work built on earlier material by Peter Coad who had developed the idea of a Feature definition and a Feature List. FDD incorporated many established best practices of software development from the previous 30 years.[1] Added to those established concepts were newer ones from Coad and advances in object oriented analysis and design, known as Archetypes, developed on the same project. Archetypes would later lead Peter Coad to develop the Domain Neutral Component (DNC) [Coad 1999], which is widely considered part of FDD.[2]

Overview of Feature Driven Development (FDD)

FDD took all of these software development techniques and wrapped them in a management control structure based on very fine grained tracking and metrics analysis. FDD is essentially a software management method, rather than a software engineering lifecycle development method. FDD does not claim to have introduced any new software development methods, but rather to have harnessed the best practices of a generation of industry luminaries through the use of an innovative management technique.

I was fortunate enough to have been one of the team in Singapore and I have worked with FDD projects in Ireland and several states of the United States over a 4-year period with 3 different teams of developers. I have run these projects using differing technologies, in different industries with a diverse set of developers from many different cultures, educational backgrounds, and experience levels.

My experience with FDD is that it supports the repeatability claims made by both Jeff De Luca and Peter Coad. It is also transferable across an organization and organizations. It is in this sense a scalable Agile method and a repeatable Agile method. There have been many FDD projects run across the world in the last 5 years. The body of evidence would suggest that there is correlation that FDD works and works predictably.

---

[1] Most of the established best practices used in FDD are taken from work by Jerry Weinberg [Weinberg 1997 & 1998], Tom DeMarco and Tim Lister [DeMarco 1999], and Fred Brooks [Brooks 1995]. These authors recognized the human nature of software development as early as 1970. Many aspects of Agile processes are not new.
[2] Archetypes and the DNC have been taught by Stephen Palmer and his former colleagues at Togethersoft as the technique for modeling in FDD. Some in the FDD community take a view that the DNC is entirely optional. However, as discussed in Chapter 32, the use of the DNC is important for reduction of variance, and FDD is therefore stronger when the DNC is used.

There is a slight bias in this section towards FDD. There are 4 chapters discussing it—more than any other Agile method. I have used the opportunity presented with this book to cover previously unpublished FDD material.

FDD has been described by some Agile methodologists as "less Agile." This is probably due to the fact that FDD looks more like and uses many established software development methods. FDD's claim to repeatability goes against the thinking of many Agilists that software development "lives on the edge of chaos." FDD involves planning and up-front modeling and design. It takes a "right first time" approach to agility. As I will go on to show, FDD is an Agile method and is an extremely Lean method that incorporates many aspects of Lean thinking.

What follows is a description of the state of the art in FDD at the time of writing. It represents a mild departure from the most recent book on the topic, *A Practical Guide to Feature Driven Development* [Palmer 2002]. It tries to incorporate some elements of what the Australian FDD enthusiasts are calling "FDD Workflow."[3]

A System Representation of FDD

FDD uses a simple five-stage model to explain its function. Figure 21–1 is drawn as a full lifecycle system to be consistent with other diagrams in this text. The five steps of FDD as shown are: Shape Modeling, Feature List, Plan by Subject Area,[4] Design by Feature Set,[5] and Build by Chief Programmer Work Package.[6]

Step 1—Shape Modeling. FDD promotes modeling as part of the requirements discovery process and includes the marketing team as part of the effort.[7] The modeling effort leads to a UML Class Diagram that models the business behavior as it is mutually understood by the crossfunctional team. The modeling step also involves a parallel activity to examine the nonfunctional requirements and develop an architectural model for the proposed system.

Step 2—Feature List. It involves use of the model from step 1 and an understanding of the basic scope or marketing requirements to develop a fine grained Feature List. This Feature List will be treated as the desired scope for the release. Traditionally, this might be called an outline for a Functional Specification. The Feature List should be prioritized in a fashion similar to that described in Chapter 16.

---

[3]At the time of writing, there is no documentation on FDD Workflow. Other advances in FDD developed in the United States have similarities to FDD Workflow, and these are reflected in the description here.

[4]Originally documented as "Plan by Feature" [Palmer 2002].

[5]Originally documented as "Design by Feature" [Palmer 2002].

[6]Originally documented as "Build by Feature" [Palmer 2002].

[7]At the time of writing, the marketing team at 4thpass-a Motorola subsidiary in Seattle, WA, is sufficiently skilled in UML modeling with Archetypes that it undertakes this process for requirements discovery before engaging the engineering team.

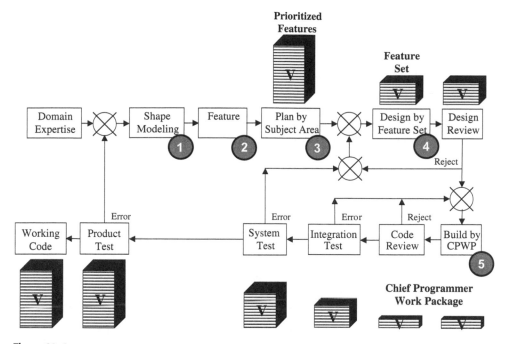

Figure 21–1
System representation of FDD.

Step 3—Plan by Subject Area. It involves planning the project by grouping Features from the list into functionally related sets and super-sets, known as Feature Sets (FS) and Subject Areas (SA). The team would then agree on a schedule of delivery for Subject Area and Feature Sets with the project sponsor. This is similar to the project planning method described in Chapter 7.

Step 4—Design by Feature Set. It involves production of a design for a Feature Set. Problem Domain (PD) Feature Sets are known as Business Activities.[8] The Features in a set are logically grouped because it makes sense to design them as a single batch. The design step in FDD involves detailed, in-depth UML modeling, including enhancement of the Class Diagram and development of a UML Sequence Diagram for each Feature in the activity.

Step 5—Build by Chief Programmer Work Package. It involves packaging a smaller batch of Features from the Feature Set in step 4 and developing the code for those Features and unit testing them. The batch of Features is known as a Chief Programmer Work Package (CPWP) and should be selected such that it can be completed by a single Feature Team in less than 2 weeks. The chief programmer leading the Feature Team is responsible for selection of the Features in the CPWP in negotiation with the project manager or project secretary and other chief programmers on the project.

---

[8]Business Activity is a replacement term for Feature Set, http://www.nebulon.com/articles/fdd/download/fddprocessesUSLetter.pdf.

The essential element of FDD is the Feature. A Feature is a small piece of client-valued functionality: a tangible result, which can be delivered in 2 weeks or less; a frequent result, with some measure of quality; or a working result. Features are listed by first developing an in-depth understanding of the requirements through modeling. Modeling is a "must have" first step in FDD.

FDD defines four layers of architecture: UI—User Interface, PD—Problem Domain (business logic), DM—Data Management, and SI—Systems Interfaces. For each of the four layers a detailed model may be developed.[9] A list of Features is produced using a language formula that leads to a definition of a very small piece of development work. A PD Feature, such as "Is the privacy option designated for a subscriber," is actually a simple Boolean check and could be coded in minutes. Each type of Feature is defined using a repeatable formula. It is this repeatable formula that makes it possible to estimate an FDD project with considerable accuracy.

A PD (business) Feature is written using this structure:

<action> the <result> |by|of|from|for|to| a(n) <object>

for example,

> total the value of a sale
>
> calculate the interest for a bank account
>
> total the hours worked for a pilot

The privacy option example above doesn't directly fit the template. Sometimes rearranging is necessary—particularly with separable verbs and present progressive tense. So "Is the privacy option designated for a subscriber" would strictly need to be written as "Is designated, the privacy option, for a subscriber." As a result, FDD does not strictly mandate the template. The rule of thumb is that the more Features that strictly meet the template style, the lower the variability in implementation. Hence, making an effort to accurately map requirements into the template will result in more accurate estimates and plans.[10]

For UI Features the formula is different. The UI is modeled using a Statechart [Horrocks 1999]. The Statechart, as shown in Figure 21–2, is a very precise blueprint for the presentation layer code implemented using the Model-View-Controller Type-II variant. Some states of the Statechart model are designated as Views, that is, they represent specific View classes to be constructed in the presentation layer code. State transitions on the Statechart are labeled with the name of the event that caused the state transition. By convention, these events are named after the behavior of a UI component represented on the Statechart model. For example, a button

[9]Sometimes it is unnecessary to model the DM because it is implemented using an automated tool that maps directly from the PD model. For smaller FDD projects it may only be necessary to model the PD and let the other layers organize themselves in Step 4.
[10]The use of the FDD Feature Template to reduce variability is discussed in Chapter 32.

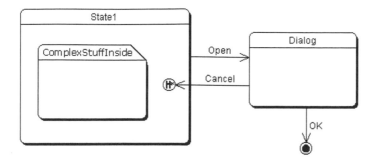

Figure 21–2
Example of a
Statechart UI model.

labeled "OK" would create an OK Event. State transitions from the same state labeled with the same event are grouped together to be implemented by a single Controller class.

A UI Feature can be one of two things:

A View Class, for example, Search Results Table

A Controller, for example, SEARCH Event

Formulas for SI and DM are similar to the PD, but the result and object terms are system-related rather than domain-related.

FDD's five main steps can be examined using theory from Section 1. The Feature List is clearly the raw material (V), (the input) for the system. The cost of acquiring the Feature List is the Investment, (I) in the system for an FDD project. The cost of operating the Plan, Design, and Build steps is the Operating Expense (OE). The number of Features delivered in a given time period is the Production Rate (R).

Agile Management Theory and FDD

The process task steps—Queue, Setup, Process, and Wait times—can be examined for an FDD project taken as a whole. The Queue time would be the time spent before Step 1, Modeling, gets underway. For example, the project may have decided to hire a mentor, such as Stephen Palmer, to assist with the modeling stage. Waiting for Steve to arrive would be Queue time. Another example of Queue time would be waiting for a project signoff or authorization.

Process Steps and FDD

Steps 1 through 3 represent the Setup time for an FDD project. The Modeling, Feature Listing, and Planning stages all represent Setup for the mainline development activity. Steps 4 and 5 represent the Process time. The time Features spend after Step 5, Build, without being delivered to the customer, would represent the Wait time.

The Lead Time for the whole FDD project would be the sum of the Queue, Setup, Process, and Wait times. However, FDD does not generally advocate delivery of the whole project in one drop. Hence, the Inventory will be broken into portions and delivered according to the plan agreed in Step 3. The Lead Time (LT) for specific Features will be lower. This is shown later.

Production Metrics in FDD

185

Estimating OE for an FDD Project

Once the scope for a given project or system release is agreed in Step 2, the engineering group can proceed to estimate the level of effort (LOE) required to design, build, and test the scoped functionality. The Bill of Materials, for the software resource planning, is the agreed Feature List of prioritized Features. A 5-point weighting technique [Anderson 2001] has been introduced to enable calculation of the LOE. Features are evaluated against a complexity metric, and the complexity is translated into an LOE for each Feature.

Exponents of FDD claim that it is repeatable. "Repeatable" in this instance means that it is transferable across teams who can repeat the process and estimate projects based on the relatively low variance associated with Features and related analysis techniques in FDD. This is a fairly unique claim amongst Agile methodologists. The others tend to advocate that repeatability is unobtainable. They lean towards the notion that estimation is impossible, but empirical data and fast feedback can be used to compensate.

The key to FDD's repeatability is its core definition of a Feature. Features are defined for different levels of the architecture. FDD partitions the system architecture and effectively chorales the development variability.[11]

The Modeling Rule of Thumb

A rough estimate technique is used in FDD to estimate the length of a project for Steps 4 and 5. This rule of thumb sounds remarkably unscientific, but there is significant correlation from projects run all over the world by numerous managers that this technique works. The rule is simple—1 week of modeling (step 1) results in 12 weeks of design and coding (Steps 4 and 5). A project that takes 3 weeks to model will take 9 months to build. The rule assumes that UML color Archetype modeling with the Domain Neutral Component is being used.

Level of Effort Estimation in FDD

Once a fine grained Feature List is derived, it is possible to calculate with some accuracy the level of effort required for these small pieces of work. Because each piece is so small, each Feature is very transparent to the developer. By adding the estimates for each Feature, it is possible to estimate the LOE for a Feature Set, a Subject Area, and a whole project.

Some FDD methodologists encourage developers to make an LOE for each Feature based on hours or days. This approach ought to suffer from the local safety problem. However, reality suggests otherwise. This could be explained by the fact that each Feature is so small that the developer has a high degree of confidence in her estimate. Hence, she does not add a local safety margin to the estimate.

To completely avoid the local safety problem, I have developed a technique that asks the developer to categorize a Feature based on a 5-point complexity rating. The developer is no longer being asked to have a confidence level in her estimate but only to apply a series of evaluation criteria to the Feature and derive a complexity rating.

[11]Reinertsen describes how to use design architecture to segregate variability [1997, p. 149]. Areas of the architecture known to be better understood have less variability and less uncertainty. They need less buffering and can be more accurately estimated.

The 5-Point Scale

The 5-point scale shown in Table 21–1 moves the level of effort estimation problem to the manager. The manager can calculate the estimate by aggregating historic data from earlier projects. The 5-point scale can be adjusted based on historic data from a single engineering location. However, a default initial set of values is required. Following lessons learned from Fred Brooks, Gerald Weinberg, and Barry Boehm [Boehm 1981; Brooks 1995; Weinberg 1997], the scale is nonlinear. It is used later for tracking actual against planned values and adjusting estimates as project progress is reported.

A planning team, which typically consists of the project manager/project office staff, some of the modeling team or analysts, plus the chief programmers will make the complexity estimates. Each Feature will be briefly discussed and a weight assigned. For a project with 500 Features, this weighting can be performed in a typical afternoon planning session. It is well worth the effort.

If a 3-person Feature Team were given three Features to design and build, all of weight 3, then it ought to take them 2 working days to develop the design material, review it amongst themselves, write the code, perform some unit tests, and review the delivered code.

In recent studies,[12] where the emphasis was on web development of presentation layer, the average complexity of Features, modeled using the methods described here, have delivered an average complexity weighting of 1.7 with a standard deviation of 0.1.

In other words, a typical web page can be built as a JSP by a single programmer in 1 day, and a typical event controller can be built as a Servlet by a single programmer in half a day.

Similar results for PD Features have yielded results with an average rating of around 3.0 with a slightly larger standard deviation. The overall Feature average for entire projects has been in the order of 2.3 with a standard deviation of 0.2.

So far this scale has proved reliable, needing only minor adjustment during the development lifecycle. At the very least, it provides a good basis for evaluating plan versus actual performance.

Table 21–1
Feature complexity versus man days effort.

Feature Complexity	Effort (Man Days)
1	0.5
2	1
3	2
4	4
5	8 (or more)

---

[12]Thirteen projects run by the author between 1999 and 2002 varying in size from 150 to 600 Features and typically taking between 3 and 9 months to complete.

Business Features and the 5-Point Scale

For PD Features assign points on the scale against the number of affected classes for the Feature, as shown in Table 21–2. During the planning, the team is only guessing at the complexity of the sequence diagramming, but a good guess is good enough. Normally, there are enough Features that errors in the guessing will average out over the whole project.

At the time this method was adopted, I was skeptical that it would work. It was purely an experiment to evaluate the variation in Features and the reliability of the Feature template technique. On an electronic bill payment and presentment system project in 1999, this scale was used to predict the resources needed for the business layer development on a medium-sized project with 153 Problem Domain. It performed to an accuracy of -10%. In other words, development actually took 10% longer than predicted. This result was sufficiently accurate for the technique to remain in use, and it has proven to be reliable ever since.

Formulae for Success

It is the precisely defined nature of FDD Features and the use of repeatable formulae for estimation that makes FDD a highly statistically predictable process. FDD produces repeatable results because the analysis and planning at a fine grained level are spelled out in an understandable, repeatable fashion. The corollary is also true. When the modeling and Feature List stages go poorly due to ambiguity in the requirements, the estimates tend to be much less accurate.

FDD provides a mechanism to accurately calculate an estimate of the operating expense figure for a project. An experienced FDD team should be able to predict OE within 10% variance.

The architectural partitioning and the analytical techniques for evaluating functionality at each level in the architecture help FDD to significantly reduce the variability and hence reduce the uncertainty associated with an estimate. The result is that FDD estimates require less buffering due to reduced uncertainty. Less buffering means that FDD is leaner and more efficient than many other methods of software development.

Table 21–2
Estimated classes involved versus feature complexity.

Estimated Number of Classes in Feature	Feature Complexity	Effort (man days)
1	1	0.5
2	2	1
3	3	2
4	4	4
5	5	8 (or more)

Adapting FDD to Nonideal Situations

FDD works best when the modeling is done using a joint team of business owners and developers as an active part of the requirements process. This allows a detailed model to be developed and accurate planning to take place. However, it is not always possible to run an FDD project under ideal conditions.

Over the last few years, my colleagues and I have learned how to adapt FDD to nonideal situations where volumes of requirements documents are not supplied and access to subject matter experts or business owners in the modeling stage is not possible.

With poor-quality or vague, high-level requirements, it can be difficult to develop an initial Feature List. Mapping Features to the classes on the model can be difficult. In this situation it is best to make the Features look as much like the template as possible and not worry too much about association with the model. Sometimes Features look coarse grained, and sometimes they begin to look like tasks rather than pieces of client-valued functionality.

When the Feature List doesn't accurately map to the model and doesn't always fit to the template, it becomes impossible to use the 5-point complexity estimating scale. In this situation, it is necessary to fall back on the LOE per Feature approach. Local safety margins do not appear to represent a significant issue. However, the accuracy of the plan does suffer. Some Features are horribly over, or underestimated. Hence, uncertainty grows in FDD projects run in nonideal conditions. The greater uncertainty must be compensated for by use of larger buffer sizes.

In a situation with poor quality requirements, the FDD LOE will not be as accurate as +/− 10%. The exact margin of variance will vary according to the domain and the degree of vagueness in the requirement document. In extreme cases, it can be +100% out, and this needs to be buffered accordingly.

chapter 22

Project Management with FDD

FDD lends itself readily to the techniques for Agile project management from Chapter 6, Agile project planning from Chapter 7, and software resource planning from Chapter 10.

Paul Szego talked about the notion of self-organizing construction within planned assembly [Highsmith 2002, p. 277]. What he means is that individual Features are left for the Feature Team of developers to plan, design, and construct, while the overall project is planned as a series of aggregations of Features for testing and delivery. These aggregations are known as Business Activities (or Feature Sets), and aggregations of Activities are known as Subject Areas. These aggregates are assembled together to produce a finished product.

In FDD, features are grouped into Feature Sets Feature Set is an abstract term for a logical grouping of Features. A Feature Set is intended as a potentially client-deliverable piece of work. It is a coherent set of client-valued functions that might be deliverable as a component. It is a grouping of related business features. PD Feature sets are named after business activities or processes—hence the term "Business Activities."

A Business Activity can be written using the following structure:

<action>ing <business deliverable>

for example,

    approving a bank loan
    updating customer details
    restocking a warehouse

A Feature Set might typically be 15 or more Features.

Features are developed in batches known as Chief Programmer Work Packages (CPWP) and typically consist of 5 to 10 Features. Therefore, with three iterations of five Features per CPWP, a typical Feature Set of 15 Features would be completed. This Feature Set could then be delivered as an interim deliverable to the test team or client. It has real business value.

User Interface Feature Sets

I have tried several strategies for grouping UI Features into Features Sets. Two make most sense: a Feature Set for each Use Case and a Feature Set for each container in the UI model.

Strategy 1: A Feature Set for Each Use Case

If the functional specification for the project was delivered in the form of Use Cases, then it may be possible to relate back to the Use Cases for Feature Set grouping. This has meaning to the business as it can easily relate the output (delivered Features) to the original input (requirements as Use Cases). A full explanation of this technique is provided in the article, "Extending FDD for UI" [Anderson 2001].

At least one FDD methodologist has suggested that Use Cases can be used to group Features across all four architecture levels, that is, building an FDD project as vertical slices. This is attractive because it means each Feature Set represents a demonstrable component with full functionality. This is useful for clients who insist on seeing regular working updates.

However, I consider it suboptimal due to the nature of the vertical slice through the architecture. Having the capability to bundle Features horizontally, that is, across a single layer of the architecture, is better. It allows the developers to work more efficiently due to the architectural partitioning and allows for variability to be segregated by architectural layer. Setup and integration time is generally reduced in a horizontally partitioned design and build stages. Using vertical slices is likely to increase variance and uncertainty requiring larger buffers. Hence, it is less optimal. Nevertheless, with a nervous customer who needs reassurance, the grouping of Feature Sets by Use Case is a useful alternative.

Strategy 2: A Feature Set for Each Container in the UI Model

Writing in early 2003, this is my preferred strategy. It relies on the development of a complete interaction model for the UI. The containers within the UI design are identified. Containers are UI components that receive and process message events and usually bind the persistent transactions or the save points. A Feature Set is built from all the finer grained views aggregated by the Container.

Depending on how large the result from this strategy, you may wish to consider the output as a Subject Area. Ask yourself whether or not the component would make business sense on its own, as an interim deliverable. If the answer is yes, then you probably have a Subject Area.

Subject Areas

A Subject Area in FDD (called "Major Feature Sets" by Coad [1999]), is a major component or subsystem. In many organizations, a Subject Area represents a single project. Several projects together make a business program. In my experience, a single Subject Area can take a team of 10 or more people at least 3 months to develop.

In FDD, Subject Areas are named with the following convention:

<object> management

for example,

Customer Relationship Management

Account Management

Inventory Management

A Subject Area should include the UI Feature Sets for the screens associated with the same business management area, for example, all the screens for Customer Relationship Management or all the screens for Inventory Management.

The Feature Lifecycle

The lifecycle of a Feature is usually divided into six milestones, with each milestone being assigned a percentage of completeness, as in Figure 22–1. These percentage weightings have been developed from experience and are designed to reflect the level of effort expended to reach the milestone.

Process Control in FDD

Feature Driven Development delivers a fine grain of control and offers opportunities for precise and frequent measurement of progress. This provides the ability to report progress with astounding accuracy, for example, 43% complete, and speed with equal accuracy, for example, work is progressing at 2.7% per week.

FDD offers the possibility to get at least six data points for progress against a single Feature. Features are very small; they can represent as few as 4 man hours of work. On a project estimated to take 20 people 9 months, you have the ability to measure progress at a level of man minutes. It is possible to sample the progress and track it on a daily basis.

FDD is designed to track the flow of value—described in Chapter 6—and the Feature lifecycle data naturally lends itself to the production of a Cumulative Flow Diagram (see Figure 22–2).

Domain Walkthrough	Design	Design Inspection	Coding	Code Inspection	Promote to Build
1%	40%	3%	45%	10%	1%

Figure 22–1
The Feature lifecycle through steps 4 and 5.

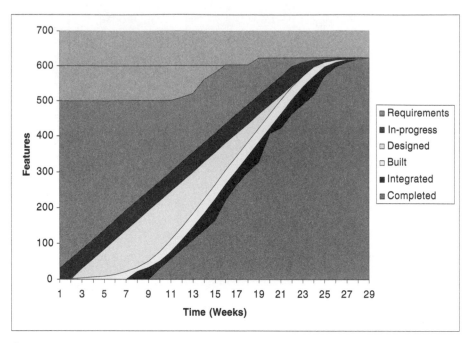

Figure 22–2
Idealized Cumulative Flow Diagram for an FDD system.

It is possible to use this information to predict the delivery of an FDD project. However, the projection is not linear. The evolution of an FDD project follows an S-curve pattern. Nevertheless, when you undertake any journey, knowing how far you have come and how fast you are going is extremely useful information.

It is possible to gain some degree of linear scaling on FDD projects. For example, if developers are added without expanding the number of chief programmers, the effect on increased production is almost linear. This effect is true as long as the number of lines of communication is not increased. The introduction of an additional chief programmer along with additional developers will produce a less than linear increase and a deeper J-curve effect.

Estimates Versus Agreed Function

Being able to measure how fast the team is going is not enough to guarantee delivery of agreed function within the planned date. The estimate could have been wrong! This is a reality of life. Until a team has been through several iterations and has accurate historical data, estimating can be problematic. The advantage of having a fine grain of control is that the manager will know early whether the team is going to be late. This gives management the opportunity to take action to elevate constraints or to negotiate the scope constraint to reduce functionality.

In today's world of rapid business change, it is important to deliver on the appointed date. It is rare that resources can be increased, because time is too

Design & Build by Feature 100 Calendar Days	Buffer 15 Days

Start   115 Days End

Figure 22–3
Estimating the "code complete" date.

short to add people or budget for staff augmentation is not available. So Features must be traded out of the scope. Being able to do this early rather than later is much better. It allows the plan to be refactored and expediting or waste to be avoided. In order to have early warning, a system that facilitates accurate measurement at frequent sampling points is required, and the manager needs to be capable of predicting the S-curve effect based on the project complexity, risk and uncertainty, and the engineering team's ability.

Scheduling an FDD Project

FDD projects should be scheduled in two pieces: steps 1 through 3 and steps 4 and 5. For a project in which modeling activity takes around 1 week, FDD suggests that the total time for the project is 3 months with between 10 and 20 developers. It will need 2 days of Feature List analysis and 1 day of planning. If the modeling phase takes 4 weeks, then plan on the project taking 1 year. You will need 8 days of Feature List analysis and 4 days of planning, that is, 6 weeks of effort for steps 1 through 3 for a 1-year project.

At the end of the first three steps in an FDD project, it should be possible to calculate the LOE for the design and build stages. This can be used to predict the "code complete" date. This date is not simply the start date plus the number of calendar days estimated from the level of effort divided by the available manpower. This would be a foolish target. There is no allowance for any uncertainty—no buffer against Murphy's Law. Critical Chain has shown that it is necessary to add a project buffer based on the uncertainties involved.

My rule of thumb is to use a 15% minimum buffer for a low-risk project, as shown in Figure 22–3. As uncertainty increases, the buffer could rise to as much as 100% of LOE.

Scheduling Subject Areas and Feature Sets

There are two important pieces of information required in order to schedule the start of Feature Sets or Subject Areas: the dependencies between Feature Sets and the level of effort for each Feature Set.

First, draw a PERT, as shown in Figure 22–4, chart showing the dependencies between the Feature Sets, and show the LOE for each Feature Set.

If there are interim deliverables or the marketing department has indicated a preference for the order of development based on marketing priorities, which could be derived out of the individual Feature priorities, use these to estimate desired delivery dates for each Feature Set. With desirable delivery dates, dependencies, and LOEs known, it should be possible to allocate manpower against Feature Sets and determine the Critical Path for the project.

Figure 22–4
PERT chart breaking out project Feature Sets.

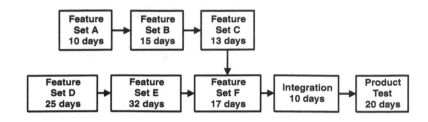

Figure 22–5
Critical Chain for a sample FDD project.

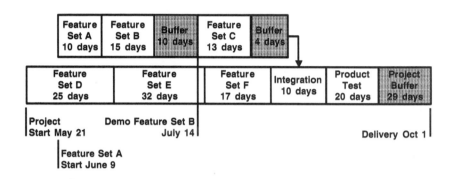

Figure 22–6
Feature process steps.

		Setup Time	Process Time	Wait Time
	Queue Time	Walkthrough DBF & Inspection	BBF Inspection	Promote

Feature Set Start	CPWP Start	Time	CPWP End	Feature Set End

With this additional information, it is possible to reverse back from the delivery date to determine the approximate start dates for each Feature Set. However, before this is done, feeding buffers must be added to the noncritical path, feeding chains of dependencies. Again, the buffer required should be based on the uncertainty associated with the Feature Sets or aggregation of Feature Sets in the chain. The revised PERT chart with appropriate buffers and dates is shown in Figure 22–5.

Now that suitable feeding buffers have been added, the approximate start date for each Feature Set can be determined. This allows manpower to be allocated across the project.

Note that the buffer is not a delay. The buffer is there to absorb uncertainty. If Feature Sets A & B are complete before July 14, Feature Set C should be started immediately.

Building a Feature—Queue, Setup, Process, and Wait Time

Figure 22–6 shows how to allocate feature milestones against process step elements. The Queue time associated with a Feature is the time between the Feature's Feature Set starting and the Feature actually being picked up for development by the developers. The Setup time for a Feature is the time for the first three milestones in the Feature lifecycle (from Figure 22–1): walk-through, design, and design review. The Process time is the time for the next two milestones: code and code review. The Wait time is the time spent while the Feature waits to be grouped with others and promoted to the build, integrated, and handed off for testing.

More than 50% of the time for processing a Feature is nonprocess time. In fact, for large Feature Sets, the Process time may be a very small percentage of the total time, with Queue, Setup, and Wait being far greater.

FDD Workflow is about software resource planning for FDD. The chief programmers work together and in liaison with the project manager and development manager to ensure that the engineering constraints are always suitably protected.

Each chief programmer is given a buffer of waiting Features known as a "virtual inbox" [Highsmith 2002, p. 280]. The CP has warning of what is coming next and can use this information to plan ahead and ensure that the correct team is available for the next Build-by-CPWP step.

Workflow includes defining the correct set of Features to pass through a given process step at the same time. This could be thought of as a Bill of Materials (BOM) for a step in FDD.

Business Activities or Feature Sets are designed together. They pass through the Design-by-Feature Set step together. This optimizes design effort by providing suitable coverage to allow a design to be complete without an overly large scope that would become cumbersome or take too long, resulting in a lengthening of the lead time for CPWP completion beyond 2 weeks.

Chief Programmer Work Packages

Features are so small that it would be inefficient to build a project Feature by Feature. The next step in FDD Workflow is to batch sets of Features that are closely related for development. A batch of Features for development is called a Chief Programmer Work Package (CPWP). The purpose of batching is to exploit the capacity constrained programming resources by optimizing overlap in the coding effort.

The code for several Features can then be written simultaneously. If several Features in a CPWP require adding code to a single class file, that file can be accessed and updated for all the Features in the CPWP at one time by a single developer. This makes for more efficient programming and reduces the process time per Feature.

Monitoring the Buffers in FDD

FDD uses a parking lot diagram, Figure 22–7, to report the project status on a single page. The parking lot diagram has a parking space for each

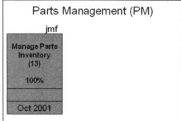

Diagram courtesy of Stephen Palmer, Copyright 2002 Step-10 Limited, all rights reserved, http://www.step-10.com/.

Figure 22–7
FDD project parking lot.

Feature Set and uses a color coding scheme to indicate whether the Feature Set is in-progress, complete, in need of attention, blocked, or late. Additional information displayed includes the number of Features in the Feature Set and the percentage complete. The Feature Sets occupy single parking spaces whilst the Subject Areas group them together into sublots.

The parking lot diagram can be enhanced by showing the buffer usage associated with the Feature Set as was shown in Figure 14–5. The status of the Feature Set should reflect the buffer remaining, as described in Figure 7–4. Feature Sets that turn red are indicating that they are impacting the Critical Path and eating into the overall project buffer.

When something is impacting the project buffer, it is of significance and should be reported to executive management. As the parking lot diagram is intended for executive management, it is right that Feature Sets should turn red when they impact the overall project.

Overall Project Status

The summary status of the project should be determined by the overall project buffer usage. No other metric is really useful for the executives. Executive status should be reported in the operations format presented in Chapter 14.

All information regarding the status of Features, Feature Sets (Business Activities), Subject Areas, Chief Programmer Work Packages, FDD Workflow, and overall project metrics should be provided in a web-based Knowledge Management System (KMS) as shown in Figure 22–8. The FDD KMS should be used every day by everyone on the project. The development manager may find that printing out the contents of the website in color and displaying it prominently in the building is useful.

Regardless of whether the KMS data is printed and displayed or is simply accessed electronically, the data is being used for visual control. It allows the self-organizing aspects of the FDD Feature Teams and individual developers to see at a glance what work is in progress, who is responsible for it, and at what stage it is at.

Visual control is a key aspect of Lean Production, and FDD has utilized this technique since its inception in 1998.

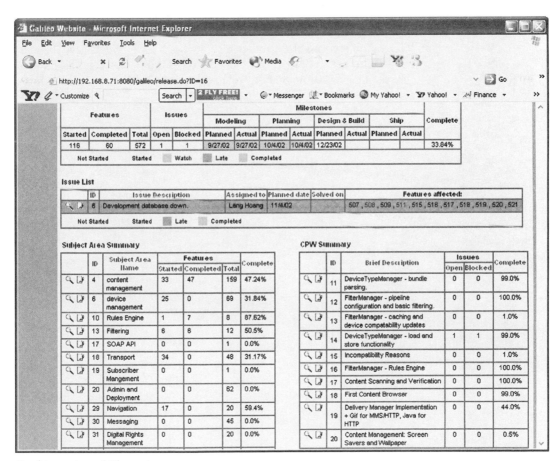

Graphic courtesy of 4thpass Inc.

Figure 22–8
An FDD KMS project dashboard.

Executive Management Metrics in FDD

In FDD, the executive dashboard includes just enough information to satisfy busy executives. It focuses on significant information that communicates the health of the project. In addition to the parking lot diagram, the following information is useful:

- The project status as green, yellow, or red (determined from the project buffer usage)
- The cumulative flow diagram
- The total number of Features completed
- The current percentage of client-valued functionality completed
- The number of issues open
- The trend in the number of open issues as a graph
- The number of Features blocked
- The trend in Features blocked as a graph

This should be enough for any executive to understand the health of a project. If more information is needed to answer specific questions, this can be obtained from the KMS. It will contain the entire Feature List along with the status of each Feature and any related blocking issues.

chapter 23

FDD Process Elements Explained

FDD is a three-dimensional software development and management method that uses process experience, analysis and modeling techniques, and, most importantly, the psychology of computer programming. This chapter examines how all three of these dimensions contribute elements to the FDD process and how each one contributes to improved Throughput.

In order to maximize the Production Rate (R) from the FDD system of software production, the capacity constrained resources must be fully exploited. The most highly prized (and priced) of these resources are the engineers. If Throughput is to be maximized, engineers must be kept busy working on production of code. Distractions and interruptions should be minimized, and issues that result in developer downtime should be eliminated.

Exploiting the engineering resources fully is more than just a software resource planning issue. Although it is true that an FDD project must execute well on project management and resource planning, issues must be resolved before they slow developers down. Software resource planning must keep the chief programmer's inbox full with well-defined work to be done and the CP in turn must ensure that individual developers are kept busy. Of even greater value, the engineering team must be well motivated. Psychology is the most useful tool for improving the effectiveness of the engineering team. It is the role of the development manager to ensure that the team is properly motivated.

FDD uses psychology in several ways to maximize the exploitation of the capacity constrained engineer: teamworking, sense of belonging, peer pressure, peer recognition, shared learning experience, safety in numbers, group confessional opportunity (if one person admits to facing a challenge or having a problem, others will follow), reward for Feature completion, and punishment for Feature misses.[1]

Exploiting Engineering Resources

---

[1] An optional inclusion in FDD is to designate teams with demerits for late delivery.

The File Access Constraint— Class Ownership

FDD uses class/file ownership as a core element of the process. This is unusual for an Agile method. FDD does not treat version control as a policy constraint but as a genuine process constraint. In FDD, strict exclusive write access to program code is considered inviolate as a part of the process. Hence, availability of a file for editing is a constraint and a potential bottleneck. FDD recognizes this as a constraint, decides to exploit it, and subordinates all other process elements to the decision. This constraint decision is a fundamental tenet at the core of FDD.

Some Agile methods have chosen to treat version control as a policy constraint and have chosen to abolish the policy with collective ownership. This will be studied as part of the analysis of Extreme Programming in Chapters 25 and 26.

Once the creators of FDD decided to accept file access as a constraint, the next step was to determine how best to exploit this constraint. It did so by designating class owners for each class in the system and then allowing class owners to form working teams with other class owners in order to complete a small batch of work. In FDD, these working teams are known as Feature Teams. They are formed for the lifetime of a Chief Programmer Work Package (CPWP). A class owner can be on more than one Feature Team at any given time, that is, a class owner can be working on more than one CPWP (batch) of development.

This mechanism allows the class owner to batch work across many Features, often from more than one CPWP, in order to write all the code that needs to go in a particular class at one time. FDD allows the class owning developer to self-organize the development of code in a class they own.

The argument for class ownership is that it leads to higher quality through the improved integrity of allowing only one developer to touch a file. Further, it prevents rework from mistakes made during the merging of multiple edits in a collective ownership environment. Hence, FDD elevates the constraint of file access through the use of virtual Feature Teams.

The Developer Resource Constraint— Feature Teams and the Surgical Team

Fred Brooks observed that effort required for software development does not scale linearly with the size of a product or project [1995]. That is to say, the level of effort expended in the system of software production increases non-linearly against the level of client-valued functionality output from the system. Brooks attributed most of this phenomenon to the growth in lines of communication as teams grow in size. He further suggested that in order to approach linear growth in software development, it is necessary to reduce these lines of communication. Brooks offered the Harlan Mills concept of chief programmer teams, which he compared to surgical teams, as the solution to this problem.

FDD adopted the use of the surgical team and adapted it for the world of object oriented programming and the existing observation that file access was a constraint and that the constraint could be exploited through use of class/file ownership.

FDD introduced the virtual surgical team known as the Feature Team. Each Feature Team is led by a chief programmer. A chief programmer is responsible for the development of a batch of working code. He forms a Feature Team based on the owners of the files likely to be affected by the development of the batch. Developers are free to join more than one Feature Team at any given time. This avoids wasteful downtime in which one chief programmer might have to wait to start development because a vital team member is engaged on another team. Balancing work between Feature Teams is left to the developer. Balancing the need for developers to work across teams can be achieved through careful selection of the batch of Features to be collected in a CPWP.

The need for the virtual surgical team, the Feature Team, came as a direct result of the decision to subordinate everything to the decision to restrict write file access to class owners only.

The Setup Time Constraint—Chief Programmer Work Packages

Having eliminated the file ownership and the developer resource constraints, where is the next constraint? It is the Feature design and build. If every Feature were to be designed and built individually, there would be a lot of wasted effort. Consider again the process stages for a Feature, as shown in Figure 23-1.

The Queue time is the time required for the Feature team (the related class owners) to assemble and be free to undertake the work. The Setup time is the time required to meet, hold the requirements walkthrough, and create a design in joint session. The Process time is the time for each developer to write the code. The Wait time is the time required for all the class owners to check-in their changes and promote the finished Feature to the integration test build.

If another Feature were to require a similar set of class owners and perhaps a similar requirements walkthrough, much of the time spent on the first Feature would be repeated on the next. This duplication can be eliminated by batching a number of related Features together. The result is that the Queue time, Setup time, and Wait time for one Feature can be amortized against all the Features in the batch as shown in Figure 23–2. The result is an increased production rate.

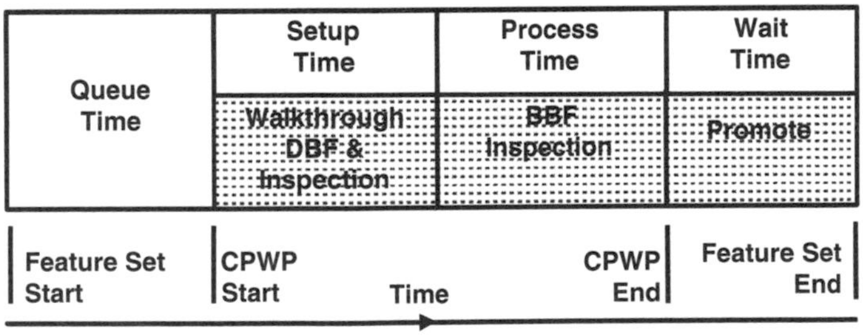

Queue Time	Setup Time	Process Time	Wait Time
	Walkthrough DBF & Inspection	BBF Inspection	Promote
Feature Set Start	CPWP Start	CPWP End	Feature Set End
	Time		

Figure 23-1
Process step time in FDD.

Figure 23–2
Process step times
for multiple Features
in a CPWP.

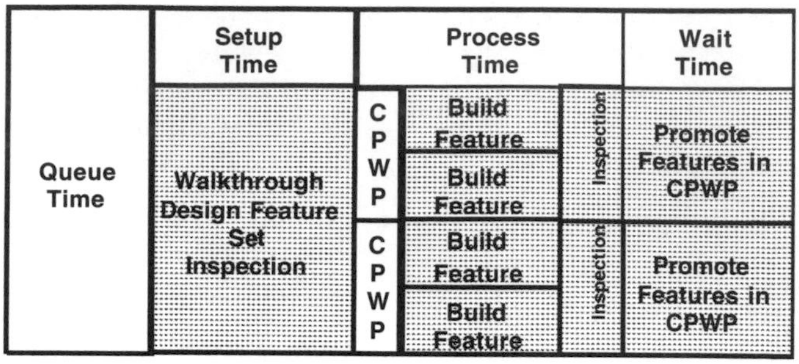

Queue Time	Setup Time		Process Time			Wait Time
	Walkthrough Design Feature Set Inspection	C P W P	Build Feature	Inspection		Promote Features in CPWP
			Build Feature			
		C P W P	Build Feature	Inspection		Promote Features in CPWP
			Build Feature			

Batch Size

The next constraint to emerge is that of batch size. If too many Features are batched together, all the problems related to high work-in-progress inventory start to appear, that is, long lead time, higher levels of investment, and more people. More people involves more lines of communication, which slows production rate, and so begins a vicious spiral. Production rate compared to the effort expended gradually falls as inventory increases and more people are added.

There is an optimum point for batch size where the waste due to Queue and Wait time is minimized and overhead related to setup and maintenance during process is optimal, and the intersection with rising OE due to increased WIP inventory and increased staffing requirements.

FDD restricts batch sizes to the amount that can be constructed by a single Feature Team in 2 weeks or less. In other words, a chief programmer work package must be sufficiently small enough to be complete within two weeks. A Feature Team should be no more than six people and usually fewer.

There are two good reasons for this choice. The team must be a single surgical team. It must have only one chief programmer, and the team must communicate through that CP. The second reason comes from psychology. The team members deserve to be able to reflect on success at least once every two weeks. They ought to be able to claim, "We completed n Features this week!" Being able to claim completion gives a sense of job satisfaction. Hence, FDD exploits the developers as capacity constrained resources by providing them job satisfaction on a regular basis. Happy developers are productive developers!

The Scope Constraint— Prioritized Feature Lists

Chapters 3 and 4 presented the concept that one way of exploiting a constraint is to protect it with a buffer. The scope constraint in FDD is the Feature List. In order to protect the scope for a given release or project, there must be additional Features to use as a buffer. What does this mean? It means there must be Features the client is willing to forego in the event of something going against plan. There must be some Features that are "nice to have," but that no one will cry over if they are not delivered.

Therefore, the Feature List must be prioritized in order to buffer scope. Ordinal ranking of Features may be possible for smaller numbers, but asking a business owner to ordinally rank hundreds or even thousands of Features is not practical. To cope with this problem, Peter Coad introduced a method of prioritizing Features in three categories. More recently, I introduced a method for prioritizing Features that involved asking the client to elect a value 1 through 5 (5 being the highest) to indicate how important it was for a particular Feature to be included. The client was then asked to elect a value 1 through 5 to indicate how annoyed they would be if the Feature were not included. This concept of "included" and "excluded" was first discussed by Peter Coad in 1997 but never published. The numbers can be totaled, and a score of 2 through 10 obtained. The Feature List can be sorted by this client value score. (The range of 1 through 5 was carefully chosen based on cognitive research on set sorting theory, which suggests that humans are challenged to sort random elements into more than 6 categories [Bousfield 1955 & 1966].)

With a ranked Feature List, it is possible to negotiate a buffer into the scope for a given release. First, the total capacity should be agreed, based on a level of effort estimate and a desired delivery date. This will provide a number of Features in the release. A bar can then be drawn across the Feature List at the point indicated by the total capacity. A percentage of the Features immediately above the bar, by definition lowest in priority, will then be agreed as the scope buffer. For example, assume the capacity constraint indicated that everything with a rank of 4 points or greater could be built in the proposed project. The client could then be asked to accept that all Features below a priority of 6 would be classified as "nice to have." These "nice to have" Features represent the protection buffer.

Figure 23–3 shows a sample of Features for an FDD KMS using prioritization for desirability of inclusion and undesirability of exclusion from a single release. For example purposes only, the shaded area represents the Features definitely agreed as included and those below in the unshaded area represent the scope buffer. The project will be planned based on the full list, but the lower unshaded part of the list will be considered for exclusion in the event of a significant impact on the project schedule.

Time-Modified Prioritized Feature Lists

This basic Feature prioritization works only for a single iteration of a software project. Often, the marketing owner or client for the system will refuse to prioritize or refuse to cooperate with buffering the scope. This refusal to cooperate may be based on a fear that deprioritized features will never be built. This fear can be overcome by introducing a two-dimensional aspect to Feature prioritization because Features also have a time value, that is, the Throughput value of a Feature is truly dependent on its delivery date. In some circumstances early delivery is of no value.

Sometimes government legislation forces a change by a given day. This is common in tax calculation systems, for example. To take into account the time value of Features, the Feature priority must be treated as a two-dimensional attribute. This is difficult for humans to visualize or to understand. An example can make this more obvious.

Figure 23–3
Prioritized Feature
List.

Feature / Release	Release 1		
	IN	OUT	TOTAL
List the Features for the Project/Release	5	5	1 0
Set the Milestones for a Feature	5	5	1 0
Set the CPW for the Feature	4	3	7
Set the Subject Area for the Feature Set	4	3	7
List the Feature Completion Dates for the CPW	3	3	6
List the Virtual Team Members for the CPW	4	2	6
Set the Feature Set for the Feature	3	3	6
List the Feature Completion Dates for the Release	3	1	4
Total the Features for a Product	3	1	4
List all Feature Sets for the Subject Area	2	1	3
List the Subject Areas for the Product	2	1	3
List Change Requests for the Release	1	1	2
Total the number of open issues in the Issue Log for a given Release	1	1	2

Figure 23–4 shows a sample of Features for an FDD KMS broken into three time-based releases using time-based prioritization for desirability of inclusion and undesirability of exclusion from each release. The shaded area indicates the Features to be included in each release.

To add a time dimension to the Feature priority scoring, the Feature analysts should ask the client the same question several times with dates associated. For example, "Tell me how important it is to have the 'calculate tax for the subscriber' Feature by end of the first quarter? Assume we can't do it for that time, how important would it be to have it by end of the second quarter and again by end of the third quarter?"

By probing for a Feature priority with a time dimension, Features can be ranked by time, which allows a plan for several releases to be constructed.

The overall effect reassures the client for the system that Features will be included. Seeing a longer term plan with several iterations builds trust. The result is that the client begins to cooperate with the introduction of a scope buffer.

Feature / Release	Release 1			Release 2			Release 3		
	IN	OUT	TOTAL	IN	OUT	TOTAL	IN	OUT	TOTAL
Set the Milestones for a Feature	5	5	10	5	3	8	5	5	10
List the Features for the Project/Release	5	5	10	5	5	10	5	5	10
Set the CPW for the Feature	4	3	7	5	5	10	5	5	10
Set the Subject Area for the Feature Set	4	3	7	5	5	10	5	5	10
Set the Feature Set for the Feature	3	3	6	5	5	10	5	5	10
List the Virtual Team Members for the CPW	4	2	6	4	4	8	5	5	10
List the Feature Completion Dates for the Release	3	1	4	4	4	8	5	4	9
List the Feature Completion Dates for the CPW	3	3	6	4	4	8	5	5	10
Total the Features for a Product	3	1	4	4	1	5	5	5	10
Total the number of open issues in the Issue Log for a given Release	1	1	2	3	1	4	5	5	10
List Change Requests for the Release	1	1	2	2	2	4	4	5	9
List the Subject Areas for the Product	2	1	3	3	2	5	4	4	8
List all Feature Sets for the Subject Area	2	1	3	3	2	5	4	4	8

Figure 23–4
Time-modified prioritized Feature List.

The Time Constraint and Buffers

As shown in Chapter 4, time should be buffered with more time. Hence, an allowance against the project must be factored in to absorb uncertainty and variance. In TOC, this is known as the project buffer. Chapter 4 described a method for calculating the necessary project buffer.

First, the ideal level of effort for the project should be calculated. This is done by multiplying out the Feature complexity weightings with the historical table of nonlinear translations for those weightings. This produces a level of effort for each Feature. Add these up, and we have the LOE for the whole project. This is more easily done with an automated tool. Such functionality can be built into an FDD KMS.

This effort does not account for integration testing and bug fixes, that is, the number of Feature equivalents produced is greater, as several Features will receive rework. Experience has shown that 15% should be added to accommodate the LOE for integration testing. The amount added for bug fixes will depend a lot on the anticipated level of quality from the development team and the anticipated acceptable number of bugs at time of shipping.

The total LOE calculated for the project is based on what are known to be sustainable levels of effort. The development manager should have confidence in these numbers. However, industry metrics suggest there is, at best, a 50% likelihood of hitting this estimate, even allowing for the fact that the estimate is accurate and the variance in an FDD system is low. Remember, if an estimating scale is accurate, around half the time the deliverable should be late [Goldratt 1997]. If half the deliverables are not late, local safety is being built into the estimate. The 5-point nonlinear LOE scale is intended to eliminate local safety. So there must be global safety through a project buffer.

How big to make the project buffer is a matter for personal experiment. For web-based projects using a team who has done it all before and with subject matter close to projects previously developed, I believe another 15% is all that is necessary.

However, a project buffer of up to 100% (or more) may be necessary depending on the uncertainty involved. Note that the size of the project buffer required will vary according to the buffers negotiated for the other key constraints of scope and resources. If the other constraints are unprotected, the project buffer must be as large as reasonably feasible. A manager should use the language heard from team members to assess the buffer size needed. Another factor worth considering is the technology to be used. Has the team used it before? If not, add uncertainty to the calculation.

In my experience, FDD project estimates, even with generous buffers, always sound aggressive to those who have lived with more traditional methods of software development. I had an individual developer mutiny after I came up with a 16-calendar-week total project estimate when he was convinced it would take 9 months. His belief was based on a "similar" project completed shortly before that was conducted using a more traditional method. It had taken 9 months. Actually, the project in question took 16 weeks and 2 days.[2]

The project buffer should be created for a whole project. Feeding buffers should be created for feeding chains of Subject Areas or Feature Sets. For feeding buffers, the same method should be used but on a smaller scale, as shown in Figure 23–5. Add the individual Feature LOEs together for the

Figure 23–5
An FDD Critical Chain with calculated feeding buffers.

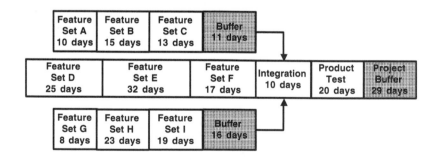

---

[2]The output of this project is commercially deployed on the website of a leading national wireless phone operator in the United States, where it provides end-user control to a business telephone service of integrated office functions, such as single voice-mail for office and mobile phones.

Feature Sets or Subject Areas in the feeding chain. Add a buffer for integration testing and bug fixing. Then, add a feeding buffer based on your confidence about the subject matter of the Subject Areas or Feature Sets in the feeding chain—the higher the confidence, the smaller the buffer. In my experience, the buffer should never be less than 15%.

FDD enables project buffers and feeding buffers to be implemented as required by the Theory of Constraints Critical Chain. This is possible because FDD enables confident prediction of the LOE for a project and for smaller component deliverables within that project.

The major element in the consumption of budget for software is direct labor costs. Even software tools tend to be very inexpensive compared to labor. As labor is the main overhead, it is the most likely element to create a budget overrun. The budget will probably overrun if the project is late, that is, the time constraint was broken, or if the scope of the project is increased, that is, the scope constraint was broken. However, by focusing the organization on Throughput, utilizing the TOC approach to constraint management, and using FDD, the scope and time constraints should be brought under control. However, it is still desirable to have direct control of the budget and to have some spare cash allocated to provide an ability to maneuver. It is impossible to be Agile without some slack.

The Budget Constraint— Inventory Cap and Buffer

The budget can be kept under control by agreeing on the Feature inventory capacity that can be maintained in the system of software production with the client. This can be set at a level that is sustainable with the current resources and budget. The theoretical maximum inventory the system can handle can be calculated:

$$\text{Inventory} = \text{Production Rate} \times \text{Lead Time}$$

$$V = R \times LT$$

For example, if 8 Features can be produced per day at full speed and the Lead Time is 35 days, then the inventory level should be 280 Features. To buffer this, we simply negotiate with the client to keep the inventory in the system below this, say 10% below—250 Features. However, the budget should be negotiated for the full amount by multiplying the cost per Feature by the inventory level:

$$\text{Budget} = \text{Inventory} \times \text{Average cost per Feature}$$

$$\text{Budget} = V \times ACPF$$

The Agile manager has just negotiated a significant financial buffer.

Should the cost of direct labor increase because some contractors are hired, then the additional costs should be absorbed within the budget buffer.

The Test Bottleneck

FDD recognizes that software test and quality assurance can be a bottleneck. FDD believes in exploiting the software testers as a constraint by focusing on improved quality in front of test. FDD is grounded in a "right first time" approach. There are several elements of FDD that address the issue of quality before the quality assurance (testing) bottleneck.

FDD believes in unit testing. Unit testing has been shown to reduce the bug count by around 35% [Wiegers 2002]. However, FDD does not stipulate when unit testing should happen. It is treated as part of step 5—Build-by-CPWP. Development could be test-driven like Extreme Programming, but it may not be. The unit tests could be written after the code, and the unit tests could be run before or after code review. FDD does not stipulate when unit tests should take place, merely that they should.

FDD also stipulates the use of peer reviews of both code and design. Peer reviews of code have been shown to reduce bug count by at least 35%. By stipulating that reviews happen for both code and design, FDD is suggesting that it is best to invest up to 15% of the available engineering time in order to improve quality. FDD proponents suggest that this investment pays off significantly in improved overall production rate for the system as a whole. The theory for this was explained in Chapter 9.

Whether the theory works in reality can be easily measured using the FDD Trend Report. A project iteration that did not perform reviews or unit tests could be compared to a later iteration in which reviews and tests were performed. The resultant figures for overall features delivered (Q) and Throughput dollars (T) could be compared.

Note that it is important that the metrics used reflect the overall system, that is, delivered and working code, not just the metrics for the development organization. Only if testing and bug fixing are taken into account will the manager be able to analyze whether measures to fully exploit the Test department as a capacity constrained resource were actually effective.

FDD also explicitly requires a modeling and analysis phase as part of the process. This is different from many other Agile methods. FDD advocates believe that modeling and analysis lead to a better shared understanding of the requirements and problem domain. The result of this is better, simpler designs, which in turn lead to better, simpler code. The overall result is a reduction in lead time, increased production rate, and reduced defect rate in exchange for a 10% investment up front in modeling and analysis. Again, whether this is truly effective can be easily measured using the FDD Trend Report. An iteration of a project could be undertaken without modeling up front. The results for overall R and T could then be compared with another iteration that did perform the modeling up front.

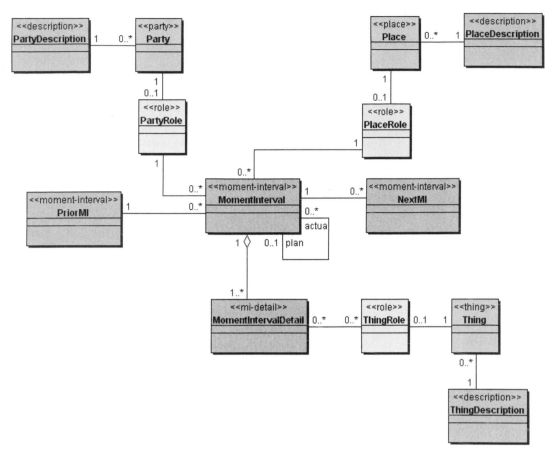

Figure 23–6
The Domain Neutral Component.

FDD advocates use of the advanced techniques in analysis and modeling developed by Peter Coad and colleagues [Coad 1996, 1997, & 1999; Nicola 2001]. The Domain Archetypes and Domain Neutral Component, shown in Figure 23–6, presents a method for modeling a business system that has proven to be repeatable across many business domains.

The use of the Domain Neutral Component (DNC) has greatly improved the speed and accuracy of object modeling. The construction of the DNC and the relationship of the Archetypes within it have been carefully constructed from years of experience in order to create an optimal model of a business domain. The model is designed to be robust to future change and potential expansion of the requirements in subsequent releases of the software.

The Domain Neutral Component and related techniques represent true Agile modeling, that is, modeling resilient to change.

Advanced Modeling Techniques

In my experience, modeling using Archetypes and the DNC can produce a ten-fold improvement in terms of reduced lead time for modeling a business system in comparison to older object modeling techniques. These older techniques typically start with a process of listing verbs and nouns found in the Use Cases and then attempt to decipher which nouns are classes and which are merely attributes of classes.

Agile methods have generally de-emphasized modeling and analysis, and there has been a trend away from research in this area. The DNC suggests that there is still considerable scope for improvement in this field, and it should not go ignored. Agility is more than just good people and shorter lines of communication.

The DNC also leads to better quality models that reduce the potential for refactoring of the code due to late changes in the requirements.[3] Consequently, the DNC and the modeling phase in FDD are used to better exploit the developers and testers as capacity constrained resources through improved quality in analysis. The potential for rework is reduced, and the potential regression effect of any necessary rework is reduced. The overall effect is to greatly enhance the capacity of the development team to deliver Features.

Inventory Management in FDD

FDD uses regular reporting of project metrics to influence management decisions and executive reporting. Jeff De Luca has written about the use of inventory management in FDD [De Luca 2001]. The metrics regularly reported are Features completed as shown in Figure 23–7, Features in-progress, Features not started, Features blocked, number of open issues; percentage of work completed, and the trend in each of those metrics. The Feature metrics directly report inventory levels. The trend in the percentage of work completed reports the production rate.

The Features in-progress metric is used to determine the need to release new work into the development team. If the trend in this metric is falling, Features are either blocking or being completed. The development manager and chief programmers should use a minimum threshold in this metric to indicate when it is time to plan the next set of CPWPs.

Similarly, if the combination of Features in-progress and Features blocked is growing, the overall work-in-progress inventory is rising. This is a clear indication that the development team doesn't have what it needs to finish work. This can indicate to the manager that something is wrong, the root cause must be identified, and the problem resolved.

Inventory tracking can be used to observe the impact of expediting on the effectiveness of the development team. When a team is asked to expedite a number of Features at the expense of others, existing work-in-progress has to be put aside. This results in stalling the percentage complete metric, while work-in-progress inventory grows slightly. The number of Features completed metric will also stall until the expedited Features are delivered.

---

[3]The quality of a model is defined by its ability to cope with change and provide an optimal, fully normalized environment for code construction. A quality model is an agile model.

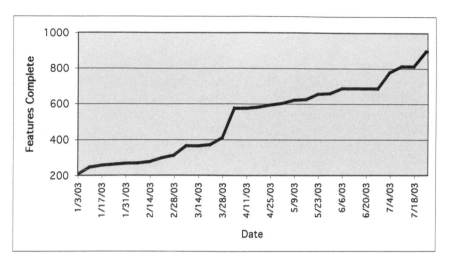

Figure 23–7
FDD Features complete graph.

Jeff De Luca reported on the effect of expediting features in the first ever FDD project.[4] The project was asked to expedite a full demonstration of work completed for the senior executives of the sponsoring business. During this time, the team had to cease work on new Features, complete bug fixes on existing development, and stabilize the code base. Team members were distracted by rehearsal for the demonstrations—demo scripts had to be written and rehearsed. The result was a drop-off in production rate, a stalling in percentage complete, a fall-off in work-in-progress as current work was finished and no new work was started.

If the percentage of work complete is rising steadily but the number of Features complete is not rising, this is also an indication that Features are stalling. The number of Features blocked should be rising, and the number of open issues should also be rising. If this is not happening, the Feature Lead Time must be lengthening. This is a good indication that the team is not being honest and is not admitting a blockage or raising issues. This tells the manager that the team needs prompting to "face the truth." A situation in which work-in-progress inventory is rising, Features completed is stalling, and Features blocked or open issues is not rising may be a good time to introduce a morning roll call meeting.

Morning Roll Call,[5] a technique I introduced into FDD [Anderson 2002], uses teamworking, peer recognition, and peer pressure to keep a team motivated. It provides a mechanism for improved communications and fine grained project management. Morning Roll Call provides a simple and effective mechanism to

Morning Roll Call

---

[4]The effect was reported in A *Practical Guide to Feature Driven Development* [Palmer 2002].
[5]A daily stand-up meeting is not new. However, its first known use with FDD was at Sprint in Kansas City, MO.

help maximize exploitation of engineering resources. Morning Roll Call is a stand-up meeting held each morning. This technique is employed in other Agile methods such as XP and Scrum. It was first introduced to FDD in 2001 on a project that was going astray. About halfway into the project, the FDD Features complete metric indicated that the project was going to be late. The project had been dependent on another team delivering infrastructure that had not materialized. Consequently, there were lots of Features stalled but not reported as blocked due to the internal politics.

For some of the team it was their first FDD project. Others had done only one project using the method. With new process, new technology, and some ambitious technical objectives, getting the project back on track was going to take an extra special effort. I needed to find a method to focus the team and raise the pulse of the project to get that extra performance.

The answer was the Morning Roll Call. I modeled this after the opening sequence in the American TV police drama "Hill Street Blues" where the sergeant would go over the recent events and allocate patrols and tasks for the day. The roll call in FDD is not a roll call of developers, but rather a roll call of Features.

Morning Roll Call Process

The Morning Roll Call was at 9:15 A.M., all hands on the project, attendance mandatory.[6] The meeting was a "huddle"—or stand-up meeting—so that people did not get too comfortable and spend more time than was necessary. It was held in an open area near the developers' cubes. The manager was not required.

The duration was 15 minutes, with a maximum of 30 minutes—never longer. The norms were honor the rules, turn up on time, keep focused, take lengthy issues and resolve them outside of the meeting, and keep things moving. The meeting was chaired by the chief programmer or the most senior of several chief programmers. In the event that the CP was absent, the process coach (or mentor) would run the meeting.

Each CP would run through the Features on the current Chief Programmer Worksheet. Developers were asked for Features they had completed since the last meeting, status of Features in-progress, when they expected to finish, and if they needed more work to do. The whole team could make an assessment of whether each Feature was on track.

Developers were encouraged to ask for help, if needed. Sometimes the team would suggest a developer might need help. If help was needed, a more senior and experienced developer was assigned to help out for that day. Technical discussion and debate about solutions were banned. The whole team would see to it that the roll call only took 15 minutes. Developers wanted to get the meeting over so that they could get to "real" work. Colleagues were asked to take debates off line.

[6]The time, 9:15 A.M., was chosen by the team as an acceptable compromise. A few team members had to get in a little earlier than usual. Everyone else was already there. Some started at 7 A.M. The idea was to be as early in the day as was reasonable and still get full attendance.

Issues with requirements, environments, test plans, or anything else out of the immediate control of the developers were noted by the CP who would have a separate discussion afterwards with the project manager/project secretary to log the issue. The PM would be responsible for chasing down the issue or assigning it to someone. When closure occurred, the CP would be informed and work could restart on that Feature.

Developers who expected to finish current work that day or the next, would be allocated more work. They always knew a day or two in advance what was coming.

How Big Does It Scale?

Obviously a Morning Roll Call on a very large project would be impractical. So, how large is practical for a Morning Roll Call? Experience has shown that a team working on a single Subject Area should meet together for a Morning Roll Call. At most, this could be stretched to two Subject Areas. What if some developers need to be at more than one Morning Roll Call? They have a clash because they are working across Feature Teams that are working on different Subject Areas. There is a simple solution—stagger the start times of the Morning Roll Calls for each Subject Area where a schedule clash occurs.

Morning Roll Call has been successful with up to 20 people. Typically, it should be used with around 10 to 12 people. If there is more than one Subject Area, but less than 12 people, it is perfectly reasonable just to hold a single meeting. Remember the ground rule—15 minutes, maximum 30 minutes!

When to Use Morning Roll Call

Morning Roll Call was initially used as a process for recovery. The FDD Features Complete metric can suggest that a project is going to be late. Morning Roll Call served the purpose of keeping people honest and making them accountable for their work. Developers had to stand in front of their colleagues each morning, look them in the eye, and state how they were getting along with their piece.

Morning Roll Call served a second purpose. It was an opportunity for education and self-help. In a situation where some of the team were new to FDD and were also new to several technologies on a project, such as XML and XSL, Morning Roll Call helped them to get over the process-related learning barrier.

Chapter 9 identified the S-curve effect. FDD has a number of elements that help to minimize the impact of the S-curve effect.

If step 1, Modeling, has been completed satisfactorily, there should be a good enough understanding of the problem domain amongst the team and at least some requirements should be agreed and satisfactory. This should enable the development team to get started. Without a successful Modeling stage, there is little point in starting because very little progress may be made due to as yet undiscovered issues with the requirements. As a result, R may be very low initially. Valuable capacity constrained development resources will not be fully utilized.

A fundamental principle of FDD is that steps 4 and 5 should represent the known and well understood. The Design and Build steps are intended to be a period of software production, not invention or experiment. That means that as much ambiguity and uncertainty should be eliminated as is humanly possible before a project gets to step 4. If the project is using a new technology, it is important that the team receive training on that technology before steps 4 and 5 begin. Failure to train staff before development starts will reduce R.

In FDD, the Modeling stage is wide rather than deep. Jeff De Luca calls this "shape modeling." If the modeling stage were both wide and deep, it might be possible to eliminate design changes and regression effects. However, this would be seen as a waterfall approach to analysis and design and is referred to as BDUF (Big Design Up Front) by Agilists. FDD does not recommend BDUF. The modeling stage in FDD is JEDI (Just Enough Design Initially). Shape modeling allows the inventory to move forward to the next step quickly. An underlying assumption is that the benefit of moving forward is not outweighed by the penalty of later changes because the design is better understood.

FDD assumes that best-of-breed modeling techniques, such as the DNC, are being used. These techniques minimize the risk from interface changes and regression effects across the wider design. Modeling techniques that lead to better encapsulation allow FDD to promote a shallow but wide modeling and move the requirements inventory along to the next stage. The DNC provides a model with a robust shape but little detail. In doing so it echoes the Lean Design techniques employed in manufacturing.

As a project matures and more code is available for system and product test, the number of bugs reported rises. As the bug database rises, the tendency on an FDD project is to gradually increase the mix of bugs to Features in each Chief Programmer Work Package. The result is that the overall speed of the team is maintained but an increasing percentage of the effort is going toward fixing bugs that are related to Features already shown as complete. If bugs were treated as new Features, the slope of the Features complete graph would not tail off so dramatically, but the project would be falsely reporting delivery of client value.

Maintaining the Critical Path

Eli Goldratt astutely observed that eventually everything hits the Critical Path on a project [Goldratt 1997]. Thus, it is important that FDD Features blocked do not remain blocked for long or they may impact the Critical Path and hence the project delivery date.

It is important in FDD that for every Feature blocked, there is an explanation for the blockage and an issue logged against it. The project manager should be concerned with resolving issues as quickly as possible in order to avoid affecting the Critical Path. The open issues in an FDD project are usually displayed and available to the whole team as an integral part of the Knowledge Management System website.

The metric for number of open issues and number of Features blocked should be used to monitor the potential effect on the project timeline. If R is dropping off, it is an indication that blocked Features are already hitting the Critical Path and the project delivery date is in jeopardy. By focusing on fast issue resolution, the project manager helps to protect and exploit the project time constraint.

It is important to prioritize issues on the Issue Log against the likely impact to the Critical Path. Issues raised against Features that hit the Critical Path earlier should be prioritized higher. Prioritizing issues helps to best exploit the project time constraint and hopefully elevate issue resolution so that it is not a constraint and does not impact the production rate or Throughput dollars from the system of software production.

Similarly, bugs reported should be prioritized based on the priority of the Features they affect and the effect of the Feature on the Critical Path. It is common for bugs to be classified by severity, but they must also be classified by priority. That priority should be calculated based on the marketing Feature priority and the position of the Feature on the Critical Path. For example, if the Feature is part of a Feature Set on which there are many other dependencies, then delaying the delivery of that Feature Set may have a significant impact on the project time constraint.

When calculating the Critical Path for an FDD project, it is important to spend time during step 3, Plan-by-Feature, to analyze the dependencies between Feature Sets and Subject Areas. It is important to plot these with a PERT chart and to understand the Critical Path for the project in terms of Feature delivery. A failure to do this may result in a project in which resources are not optimally exploited and unnecessary Wait time is incurred because Features were worked in the wrong order. A failure to properly analyze the Critical Path, can result in a suboptimal use of capacity constrained resources and lead to an overall impact to the project time constraint.

The Student Syndrome

Goldratt also identified a problem with project and task estimating that he called the "student syndrome" [Goldratt 1997]—the latest possible start of tasks in which the buffer for any given task is wasted beforehand, rather than kept in reserve. The observation was made that many students do not complete assignments early, but wait until the last minute before starting, often having to rush to submit their assignment minutes before the deadline. A similar phenomena is seen every year in the United States when personal tax returns are due the—Post Offices remain open until midnight on the final day as people queue to get their tax return postmarked.

FDD avoids the student syndrome problem by never estimating individual Features. However, there is a possible problem with Chief Programmer Work Packages in previously published FDD. The Feature Team is asked to estimate the completion dates for milestones for each Feature on the worksheet. If these projected completion dates are overly generous, student syndrome could be a problem. This can be avoided by focusing the team on the overall production rate and Lead Time. If production rate and Lead Time trends are falling, there may be a student syndrome problem.[7]

Multitasking

It has also been well documented that multitasking leads to a reduction in production rate [Clark 1992]. If a schedule is estimated using an aggregate technique based on average times for Features of a particular complexity, that metric does not take into account any downtime caused by multitasking.

Switching from one task to another incurs a Setup time and a reimmersion time for the developer. This will reduce the production rate and increase the Feature Lead Time. The effect will be to eat away any buffer in the schedule because the level of effort estimate against incurred Lead Times will be out of sync.

If the developer as a capacity constrained resource is to be fully exploited, the manager must minimize or eliminate requests that require the developer to multitask between projects. Chief programmers must also be aware of the effect of this when scheduling developers who are involved on multiple virtual teams.

Dependencies and Cumulative Delays

Another identified problem in project management is failure to report early finish. The result is that downtime is incurred by the capacity constrained resources because they have no new work to start. The time delay between early finish and reporting completion can never be regained. Successive early finishes without early reporting creates a cumulative delay that is not accounted for in the plan and can use up the overall project buffer.

FDD could suffer from this problem if the manager is not careful. Generally, FDD recommends a weekly project tracking meeting with the project secretary. CPWPs that finish earlier in the week may not get reported until the secretarial meeting. The chief programmer is expected to have anticipated a CPWP finishing and to have allocated more Features into his virtual inbox. Use of FDD workflow techniques avoids the chance of the early finish problems in FDD.

A second line of defense against early finish is the Morning Roll Call. Effectively, no Features should go more than 1 day without reporting completion. If Morning Roll Call is being used properly, Feature completion should be anticipated and new Features lined up in advance.

---

[7] I have abandoned the use of interim milestones in FDD and do not use planned dates for interim Feature milestones. I find that there is still some value allocating a planned completion date for a CPWP.

Goldratt also identified the local safety problem as a potential threat to the time constraint of a project. Given a small task, people will tend to build in a lot of safety, based on knowledge of how likely they are to complete. With an 80% chance of completion, the estimate can be as much as 200% of what is really needed.

In each CPWP, the CP is asked to estimate the completion dates of milestones. Features in a CPWP are shown as late if a milestone date is missed. Feature misses (demerits) can be awarded for missing a milestone. Hence, CPs may be inclined to build in a safety margin to avoid being awarded a demerit. This would seem to fall into the local safety trap, and the development team will not run at full speed.[8]

Over time, the safety inclusion will fall because the CP becomes more confident that the team can deliver. The effect of feedback in the system reduces any local safety margins. This is true for all Agile methods. Higher confidence of completion leads to shorter estimates with less safety. This could be one reason for the speed up of Features completed at the bottom end of the S-curve. There are other reasons why R will increase, such as familiarity with the domain, familiarity with the tools and architecture, and increasing confidence amongst the team members. Increased confidence leads directly to lower estimates for CPWPs because confidence is the flip side of uncertainty. Increasing confidence means less uncertainty, and less uncertainty means less buffering.

If approximately 50% of small tasks should be slightly late when the estimates are accurate, it follows that, if most CPWPs are delivered on time, the CP is probably including too much safety in his estimates and should be encouraged by the manager to feel more confident. This should lead to shorter estimates.

Goldratt has suggested a solution to the local safety problem, a solution easily implemented with FDD. Critical Chain asks the manager to focus the team's effort on the total completeness and the rate of production, that is, Features completed per week/month/quarter for the whole project. Hence, the team members must be encouraged to focus on the metrics for Features completed over the last week and percentage of work completed during the last week. By encouraging them to keep the production rate high, they will be encouraged to avoid local safety margins when estimating CPWPs.

FDD assumes that in the real world it is usually impossible to negotiate a scope buffer. This is certainly true for most organizations on their first few passes through an FDD cycle. As sufficient trust hasn't been established between the customer and the engineering team, the customer is reluctant to agree to any "nice to have" Features that would represent a buffer.

Hence, the scope is a fixed constraint without protection. The delivery date is often fixed and cannot be easily moved. The development manager only has resources and people as elements that can be adjusted to cope with uncertainty.

---

[8]It is primarily for this reason that I have abandoned the interim milestone planned dates and eliminated the need for demerit issuing.

10% Rule

Jeff De Luca has observed that if scope creeps more than 10%, the project will be late. There is an explanation for this. If the schedule and the original scope are fixed, unprotected constraints and if 10% more scope is added through discovery of additional Features during the Design-by-Feature Set stage[9] or through additional customer requirements delivered through the change control process, the only way to address this increment in inventory is to elevate the resource constraint.

J-Curve Effect

As Fred Brooks pointed out, adding more people to a late project makes it later. The production rate decreases due to the added communication effort on the existing development team to educate the new developers and get them up-to-speed.[10] The Features completed graph will suffer a localized J-curve effect, in which productivity will decline until the new developers are fully familiar with the project. Brooks' observation is based on the assumption that the team will not emerge from the J-curve on a steep enough trajectory to make up for the lost productivity before the project deadline arrives. Hence, an FDD project manager may be reluctant to add people for fear of the J-curve effect. The FDD project may also be budget constrained. OE may be capped, making it impossible to add more people, even if the development manager wanted to.

Elevate with Heroic Effort

This leaves only one alternative—obtain more productivity from the existing team, that is, elevate the developers as a capacity constrained resource by asking them to work longer hours. Examining the likely effect of working overtime, it can be shown that a 10% to 35% increase in R may be possible. If the team works 9-hour days and this is increased to 11-hour days for a short period, a 25% increase in production may be possible. Assume that this extra effort in not introduced until after 50% of the project is completed. It becomes obvious that it is hard to cover any more than a 10% overrun in scope. Hence, De Luca's 10% rule seems to be the reasonable limit that can be recovered through heroic effort on the part of the existing team.

However, it is best to avoid heroic effort altogether through use of Critical Chain project management and a combination of buffer and Issue Log monitoring from the inception of the project.

[9]Unforeseen Features are referred to as project "dark matter."
[10]This phenomenon, Brooks' Law, is explained in Chapter 31.

chapter 24

Financial Metrics in FDD

The unit of Inventory in FDD is the Feature. The Inventory in the FDD system of software production is the total Inventory being held in the Feature List. This includes Features not yet started, Features in-progress, and Features completed but not yet delivered in a release.

Inventory in FDD

In Chapter 2, Investment (I) was defined as the money sunk in the total Inventory of raw material. In software terms, I is the cost of acquiring the ideas for the product to be developed in the form of requirements. In FDD, Investment is defined as all the costs pre-step 1 plus the costs of step 1, Modeling, and step 2, Feature List.

Investment in FDD

Pre-step 1 represents any upfront activity conducted by the business to generate ideas for a new product plus any validation, such as market research, focus groups, prototyping, usability studies, user interface design, business reengineering, requirements engineering, and analysis. The outcome from pre-step 1 could be as simple as a broad domain understanding held by a single subject matter expert (SME), or it could be an elaborate set of requirements documents or Use Cases. Regardless of the delivery mechanism involved, all costs associated with the activity of idea generation must be accounted for and logged as Investment.

In step 1, Modeling, the engineering team meets with the business owners who created the ideas and explores the domain subject matter through a modeling exercise. The result is a better, and now shared, understanding of the subject matter and the ideas for the new product.

In step 2, Feature List, a team involving both engineering and business people use the shared conceptual understanding they gained through modeling to write down a precise list of the client-valued functionality contained in the ideas (and requirements) for the new product. That list is then prioritized, and a scope for the current project agreed. It is not until this stage that an accurate prioritized list of requirements is obtained in FDD. Hence, the costs incurred in and prior to step 2 represent Investment rather than Operating Expense, for the purpose of evaluating the FDD process.

The output of step 2 is a clearly defined set of raw material for the system of software production. At this stage, the Inventory for a single release has been acquired, and the cost involved in creating that Inventory is known. This cost is the Investment.

$$\text{Investment}_{\text{Release}} \, (I_R) = OE_{\text{Pre-stage1}} + OE_{\text{Stage1}} + OE_{\text{Stage2}}$$

If any of the activities to create the requirements had been outsourced and consequently incurred direct costs, those would also be attributed to the Investment figure. For example, if a management consultancy was retained to define the market and develop in-depth market research analysis, the cost of that would be classified as Investment. If an experienced mentor was hired to facilitate the modeling in step 1, then the cost of this too would be Investment.

Investment Across Multiple Releases

If the FDD system of software production is sophisticated and capable of working on more than one software release at a time, the costs of the Inventory throughout the system must be traceable. Features from different projects or releases will have different levels of Investment associated with them. Therefore, it is necessary to know the carrying costs of the individual Features being delivered as raw material into the system. This can be calculated by dividing the Investment for a given release by the number of Features in that release. This cost then becomes the Average Investment per Feature for that release.

$$\text{Average Investment per Feature (AIPF)} = \frac{I_R}{V_R}$$

When there are Features from multiple releases being tracked through the system, they can be tagged with the original AIPF for the release of which they are part. This is the FDD implementation for tracking the flow of value. Hence, the sum total for current Investment in Inventory can always be obtained for the entire system of software production.

If the system of software production is thought of as a continuous process rather than a one-off system to build a single project, then it makes more sense to use a time-based metric for reporting, that is, the average Investment level for a given time period, for example:

$$I_{\text{Quarter}} = \text{AIPF}_{\text{Quarter}} \times \text{Average Inventory}_{\text{Quarter}}$$

Operating Expense in FDD

All costs, including direct labor, for steps 3 through 5—Plan-by-Subject-Area, Design-by-Feature Set, and Build-by-Feature—must be treated as the total OE in FDD.

For a single release, this can be directly attributed against the Inventory of Features. Hence, if a release is expected to take 16 weeks to complete steps 3, 4, and 5 and the total costs of running the system of software production for a single week (or day) are known, the total OE for a release can be easily calculated.

$$OE_{\text{Release}} = \text{Estimated Delivery Time (Weeks)} \times OE \text{ (per Week)}$$

Operating Expense Across Multiple Releases

It becomes slightly more complicated when a system processing multiple releases simultaneously is considered. There are Features carrying different levels of Investment throughout the system. It is tempting to try to track the input against each class of Feature and try to attribute costs to these. At this point, the system has degenerated into the world of cost accounting. The attempt to attribute costs will almost certainly be wrong.

It is better simply to think of the system as a continuous process. Hence, the OE for a given period can be reported.

$$OE_{Quarter} = \text{Total Costs for FDD steps 3 thru } 5_{Quarter}$$

Total Costs involves all direct labor costs, including contract labor. Why include contract labor which might justifiably be thought of as a direct cost? It is very difficult, though probably not impossible, to track the direct contribution of the contract labor. In an Agile method such as FDD where team work is continuous and ubiquitous within the method, it is hard to attribute the contribution of contract labor versus that of salaried staff. Hence, it should not be attempted. It is better to treat all direct labor as purely an Operating Expense.

Throughput in FDD

Throughput is defined as the value of the delivered Features. The value should be calculated using the techniques in Chapters 15 through 17 and any direct costs, such as middleware, Operating Expense involved in delivery and commissioning, database licenses, and hardware, should be deducted. The sum left after direct costs are subtracted is the Throughput value of the delivered Features.

Across multiple releases, it is always better to think of the system as a continuous process. Again, the methods from Chapters 15 through 17 should be used to assess the appropriate Throughput value for the Features delivered.

Value-Added in FDD

Value-Added is shown by calculating the Net Profit figure. This financial construction assumes that everything upstream of FDD steps 3 through 5 is a supplier business and everything downstream is a customer. The financial results allow for a normalized comparison of software engineering businesses. The equation looks exactly like those from Chapters 15 and 16. For a single release

$$Net\ Profit_{Release} = T_{Release} - OE_{Release}$$

In a system working on multiple projects simultaneously as a continuous process, the equation would read

$$Net\ Profit_{Quarter} = T_{Quarter} - OE_{Quarter}$$

Return on Investment in FDD

The Net Profit figure can be used together with the earlier equations for Investment in FDD to calculate the ROI. The ROI can be used as the ultimate normalized metric to compare one system of software production against another:

$$ROI_{Release} = \frac{T_{Release} - OE_{Release}}{I_{Release}}$$

$$ROI_{Quarter} = \frac{T_{Quarter} - OE_{Quarter}}{I_{Quarter}}$$

Accounting for Change

When a change request arrives in an FDD project, the change must be understood and prioritized. Change requests involve additional Modeling and Feature Analysis—steps 1 & 2. The cost must be added to the Investment (I).

Some change requests, rather than extending the scope, obviate some of the existing scope of a project. This will result in obviated Features from the Feature List. In Lean terminology, these obviated Features are Inventory waste. They must immediately be written off from I and assigned to OE. This is done by reducing I by the AIPF multiplied by the number of Features affected by the change:

$$I_{Post\text{-}change} = I_{Pre\text{-}change} + I[change]_{step1 + step2} - (AIPF \times \#Features\ Obviated)$$

Accounting for Rework

Rework generally means bug fixes and possible regression effects across the design and code due to an incorrect decision at an earlier stage. Rework can be ignored, for accounting purposes, in FDD because rework will reduce the Production Rate (R) and Throughput (T). Rework should not be shown as new Features. It requires marking existing Features as unfinished. Hence, R and T are impacted, and this is reflected naturally in the financial equations.

Avoid Double Counting

It is important to avoid a double-counting mistake when accounting for I and OE. If, for example, 20% of the engineering workforce spends 1 week per quarter performing Modeling and Feature Analysis, this should be accounted for as Investment. It is important that this figure is subtracted out of the OE figure. The side effect of this requirement is that it is not entirely possible to eliminate the hated time sheet for developers!

chapter 25

Production Metrics in Extreme Programming

Extreme Programming, or XP, is an Agile method that emerged from a project at Chrysler Corporation in the late 1990s. It was devised by Ward Cunningham, Kent Beck, and Ron Jeffries. Beck introduced the basic principles of the method in *Extreme Programming Explained*, published in 2000. XP has grown in popularity and has seen wide coverage in the press and at software development conferences. It is best known for pair programming, continuous integration, no analysis or design phase, and no explicit system test and quality assurance department or phase, though there is a user acceptance test stage for each completed iteration, as shown in Figure 25–1.

There hasn't been much written about metrics for XP.[1] Conservative businesses tend to be afraid of XP because of the lack of visibility into the development process. However, when the XP Planning Game is used properly, XP does lend itself to Throughput-based measurement and control and can be used with Throughput Accounting to calculate profitability and return on investment.

Metrics in XP

The raw material of XP, taken to extreme, is the knowledge of the customers. In its most extreme form, XP doesn't even involve producing requirements in written form. Instead, the customer must work with the developers to create User Stories at the beginning of a planned release. Hence, the raw material of XP is intangible. However, the inventory of the system—Story Points—can be measured.

Raw Material

XP asks the customer to tell the Story of what the new computer system should do. The Story should be written down in small chunks—ideally on

Inventory

---

[1]Beck does include a chapter, "Visible Graphs," that discusses displaying metrics, though little is said about gathering them [2001]. In XP, parlance metrics are known as "smells." Smells come in various forms, including Code Smells and Project Smells. Both have subjective and objective measurements. More is being published about smells in XP, and doubtless new material will appear between the time of writing and publication of this text.

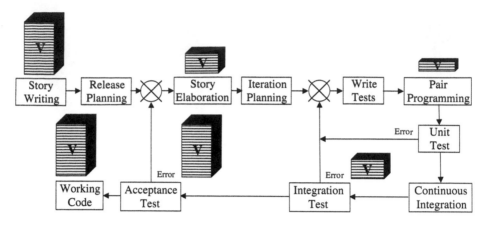

Figure 25–1

A system representation of Extreme Programming.

index cards—by the customers, though often it will be the developers who do this. The problem with measuring Stories as a unit of Inventory is that there is no set format for Stories. They are of no given size. They can vary from as small as Features in FDD to as big as Use Cases in UDP or perhaps be as big as Feature Sets in FDD. Larger Stories are known as Epics.

The important point is that Stories are recognized as the correct basis for Inventory—they are units of client-valued functionality. Stories are a measure of system output.

Therefore, to avoid problems with the standard deviation in Story size, it would be best to use Story Points as the unit of inventory. As part of the planning cycle known as the Planning Game, Stories are assessed for size and risk [Mayford 2002]. Both are assigned points on a three-point scale. Hence, a high-risk, large Story will have a score of 6 points and a smallish, low-risk Story will have a score of 2 points. Story Points are, therefore, the best and most repeatable way of assessing the amount of work-in-progress in an XP system.

Tasks

During the planning stage, Stories are analyzed and broken into Tasks. Tasks look very similar to those in Scrum and may resemble Features in FDD. However, unlike Features, there is no guarantee that they are client-valued, and as there is no template for Tasks, it is hard to control the variance between them. Although Tasks are undoubtedly useful for measuring the velocity of the team, they do not necessarily represent the delivery of completed Inventory. Hence, it is better to use Story Points.

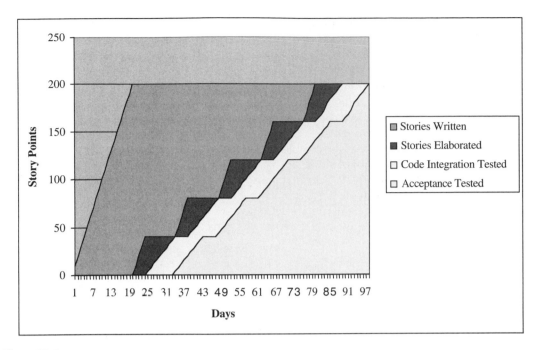

Figure 25–2
Cumulative flow in XP.

If Throughput is the value of a delivered unit of Inventory, then in XP, Throughput is the dollar value of a User Story.

XP practitioners talk a lot about the "velocity" of the team. Velocity as defined in XP is the Production Rate (R) as described in this book. R would be the rate of completion of Story Points. It is probably best measured over each two-week iteration[2] that is, how many units of Inventory (Story Points) were delivered in each development-iteration. See Figure 25–2.

Within XP, Inventory can be tracked at two levels of granularity—within a release and within an iteration. Within a release we have three phases: work-in-progress, Story Points associated with the current iteration, work completed is Story Points associated with iterations already complete but not yet released, and work yet to be started is Story Points associated with a prioritized list of Stories in the release but not yet allocated to an iteration.

[2]At the time of writing, Kent Beck is introducing the notion of 1 week as the canonical iteration in XP and 1-day iterations during an initial 2-week period.

Within an iteration there are two smaller stockpiles and one set of WIP: Story Points associated with Stories yet to be started, Story Points associated with Stories already completed, and Story Points associated with the Stories in development. It is possible to track these during a development-iteration by monitoring the completion of Tasks that relate to any given Story.

The Stories yet to be started are represented by the cards in the pile which haven't been taken by a developer. Stories completed can be easily tracked through the morning stand-up meetings. For this iteration, the difference between the completed Stories and those not yet started represents the work-in-progress. The Tracker in XP should be able to monitor these three inventory statistics on a daily basis and report them to management. Software tools are becoming available to support the XP Planning Game.[3] These can be used for electronic tracking of Stories, Story Points, and Tasks. They are, in essence, inventory resource planning programs for XP.

Lead Time[4]

In degenerate XP, LT is fixed to 2 weeks—a single iteration.[5] It is more likely that an iteration will be part of a release that involves several code iterations and perhaps takes 3 months. XP limits Lead Time to 2 weeks for design and build of any given Story. The total Lead Time is limited to the length of the release, which is likely to be time-bound to 3 months or less.

Process Step Time

In a strict 2-week iteration with XP, the Setup time is the time to conduct the iteration planning and Story elaboration, including defining the Tasks required to complete a Story. The Queue time, is the time for the Story to be called off by a programmer. The Process time is the time it takes to write the code including Unit Tests. The Wait time, is the remainder of the 2-week iteration.

In a situation in which the code releases are on a longer cycle, divided into 2-week iterations, it might be more appropriate to think in these terms: the Setup time is the time to write the Stories; the Queue time is the time before a Story gets included in a 2-week iteration; the Process time is 2 weeks—a development iteration; and the Wait time is the remaining time after coding before the release happens.

It should be possible to measure the inventory levels of Stories in each of the four basic process steps: Queue, Setup, In-progress, and Wait.

---

[3]A web-based tool for the XP Planning Game developed at the University of Calgary was shown at OOPSLA 2002.
[4]Kent Beck published a paper, "Software-in-process: A new/old project metric," in December 2002 in which he uses the term SIP in the same context as Lead Time in this book.
[5]This may have been "officially" changed to 1 week by the time of publication.

A key to the success of XP is the fact it caps inventory levels. In a strict 2-week iteration XP does this highly effectively. Inventory is capped at a level that can be processed by the developers in only 2 weeks. When using XP in a longer release cycle, the inventory level is still capped at a very low level, typically 1 month to 3 months worth of WIP.

Inventory Cap

The cost of acquiring inventory is very low in XP. Again, looking at XP strictly, inventory is acquired at the start of each development release or iteration by having the customers write Stories or having the developers write them on behalf of the customer. Writing these Stories may take less than 1 day for a single development-iteration. For a longer release it would take a few weeks at most. Hence, the investment in inventory within an XP project is incredibly low.

Investment

The time spent on the XP Planning Game at the beginning of each iteration must also be considered as Investment. The Planning Game seeks to analyze Stories, divide them into Tasks, and determine the anticipated level of effort for each Task. In addition to the Planning Game, the customer will be asked to write acceptance tests for the Stories in the iteration. The cost of writing these tests should be accounted for as Investment.

XP exhibits an interesting approach to Investment. The Investment is made over the duration of the release. The entire Investment is not committed at the beginning; instead it is fed into the system as results are achieved. XP, in this sense, is a useful risk management tool.

A key attribute of XP is its philosophy towards risk. XP says software development is hard. Therefore, do it in small batches. If you get a batch wrong, you don't lose very much. This also means the Investment to get started is very low. Hence, the risk is low, and the cost of change or abandonment is also low. This is certainly true if you can treat a 2-week iteration in isolation.

Risk Philosophy

XP also suggests that you should attempt the riskiest parts of an iteration or release first. This "fail early, fail often" approach is based on the belief that Operating Expense (OE) can be minimized by not developing pieces of a system that may never get delivered because a vital piece proves too difficult to implement.

There is no testing phase in XP. XP code is tested by the developers during the iteration. It is then handed to the customer for acceptance testing. Ideally, the acceptance testing time should be added to the Lead Time because Throughput cannot be realized until after acceptance.

Testing

While the acceptance testing is taking place, the developers will have started on a second iteration. Hence, the total inventory level and inventory cap figures should reflect this. There are really two iterations in the system at any given time.

Pipelining

Refactoring

Bugs discovered in the acceptance test in XP code are returned to the system for fixing through a bug or refactoring request. This is normally accepted into the next full 2-week iteration. As bugs and refactoring do not count as Stories, they should not be counted as Inventory (V). The delivered fix should not be counted as Production Quantity (Q).

The effect on the metrics of bug fixes and refactoring should be to reduce the production rate. This is the correct effect. A fall in the production rate metric will indicate a drop in quality from the development team.

This highlights the purpose of not using Tasks to track R. A Task might be to fix a bug. Recording the completion of this Task would falsely report production rate. As was shown in the analysis of the S-curve effect in Chapter 9, the velocity of a team is often greater than the client-valued production rate. This is often because the team is engaged in quality-related rework.

XP will exhibit an unusual trend in total Inventory, specifically in Queue time Inventory and WIP Inventory, due to the effect of bug fixes and refactoring. Most methods would see Inventory levels rise as stockpiles are built up due to the backlog created as bugs are fixed and code refactored. However, XP doesn't allow Inventory into the system to accumulate. This helps XP to keep costs under tight control.

At the start of a 2-week iteration, the development team decides how much refactoring to undertake and how many bugs they want to fix. They then only take on board enough Stories to fill the remainder of the 2-week iteration. Hence, Inventory cannot build up in XP. In fact, as the production rate falls due to bug fixing and refactoring, the Queue time Inventory and WIP Inventory levels should fall with it. This is a unique signature of an XP project. Falling quality is indicated by a falling production rate and falling WIP Inventory. The number of Stories in the system falls with falling quality because that Inventory is not being released into the system from the release planning step.

Metrics for Up-Management in XP

If tangible results from XP are to be communicated to senior executives so that they will be convinced that XP is a valuable method of software development and can be objectively compared against other methods, metrics must be collected. They must not be reported as "smells." Appropriate language should be used when communicating up inside a large organization.

The XP community has argued that delivering working code regularly is enough to convince people, arguing that "the proof is in the pudding." However, the organization has to eat the pudding first. How is a CIO to be convinced that XP is better than other methods, assuming that other projects are being delivered using those other methods? The answer is to use language that appeals to his wallet—profitability and return on investment.

By demonstrating that an XP project delivered better value-added and greater ROI than another project built using another method, a CIO may be convinced. However, to do this, there must be objective data. Enterprise XP projects must run with measurement collection as a fundamental part of the process.

The Tracker must gather the inventory, production rate, and Lead Time (LT) numbers. Ideally, you will also want to gather the Throughput—the value of the inventory delivered—and the investment—the cost of acquiring the inventory.

The Tracker would require colleagues on other projects to do the same. Their metrics for inventory will be different because they won't be measuring Story Points. However, it should be possible to normalize this by studying the Throughput and calculating the NP and ROI figures. Units of currency provide a normalized platform for comparison. To be very scientific, a small project should be used to create a baseline. The company would write Stories, Use Cases, Features, or Function Points for the same requirements. Compare them and establish a baseline translation between one metric and the other.

As Function Points can be easily analyzed from finished work and there is a widely established body of data about them, it may make sense to use Function Points as the standard baseline metric. This could be counted historically. An external vendor could even be used to perform the work. As it is being done on historical data, it is not vital that the work be completed within a given time. Using historical data will be much more accurate.

Hence, a CIO in a large organization could afford to run several different methods in different teams over a longer period of time, for example, 9 to 12 months, and then decide which method is producing the best results.

chapter 26

XP Process
Elements Explained

There isn't nearly enough written about techniques for writing User Stories. However, the best practices suggest that Stories must be contained on a single index card. If the organization is interested in reducing variance across teams and scaling XP across a large organization, developers should assess each Story for risk and complexity. Risk is assessed on scale of high, medium, or low. Complexity is assessed on a 3-point scale.

Assessing risk and complexity allows estimating of Stories to become more scientific and predictable. The estimated LOE for Stories, in each of the 9 possible weightings of risk versus complexity, should converge within a single organization over time. An estimating scheme based on codification is considered "anticipatory" in control terms. Anticipatory controllers are generally more responsive than reactive controllers.[1]

**Assessing
User Stories**

Accurate estimating helps to protect the Critical Path resource. Risk assessments help exploit the Critical Path by allowing less risky stories to be undertaken early. This is part of the use of Option Theory, which is a key tenet of XP.

Generally, XP relies on a feedback mechanism for analysis of the accuracy of estimates. In control terms this is known as a "reactive" control system. An XP team learns from experience whether they underestimated or overestimated the level of effort for a given set of Tasks that make up a Story. They use this learning to improve in the future.

The lack of a standard for the style and size of stories is perhaps less of an issue within an organization. If a codification scheme for Stories is not in use, it is still possible to reduce variance within an organization through the use of the feedback loop. Because software development is an innately human activity and humans are creatures of habit, it is likely that the style and size of Stories within a given organization will trend towards a norm. In a mature XP organization, the size of a Story this month should be pretty

---

[1]This is the same effect as Reinertsen's "leading" versus "lagging" metrics. Processes controlled entirely by feedback do not react fast enough to be competitive against process control that is anticipatory.

similar to the size of a Story last month. It should be possible to prove the convergence of Story size variance by measuring the LOE required to complete the Tasks associated with a Story and the number of Tasks for each Story.

Prioritizing Stories

User Stories should also be prioritized by the customer. Without prioritization it is impossible to protect the scope constraint. Ideally, prioritization should be done using an estimate of the business value for the Story—its anticipated Throughput. Prioritization should be used along with risk and complexity to properly schedule the order in which Stories will be converted into code. By prioritizing Stories that will deliver the highest Throughput, the value added by an XP software production system is maximized.

Option Theory

XP espouses the use of Option Theory. The idea is that something likely to cause disruption should be delayed until as late as possible. The option is held open, and the Story may never be developed.

Hence, Stories that are likely to change should be delayed as late as possible—until such time as the customer has indicated that it really must have that Story included and it is more certain of the precise requirement. Stories of lower priority should also be delayed as late as possible. A low-priority Story may turn into an unnecessary Story.

Once it is determined that a Story must be included and requirements are as certain as can be determined, the high-risk Story should be undertaken immediately. In other words, it should go from the end of the queue to the front of the queue. This follows the "fail early, fail often" approach of Option Theory.

Option Theory allows XP to fully exploit the capacity constrained resources by not asking them to expend effort on units of inventory that might require rework or end up as waste. XP uses Option Theory to reduce rework and waste in the system. Reduced rework and reduced waste increase the production rate of the whole system. Reducing waste and rework through use of Option Theory elevates the capacity constrained resources, such as developers and testers.

Option Theory also allows maximization of investment and minimization of the risk to that investment. Option Theory asks the engineers to prove that high-risk elements of a system can be built and made to work to the customers' satisfaction. If this is not the case, the project can be abandoned with a minimum waste of investment capital.

The Planning Game

Agile Management
for Software
Engineering

The Planning Game is used to protect the scope constraint. The customer is asked to prioritize the order it would like the Stories delivered. The customer is likely to prioritize based on the potential value a Story can deliver. The development team can counterbalance the prioritization with complexity and risk points. This may result in a reshuffling of the priorities to minimize the complexity and risk against an optimal Throughput value for Stories accepted in the release. The optimally sorted list will be prioritized by Throughput dollars per Story Point.

How often a project is integrated in a build is a policy decision of the organization. Policies are constraints. For example, a policy to build once per week may mean that completed code waits for up to 1 week before it is released to integration testing. XP recognizes that build policy is a constraint and seeks to eliminate it altogether. It elevates the build process through use of automation tools, such as Ant. It is suggested that Ant scripts for the project build be scheduled for as little as 15-minute intervals. This produces near continuous integration of the latest code.

Continuous integration is good for the development system performance because it eliminates Wait time for completed coding tasks. Therefore, it reduces the Lead Time between coding and integration testing. However, continuous integration is not without its problems. It is possible only on the assumption that conflicts in interface definition will not occur between different developers' code. The XP community argues that conflicts are always small and that they are quickly and easily resolved. However, it is true that when a conflicting piece of code is checked in, the build will fail. The whole team is then halted until the conflicts are resolved.

XP advocates argue that halting the code production line is acceptable[2] and is better than the Wait time lost trying to synchronize on a specific integration point. In traditional approaches to integration, the team agrees to a set of changes that are synchronized and have an agreed updated interface. If all the new pieces of code are delivered together, the new build should complete. As everyone knows, this rarely happens, and some effort is required each time to fix the broken build. XP suggests that as broken builds are going to happen anyway, it is better they happen often with small consequences.

It is hard to assess this belief from subjective dispositions. It would be better to test it in practice using the production rate metric to determine whether continuous integration is indeed the best practice.

The use of continuous integration may be one of the constraints on the size of a single XP team. In his recent book, *Agile Software Development*, Alistair Cockburn suggested that XP does not scale beyond 12 developers [2002, p. 169]. Beyond 12 developers, there are simply too many moving parts. It becomes inevitable that the build will break and that several coders will need to work on the same piece of the system. To break this barrier may require a new breed of configuration management tools that understand the model of Story-based (or Feature-based) development and are not class file centric, as is normal in current tools.

There are no testers in XP—only developers. As developers want to be coding, testing is automated. If there are any testers on an XP team, their job is to write automated tests. Traditional testing is done by a team that belongs to the customer and is called "acceptance testing." In point of fact, the term is not used in the traditionally accepted sense. In XP, acceptance testing is all stages of black box testing, such as product, stress, regression, and acceptance testing.

---

[2]Halting the line to fix a problem is a common practice in Lean Production.

Integration testing is a potential constraint, or bottleneck, in any software development system. XP advocates that it is better to completely automate it, assuming complete automation is possible. XP elevates the integration testing constraint through automation. To do this properly, integration testing must go beyond ensuring the build compiles properly and the code will run. Rather, there must be a whole suite of integration test scripts written that are based on real user tasks. This is extremely nontrivial to do properly. Often, basic method signature compliance passes for integration testing, and all the real testing is delegated to the acceptance tests.

Elevating integration testing properly should produce several global system improvements. The Lead Time for integration testing is reduced to almost zero. If integration is scheduled every 15 minutes and the automated tests take 45 minutes (assume we have a pipeline of 4 test environments), the Lead Time through integration testing is only 1 hour.

Operating Expense is greatly reduced with XP. There are no testers (in the engineering department). As discussed in Section 1, the best way to reduce Operating Expense is to use fewer people. The cost of people is the largest, contributor by far to Operating Expense in software development.

If the customer is in a different organization, that is, an organization with a different goal, a different set of accounts, and a different set of stockholders, then the cost of testing in XP has been partly offloaded to the customer. The side effect of this is that there is no assessment of whether or not the software is truly client-valued. Hence, it is difficult to record a value for T until the customer testing is completed. This is an example of moving the system constraint outside the organization and out of control.

Pair Programming

Pair programming seeks to exploit the developer as a capacity constrained resource in the software development system. If developers can be made more productive, that is, their capacity can be increased, the system will be more productive.

Chapter 9 demonstrated how time spent to produce quality code makes the system more productive. The overall production rate increases when fewer defects are found. XP is founded on the concept that it is worth the cost of effectively halving the work force, in order to improve quality. The premise is that improved quality will increase Throughput despite the reduced labor force. The anecdotal evidence suggests this is true.

In pair programming, one developer sits and enters the code into the editor, the other watches over his shoulder and points out errors or makes suggestions for improvement. This could be thought of as continuous inspection. Arguably, pair programming elevates the code inspection process of other methods to a continuous process.

Karl Wiegers has data that suggests pair programming is not as effective as code inspections at eliminating defects [2002]. Wiegers' data suggests that perhaps 25% to 35% of defects can be reduced through informal over-the-shoulder checking. However, continual side-by-side pair programming is more rigorous than Wiegers' documented peer checking. Hence, the defect reduction may be higher, perhaps 50% overall.

In a world where only 1 significant defect is created for each unit of inventory, then a 50% defect reduction might pay for the cost of pair programming. However, it would be marginal. The numbers suggest pair programming pays off when the defect rate is higher to start with, perhaps 4 defects per unit of inventory. If this were halved, system Throughput might rise by 50%. Hence, pair programming does improve the overall performance of the system and is particularly effective in teams that have a poor starting position. This implies that XP is most effective at improving very immature teams in smaller organizations. A supposition such as this could be tested by gathering data across various teams, using the metrics in this book.

There may be two more reasons why pair programming improves system performance: substitution and positive peer reinforcement. Both of these lower the barrier to entry for pair programming by increasing its effectiveness, making pair programming cost effective at a lower defects eliminated rate, or at a lower level of defects per unit of inventory.

Substitution occurs because the two developers can swap places. Software development is a tiring business. Five hours per day might represent the useful optimum for a given software engineer. Assuming the backseat position in pair programming is less tiring, it should be possible to extend the productivity of the pair for longer in the day, through substitution of the developer driving the editor.

If individually two engineers could program 5.5 hours per day, that would be 11 hours in total. If together they can program 4 hours each, with 4 hours of back seat reviewing, that is a total of 8 hours. Hence, there is only a 35% improvement needed in order for pair programming to pay off against individual programming, assuming a similar level of quality.

Positive peer reinforcement increases productivity. The energy level of a developer can be maintained throughout the day through the constant reassurance from his pairing peer that he is doing a good job. Instant positive feedback should invigorate the developer and allow a high state of productivity to be maintained longer.

Another hidden benefit of pair programming is skills transfer. It is for this reason that XP suggests that programmers swap pairs regularly. Skills transfer improves the effectiveness of the whole team and increases the production rate.

Possible downsides to pair programming reflect the truly human nature of software development. Pairs that get along too well may spend too much time gossiping and goofing off and fail to pay attention to the work on hand. Pairs that do not get along may also be ineffective because they do not try to help each other.

Stand-Up Meeting

The stand-up meeting is another tool designed to maximize the exploitation of the developer as a capacity constrained resource. The stand-up meeting allows developers to request more work and ask for help if they are struggling with an issue. It helps eliminate or significantly reduce downtime for developers. Problems can also be caught and fixed early and not allowed to fester. A festering snag in code production reduces the production rate of the system and may affect the Critical Path.

The stand-up meeting also uses psychology to exploit the developer. Developers can report completion of work and receive instant recognition from their peers—on a daily basis. Being recognized for work completed reassures the developer and makes her feel good about working. A happy developer is a productive developer. The stand-up meeting also creates a peer pressure from team members to pull their own weight. They are all expected to perform and keep the team's performance strong. The team spirit created through stand-up meetings coupled with collaborative working practices, such as pair programming, creates a self-help structure that increases productivity. The productivity of the combined team is greater than the sum of the individual parts.

Unit Testing

XP elevates Unit Testing to an art form. XP and a close relation, Test Driven Development (TDD), advocate writing the Unit Tests before the code is written. Unit Testing is intended to improve quality. In other methods that have testers, Unit Testing exploits the tester as a capacity constrained resource by reducing the quantity of inventory that will fail and require rework. Unit Testing increases the capacity of test and development by reducing rework. XP does not have any formal testing group within engineering and thus Unit Testing exploits the developers as a capacity constrained resource by reducing the need for developers to spend time testing.

As a general factor in improved quality, Unit Testing will decrease the likelihood of failures downstream in user acceptance testing. Reducing defects in user acceptance testing improves the overall Throughput of the system because it reduces the number of bugs to be fixed in a 2-week iteration. This allows for more new Stories to be developed.

XP has created a whole industry that seeks to elevate the Unit Testing constraint. There are many tools designed to make testing easier to do and to automate. The most popular tool is JUnit, which is used in Java development. Such tools are finding their way into other Agile methods and mainstream development shops. Elevating Unit Testing to better exploit the developer and testing constraints is not limited to Extreme Programming.

XP recognizes that permanent or temporary class ownership can create bottlenecks and leads to increased Queue time while Stories, which need a given class in order to be completed, wait for it to become available.

XP treats class ownership as a constraining policy and simply eliminates it. It is replaced with a free-for-all collective ownership approach. This allows more than one developer access to a file at the same time to make their changes. When the code is checked into the version control system, the differences between the two sets of edits need to be merged. XP advocates that the cost of merging changes is minimal and is a cost worth paying. The argument is that the removed Queue time is greater than the time spent merging edits.

Because XP uses coding standards and pair programming, it is believed that the quality of any given file does not decrease through use of collective ownership. This is an area of disagreement amongst Agilists. FDD, for example, argues the opposite case. FDD is based on the notion that the quality of a class file is more than just the adherence to coding standards, it is also the design integrity of the class as a whole. This is best maintained, so the argument goes, when one developer keeps control of the file.

The contention here cannot be judged subjectively. It is important to understand the essence of the argument—Queue time is greater than edit merging time. This could only be proved through formal experiment.

Once again, the answer may depend on scale. Cockburn suggests that XP is limited to 12 developers. It may be that collective ownership breaks down beyond this size. Because FDD is a method intended to be used on teams of 10 to 50 people, it may be appropriate for FDD to take a completely different view of class ownership. Detecting the appropriate inflection point and proving or disproving Cockburn's observation would require an experiment using real projects gathering real metrics.

Collective Ownership

Refactoring is used in XP to make up for a lack of up-front effort in architecture, analysis, and design. This is a deliberate policy design that helps to keep WIP Inventory low. Ideally, refactoring should happen all the time and be invisible to the outside observer. This may be possible on small, highly skilled teams who aren't under constant micromanagement and time pressure. However, for most teams, refactoring requires dedicating an iteration out of every three or four iterations.

It should be obvious to the reader that it is important to refactor often. Flow is achieved through continuous refactoring. Even interrupting development once every 2 months for a refactoring iteration seriously interrupts flow.

Allowing large amounts of completed work to collect before a refactoring increases risk, increases Lead Time, and will ultimately produce a negative effect on the production and financial metrics for the release.

Refactoring

40-Hour Week

XP advocates a regular work week, just like any other regular occupation. This would seem to be counter to the notion of elevating the developer constraint. If more capacity is to be delivered from developers, surely they should be asked to work longer hours? XP treats the 40-hour week as a desirable policy constraint intended to maintain high quality. XP contends that the long-term effect of overtime working is that quality drops off and, as a result, the overall production rate of the system decreases. This could be easily measured.

On-Site Customer

Having a customer on-site allows the exploitation of the developer as a resource by reducing downtime caused by issues. When the production of the code for a Story is halted due to an ambiguity or issue with the requirements, it can be resolved quickly. There is no need to keep an Issue Log and to hold issue resolution meetings with the customer.

On-site customers can also be shown demos of partially completed code, and they can provide fast corrective feedback to the developers. This exploits the user acceptance testing as a resource and elevates developers. The result should be higher quality, resulting in fewer defects, that will increase the overall production rate of the system.

Two things should be obvious from this: The customer must be fully empowered to make decisions, and the customer must have full domain knowledge over the whole subject matter. Otherwise, more than one on-site customer may be necessary. Again, this observation points towards Cockburn's observation that XP doesn't scale above 12 people. On larger projects, finding an on-site customer who can spend 40 hours per week with the team and who has the status to make empowered decisions without consulting colleagues is unlikely.

Chapter 13 discussed the use of outsourcing for software development. Due to the need for an on-site customer, it is difficult to run an Agile project with outsourced development. Agile methods such as XP must be seen as a valid alternative to outsourcing.

Generalists

XP eliminates specialists. There are no analysts in XP, no designers, no UI designers, or architects. XP encourages the virtue of the highly talented, highly skilled, highly educated generalist. By eliminating specialists, XP eliminates a large number of potential bottleneck points or constraints. However, this is a double-edged sword. Capers Jones has metrics to suggest that teams of specialists outperform generalists [Yourdon 2002]. Constantine has suggested that XP is bad for usability [Constantine 2001a]. Would the customer, for example, want a programmer to design the UI or would they prefer a skilled interaction designer and usability engineer?

However, eliminating specialists does eliminate constraints. There are no specialists to be scheduled on the PERT chart and no specialists to be protected with buffers. There is no need for Critical Chain in XP.

In many cases, XP seeks to deny the Theory of Constraints whilst accepting that traditional software development is constrained. XP simply eliminates the constraints and moves on, for example, version control lock and technical specialists are eliminated through collective ownership and developers as generalists. This may, in fact, be appropriate on small-scale projects with highly talented people. It may be possible to ignore constraints because the people take care of everything and don't get into trouble. However, as projects get larger and the talent level of the team begins to vary, it may be necessary to look at other methods that seek to accept constraints for what they are. Rather than ignore constraints, they will identify, exploit, subordinate to, and ultimately elevate them. Denying constraints exist and denying the need for specialists in a large-scale system of software production may hold back the adoption of XP in larger enterprises.

Another approach to the denial of constraints could be to declare them paradigm constraints. XP could be viewed as a paradigm shift in software engineering. Hence, in a new paradigm, why should existing constraints be considered? Specialialists are merely part of the old paradigm. They vanish with a switch to a Lean paradigm. Version control lock is equally part of a paradigm. By changing the working practices of development to a Lean interpretation perhaps version write lock dies with the old mass production, specialist paradigm. These are issues of active debate in the Agile community. I cannot provide the answer, only illuminate the debate.

Elimination Versus Protection, Subordination, and Elevation

chapter 27

Financial Metrics in XP

The unit of Inventory in XP is the Story Point. The Inventory in the system of software production is the total Inventory being held in the set of Story cards for the project: Stories waiting to be started, Stories in-progress, and Stories completed but not yet delivered.

In Chapter 2, Investment (I) was defined as the money sunk in the total Inventory (V) of raw material. In software terms, Investment is the cost of acquiring the ideas for the product to be developed in the form of requirements.

In XP, Investment is defined as all the costs involved in creating the working set of Stories. Any upfront activity conducted by the business to generate ideas for a new product plus any validation, such as market research, focus groups, prototyping, usability studies, user interface design, business reengineering, requirements engineering, and analysis, should all be treated as Investment.

A set of Stories is the raw material for the system of software production. The cost of creating the Inventory for the release is the Investment value for the release (I_{Rel}):

$$\text{Investment}_{\text{Release}} (I_{Rel}) = OE_{\text{Story generation}}$$

However, the added Investment in Story elaboration made at the start of each iteration must also be considered. The time spent on the Planning Game and the time invested in creating acceptance tests must also be treated as Investment.

$$\text{Investment}_{\text{Iteration}} (I_{It}) = OE_{\text{Planning Game}} + OE_{\text{AcceptanceTest Writing}}$$

The final equation for the Investment in a given XP release is

$$\text{Investment} = I_{Rel} + \sum_{n=0}^{\text{Iterations}} In$$

If any of the upstream activities were outsourced, the direct costs incurred would also be attributed to Investment. For example, if a management consultancy was hired to define the market and develop in-depth market research analysis, the cost of this would be Investment. If an experienced mentor was retained to facilitate the face-to-face Story generation sessions with the customer, the cost of this too would be Investment.

Operating Expense in XP

Operating Expense in XP can be counted as all costs, including direct labor, for the iteration or release, less any costs attributed to Investment. For a single iteration, OE can be directly attributed against the Inventory of Story Points. Hence, in a 2-week iteration it is very easy to calculate the OE figure:

$$OE_{Iteration} = \text{2-week Iteration (Weeks)} \times \text{OE (per Week)}$$

For a release, this would look like

$$OE_{Release} = OE_{Iteration} \times \text{\# Iterations in Release}$$

Total costs for OE include all direct labor costs, including contract labor. In an Agile method such as XP where team work is continuous and ubiquitous in the method, it is hard to attribute the contribution of contract labor against that of salaried staff. Hence, no attempt should be made. The cost of contract labor should be seen as OE and not as a direct cost that can be deducted from T.

Throughput in XP

Throughput is defined as the value of the delivered Stories. The value is the sales price (or budget) less any direct costs such as middleware, Operating Expense involved in delivery and deployment, database licenses, and hardware. The sum left after direct costs are subtracted is the Throughput value of the delivered Stories.

For a single iteration in an IT department, it is possible to use the Budget Basis from Chapter 15—take the system budget as transfer price and then deduct the direct costs.

Across multiple releases, it is always better to think of the system of software production as a continuous process. The financial assessments should be based on time periods. T should be determined by evaluating the true value of Stories delivered in a given period of time, such as a calendar quarter. Any direct costs that can be attributed to the commissioning of the working software in this time period must be deducted. The remainder is the True Basis Throughput value.

Net Profit in XP

The Net Profit equation looks exactly like those from Chapters 15 and 16:

$$\text{Net Profit}_{Iteration} = T_{Iteration} - OE_{Iteration}$$

$$\text{Net Profit}_{Release} = T_{Release} - OE_{Release}$$

A system of Extreme Programming production that produces several iterations before releasing them is better thought of as a continuous process and would produce this equation:

$$\text{Net Profit}_{Quarter} = T_{Quarter} - OE_{Quarter}$$

The Net Profit figures can be used together with the earlier equations for Investment to calculate the ROI for an Extreme Programming system.

$$ROI_{Iteration} = \frac{T_{Iteration} - OE_{Iteration}}{I_{Iteration}}$$

$$ROI_{Release} = \frac{T_{Release} - OE_{Release}}{I_{Release}}$$

$$ROI_{Quarter} = \frac{T_{Quarter} - OE_{Quarter}}{I_{Quarter}}$$

There are two possible ways to treat change requests in XP. In a strict system where valued working software is being delivered on every 2-week iteration, change requests should be disallowed during an iteration. In this case, they do not have to be accounted for.

However, where the iteration is part of a release, change requests will be allowed and must be accounted for. A change request will require the writing of one or more Stories. The cost of this must be accounted for as additional Investment.

Some change requests, rather than extend the scope, obviate some of the existing scope of a project. This will result in obviated Stories. In Lean Software Development, these obviated Stories are waste. Whether or not the Story has been coded, it must be treated as waste if it has not been delivered to the customer. The Investment in waste Stories must be written off. Hence, the Investment figure must be reduced by the Average Investment Per Story (AIPS) multiplied by the number of Stories affected by the change. Note that this figure can only ever be seen as an approximation, though it may be relatively accurate and consistent within a single team.

$$I_{Post-change} = I_{Pre-change} + I[change]_{Stage1+Stage2} - (AIPS \times \#Stories\ obviated)$$

Rework generally means bug fixes and possible regression effects across the design and code due to an incorrect decision at an earlier stage. However, in XP, rework also means refactoring.

Some XP advocates suggest that refactoring is continuous and invisible. This may be possible with a highly skilled team. With other teams it is more likely that a whole iteration is set aside for refactoring. Ideally, this would be every third or fourth iteration. This refactoring can use the learning from the recent iterations and create more robust code that will be tolerant to future change, that is, more Agile code.

The cost of refactoring must be treated as pure OE. A refactoring iteration will deliver no client-valued functionality. The Throughput from a refactoring iteration Is $0. Hence, a refactoring iteration can only ever produce a negative Net Profit and a negative ROI, if viewed in isolation.

The nature of XP and its refactoring iterations means that it is not suitable to account for XP on an iteration by iteration basis. XP can only ever be treated as a continuous process. By aggregating the accounting for XP over a period of time, such as a calendar quarter, the true cost of refactoring will be accounted for and smoothed across the whole period.

The Cost of Change Curve

One of the great myths with XP has been its claimed cost of change. Beck has suggested that the cost of change performs more like an 1-log(n) type curve, Figure 27–1. This flies in the face of the established theory of change that the true cost can be exponential [Boehm 1976], Figure 27–2.

It is important that this concept be examined carefully because the Beck curve is often quoted and used to argue the improved ROI for Agile methods—particularly XP. This claimed improvement is never backed with tangible objective data and metrics.

Shortly after publication of Beck's *Extreme Programming Explained*, Alistair Cockburn pointed out that Beck's change curve was probably incorrect [Cockburn 2000]. However, he did not suggest a better model. There is a better model, but first I would like to look at why Beck's suggested curve is both right and wrong.

Figure 27–1
Beck's cost of change curve (2000).

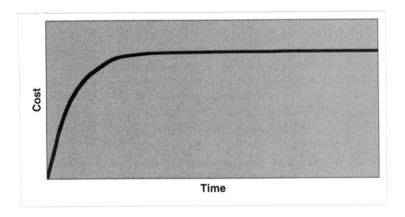

Figure 27–2
Boehm's cost of change curve (1976).

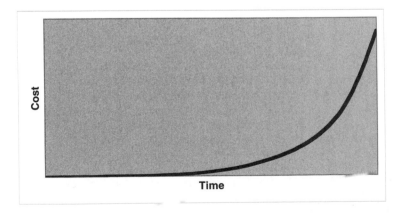

The Beck change curve is correct if each piece of client-valued functionality can be delivered in isolation. If there is such a thing as maximum cost per Story, then the cost of changing a Story should never exceed that maximum cost. The cost of change would increase depending on whether the Story was started or not and how complete it was before change was introduced. However, the Beck curve completely ignores the possibility of regression effects across other parts of the system. The typical XP developer's response to this is that the team members simply roll up their sleeves and quickly refactor the code affected. During this time, they should work as much overtime as necessary in order to complete the task without too much impact on the overall schedule (that is, the project constraints). However, it becomes apparent that Beck's cost of change curve relies on the breaking of the 40-hour-week practice in XP. So the true cost of change is not really as suggested because the production rate and quality will be affected for a considerable time to come as a result of the refactoring for the change.

Further, it is unlikely that a change that creates significant rework to core pieces of a software system can be recovered through overtime working alone. The truth is that a change that requires a new architecture and creates regression across many other pieces of client-valued output will require those other pieces to be reworked. The true cost will begin to look more like the Boehm curve. However, the Boehm curve cannot be truly accurate. The idea that cost of change spirals exponentially to infinity must surely be wrong, too. There must be a maximum cost, which would surely be the cost to rewrite the entire system.

Hence, I believe that the true cost of change curve is actually an S-curve, Figure 27–3.

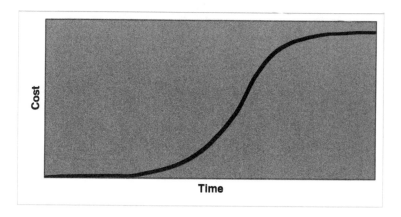

Figure 27–3
Suggested cost of
change curve (2003).

If an S-curve is observed from a long distance away, that is, over a greater time window, then it resembles the Beck curve, Figure 27–4.

Figure 27–4
S-curve seen from a distance.

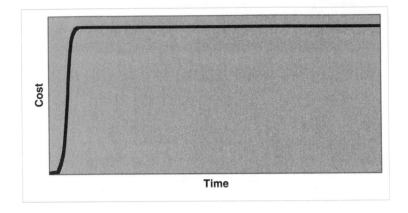

If it is observed from a close distance, that is, over a short time window, it looks like the Boehm curve, Figure 27–5.

Figure 27–5
Bottom of the S-curve seen at close range.

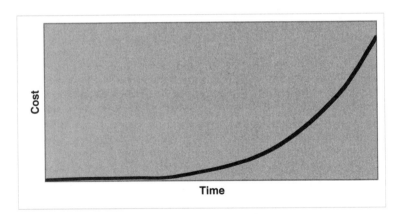

Seen at a microscopic range where only the effect on a single story can be observed, it once again looks like the Beck curve, Figure 27–6.

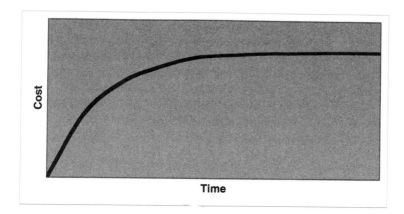

Figure 27–6
Bottom tip of the S-curve seen at microscopic range.

Hence, Beck and Boehm could both be correct, but neither went far enough. It is safe to say that XP is not a silver bullet to reduce the cost of change. Agile methods generally reduce the exposure and risk involved in change. An Agile project will have a lower sum sunk as Investment, and hence the effect of losing that Investment is lower than in a heavyweight, high-inventory traditional Waterfall project.

chapter 28

Production Metrics in Scrum

Scrum is a software management method that can be applied to other Agile methods, such as XP. It can be used as a management wrapper for other software development lifecycle methods because it is agnostic to the particular software development lifecycle method. In other words, Scrum defines how a software project is controlled, not how the software is written.

Scrum is based on the theory of empirical process control, and its foundations originated in Japanese manufacturing industry. It lends itself to acquisition and processing of metrics.

Scrum incorporates a daily stand-up meeting to discuss issues interfering with productivity. Developers are encouraged to list what they are working on, what they have completed, and what they might have issues with. The members of the Scrum meeting quickly decide on any action to give them assistance with issues. Issues are not debated in the meeting itself, which should last no more than 15 minutes. In this regard, Scrum is founded on a technique—a daily stand-up meeting, or Scrum which has also found favor in XP and FDD.

Background

Scrum organizes development work into three levels: Sprints, Releases, and Products. A Sprint is strictly 30 days (or 4 working weeks). A Release is typically a number of Sprints and may be as many as 6 to 9 Sprints. A Product is a series of Releases.

The requirements are converted into a list of client-valued functionality known as the Product Backlog. The Product Backlog can be added to over time and is not necessarily fixed at the start of a project. For each Release, a subset of the Product Backlog is called off and becomes the Release Backlog. For each Sprint, a subset of the Release Backlog is called off and becomes the Sprint Backlog. The Sprint Backlog is indivisible and cannot be altered once agreed. The development team can then work with absolute certainty on the 30-day Sprint knowing that the Sprint Backlog cannot change. Figure 28–1 provides a diagramatic representation of the Scrum system of software production.

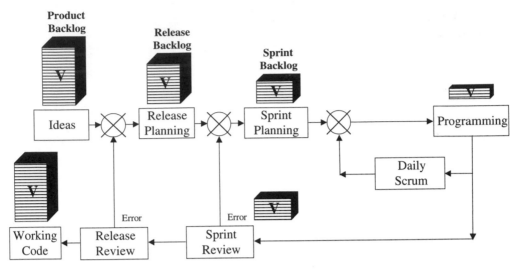

Figure 28-1

A system representation of Scrum.

The raw material in Scrum is the requirements statements. It is turned into Inventory through an analysis stage that identifies items for the Product Backlog. The Product Backlog consists of a list of functional requirements, nonfunctional requirements, defects, and other tasks to be completed in order to deliver the product [Schwaber 2003]. This analysis stage to create the Product Backlog would appear to be similar to steps 1 through 3 of FDD, though there is no explicit description of an analysis phase in the Scrum literature. The analysis stage should be considered part of the cost of acquiring the Inventory, that is, the Investment.

Inventory

Strictly speaking, Scrum as documented does not track Inventory (client-valued functionality), but instead a series of tasks. The tasks are not always directly related to client-valued output and hence may not be a good indication of the true Inventory level. The recommended method for tracking in Scrum is time-based. The number of hours for a given Sprint cannot be considered Inventory. Hence, Scrum does not naturally lend itself to the use of the techniques in this book. Nevertheless, there is little reason why the techniques for software inventory control and release planning could not be used with Scrum.

There are two alternatives available: The Inventory can be considered the subset of the task list that relates purely to client-valued functionality, including Throughput generating differentiating nonfunctional requirements, or the Inventory can be considered the entire task list. If the second option is adopted, it is not consistent with the approach taken for XP. Where Scrum is

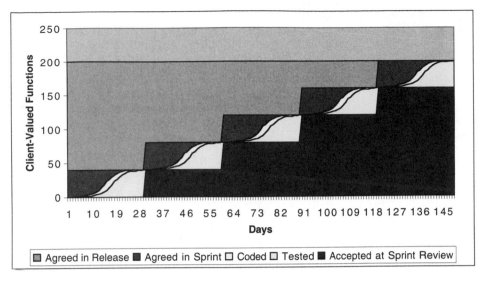

Figure 28–2
An ideal cumulative flow for Scrum.

being used in conjunction with another method, such as XP in XBreed,[1] it would be better to adopt the XP inventory tracking method of stories rather than the specific Sprint Backlog task list.

Figure 28–2 shows an ideal cumulative flow progression for a Release with 200 client-valued functions in 5 Sprints. This ideal graph assumes no changes in the Release Backlog, no scope creep, and no defects feeding from one Sprint to another.

Throughput

Throughput in Scrum is the value of a delivered Release or a delivered Sprint. There is no direct correlation to the number of tasks in the Release—the Release Backlog—or tasks in the Sprint—the Sprint Backlog. When selecting the Sprint Backlog, it is assumed that the agreed task list is optimized to maximize the delivered value at the end of the Sprint. Delivered value is Throughput.

Production Rate

Scrum provides a mechanism known as the burn-down rate. This is the rate of tasks completed in the Sprint Backlog. The burn-down rate is not the true Production Rate (R) as defined in this text. To determine R, the rate of client-valued functionality being delivered must be tracked. Hence, it may be necessary to track this in another way, for example, Stories completed or Use Cases completed.

---

[1]XBreed is a hybrid method developed by Mike Beedle in which Scrum provides a management wrapper for XP.

Metrics

Scrum actually reports the anticipated level of effort remaining for the Release at the start of each Sprint. Within a Sprint it appears that the burn down of tasks and the state of the Issue Log are the main metrics reported daily. This is compatible with the project management metrics presented in Chapter 6.

Sprint Planning and Project Management

There is no planning in Scrum Sprints. The tasks are called off by developers on a daily basis in a self-organizing, volunteer fashion. There is no delegation or management control in task allocation. Scrum is entirely self-organizing within a Sprint. The team itself knows the burn-down rate because they are reporting task completion at each daily stand-up meeting. There is also an underlying assumption that it is not necessary to plan the order of the tasks in the Sprint Backlog in any formal manner.

All that truly matters is that all tasks are completed before the end of the Sprint. In this respect, all tasks will hit the Critical Path within a 30-day period. Any issues blocking a task from completion must be eliminated quickly. Tracking issues is a good way of ensuring that the Critical Path remains unaffected. The health of a Sprint could be measured by the size of the Issue Log, and the trend in number of issues, and the typical time to close issues—the issue Lead Time.

Inventory Tracking

There are three clear inventory sources in Scrum: the Sprint Backlog, the Release Backlog, and the Product Backlog. We need a mechanism for relating backlog tasks to client-valued functionality. It may be possible to flag appropriate tasks, or it may be necessary to create a separate tracking mechanism for client-valued functionality relating to the requirements. In this respect, use of XBreed, in which Scrum is a management wrapper for Extreme Programming, would allow the Scrum backlog to be ignored as a source for inventory tracking and instead focus on the Stories defined as requirements.

Lead Time

In the small, Scrum adopts a RAD approach to Lead Time—the delivery date is fixed and the scope and budget are moderated around the agreed delivery dates. For a single process step—a Sprint—the Lead Time is 30 days.

In the large, Scrum is somewhat more flexible. The scope can be fixed for a given Product Backlog in which case the number of required Sprints will vary. Alternatively, the delivery date for the Release is agreed as a fixed number of Sprints, and the scope will vary.

For a Release, the process step time can be broken down as follows: Queue time is the time that tasks stay on the Release Backlog before being allocated to the Sprint Backlog, Setup time is 1 day at the start of each Sprint, Process time is strictly 30 days–1 Sprint, and Wait time is the time spent following the Sprint until the Release is completed.

For a Sprint, the process step time can be broken down as follows: Queue time is the time the tasks stay on the Sprint Backlog before being claimed by a developer at a daily stand-up meeting; Setup time is the time taken by the developer to review the work involved in the task, read requirements, and perform any analysis work; the Process time is the time spent designing and coding for the task; Wait time is the time spent once the task is completed until the end of the Sprint.

Adding to the Sprint Backlog during a Sprint is banned in Scrum. Scrum is founded on the recognition that expediting increases Lead Time, as other tasks are slowed to make way for the expedited request. Chapter 10 explained how expediting increases WIP Inventory. As Little's Law explained, increases in WIP Inventory, directly result in increased Lead Time. As LT is fixed in Scrum, anything that results in lengthening it, breaking the steady 30-day heartbeat of Scrum, cannot be allowed.

Scrum tightly controls the inventory in the system. The total inventory is capped by the number of tasks that can be undertaken in a Release or Sprint. However, this is difficult to know in advance because requirements have not been thoroughly analyzed into tasks and estimated for level of effort. Hence, there is uncertainty about cap accuracy. However, an experienced Scrum team should be relatively good at estimating, and the inventory level in the system is effectively capped within an acceptable tolerance of uncertainty.

In the event that a Scrum team overestimated, unfinished scope is added back to the Release or Product Backlog and will be reconsidered during the next Sprint planning meeting.

The cost of acquiring inventory is the sum of the cost of acquiring the traditional requirements documents plus the cost of the analysis to create the Product Backlog and extend the Backlog periodically. As such, this is out of scope of Scrum as documented, but an organization using Scrum must be aware that it has to measure the requirements gathering effort in order to be able to show the financial metrics.

Risk Philosophy

Scrum has a risk philosophy similar to XP. Scrum does not prescribe a method for how the software is built. Scrum assumes, like XP, that software development is hard. Therefore, it is done in small batches of no more than 30 days. Scrum fixes the batch processing time to 1 month and thus fixes the Operating Expense for any given iteration. If the Sprint goes wrong, the customer stands to lose only the 30 days of OE expended. Hence, like XP, risk is low, and the cost of change or abandonment is also low. This remains true if a Sprint can be seen in isolation from a Release. However, a lost Sprint may put a Release in jeopardy, and the effect of that loss exceeds the OE expended on the failed Sprint.

Scrum also allows for Sprint abandonment before completion. Hence, if a Sprint becomes unmanageable due to excessive growth in the Issue Log, that in the sole opinion of the Scrum Master cannot be overcome, then the Sprint can be abandoned. In theory, this reduces the financial risk exposure, but this is a cost accounting trick. The reality is that the Operating Expense costs are really fixed costs and the money has been spent whilst time was lost on the project.

Testing

Testing in Scrum is done during the Sprint. Scrum expects testing to be performed by the Sprint team and to be completed within the 30 days of the Sprint. Like XP, the acceptance testing time should be added to the Lead Time, as it can be assumed that payment is not received until after acceptance, that is Throughput cannot be recorded until a development-iteration is accepted or a full Release is accepted.

Scrum suggests that the acceptance be performed in a single day during a demonstration of the output of the Sprint. However, this is unlikely to impress professional organizations that will want to perform proper acceptance tests before handing over the money. It is likely that LT should increase by 1 month while the acceptance test on the previous Sprint is conducted.

Pipelining

While the acceptance testing is taking place, the developers will have started on the next Sprint. Scrum prefers that the Sprint Backlog not be touched during a Sprint. However, it can happen. This breaks the expedite rule. This has been referred to as "following common sense" [Schwaber 2003]. If bugs found in the acceptance testing need to be scheduled for the subsequent Sprint, a Queue time delay for bug fixes is introduced. It may be preferable to fix these in the current Sprint.

Sticking strictly to the no-expediting principle will increase the inventory in-progress in the system from a single Sprint to at least two Sprints. It is important to count this and not disguise reality by treating code in acceptance test as finished product.

Recorded bugs and refactoring tasks can be added to a Sprint Backlog. The result of doing so will be to reduce the number of tasks being called off the Release Backlog.

Scrum makes it very difficult to see the rework being undertaken because bug fixes and refactoring are added to the Sprint Backlog as tasks. These tasks were not on the client-valued list of the Release Backlog and are essentially phantoms—tasks emergent from the process itself rather than input to the process. However, if the metrics only measure the number of tasks being completed for a Sprint, the organization will continue to look very effective. It is precisely for this reason that it is important to adopt a method of tracking the client-valued functionality rather than Sprint Backlog tasks, that is, track the completion rate on the Release or Product Backlog.[2]

Refactoring

If tangible results from Scrum are to be shown to senior management so that they will be convinced Scrum is a valuable method of software development and can be objectively compared against other methods, then different metrics from those advocated by the Scrum methodologists must be collected.

The Agile manager must collect Throughput, Inventory, and Lead Time metrics that remove phantoms and accurately account for value being delivered, rather than reporting the number of hours remaining in the Scrum. Reporting using an input-based metric such as level of effort[3] (man hours or days remaining) leads to strange results in which the estimated time to completion can rise without additional scope being added to the project. This does at least provide information to the management. It shows that there is new insight on the project deliverable and the new estimate is likely to be more accurate than the older one.

Like XP, Scrum offers to deliver working code regularly. Advocates say that this should be enough to convince people that Scrum is a useful and effective management technique. Again like XP, this is arguing that "the proof is in the pudding." In order to up-manage the CIO and other executives, it is necessary to produce more than "proof is in the pudding" claims. The arguments must be couched in financial terms.

There must be objective data to show the CIO that a Scrum project was more effective than another project built using another method. The appropriate Throughput-related metrics for the Scrum project must be collected, and the financial metrics from Section 1 should be used to create a financial justification based on valued-added shown as Net Profit and ROI.

Metrics for Up-Management in Scrum

---

[2]There appears to be some differences amongst Scrum implementations, with some advocates using task lists and others using client-valued functionality instead. This text assumes that the Product and Release Backlogs only contain client-valued functionality whilst the Sprint burndown list contains an elaboration of tasks that include bug fixes and refactoring work.
[3]The standard method of reporting the remaining work on a Scrum project [Schwaber 2002].

chapter 29

Scrum Process Elements Explained

The role of the Scrum Master is to implement the Scrum method and insure that its introduction is effective and it continues properly. The Scrum Master is both a coach and a coordinator.

The Scrum Master can be compared to a sports coach. Most athletes need a coach to observe their techniques and to offer interpretation and suggestions for improvement, but the true value of a coach is psychological. The coach must be responsible for the mental well being of the athlete. It is up to him to make the athlete feel assured and confident of a good performance. The coach coaxes the best performance from the athlete. He pushes the athlete out of his or her comfort zone and into a zone of optimum performance. The Scrum Master performs a similar role. By ensuring that the Scrum process is executed properly, the Scrum Master both exploits and elevates the developer as a capacity constrained resource. By getting the best out of the developers through effective use of Scrum, higher productivity and throughput are achieved.

The Product Backlog is the inventory stockpile waiting to be fed into the system of software production. The Product Backlog represents the raw material for the system. Scrum includes tasks and activities in the Product Backlog, not just deliverables. Hence, the Product Backlog is not such a clean indication of inventory as some of the other methods studied in this book. The Product Backlog is more an indication of the effort involved to produce the output, rather than a measure of the investment required to describe the requirements. As explained in Chapter 6, tracking tasks is less desirable than tracking client-valued functionality.

The Product Backlog is broken down into the Release Backlog, which describes the expected tasks for a Release, and a Sprint Backlog, which is only the agreed tasks for a single 30-day development-iteration.

The 30-day Sprint limits the raw material actually in development and test. A Sprint is intended to release working output at the end. However, it won't represent true Throughput unless it is released to the users or paying client.

Nevertheless, the 30-day Sprint limits the inventory in the develop through test cycle. It provides an effective local inventory cap—just as much inventory as can be processed by a Scrum team in 30 days. Capping inventory at a low level reduces the investment and consequently reduces OE. Fewer people are needed to process a smaller quantity of inventory. Less finance is need for investment in the requirements.

A Sprint also locks the functionality to be built in the 30-day cycle. The development team have absolute certainty that the requirements for a Sprint will not change during the Sprint. This is incredibly useful for exploiting the capacity constrained development and test resources. There are no change requests during a Sprint—no uncertainty. By removing uncertainty and outside access to the developers, Scrum enables software development to move forward at an optimal speed.

The Sprint eliminates the possibility of expediting. There is no expediting in Scrum and hence no chance of lost productivity through the slowing effect of expediting described in Chapter 10.

A Sprint involves a 1-day planning session where the Sprint Backlog is agreed. This represents a setup time overhead for a Sprint. However, as only 1 day in every 22 (approximate) working days, the overhead is less than 5%. This 5% overhead is probably recouped through the increased efficiency gained through the "no interference" Sprint. And, in fact, this overhead **may be even less.** Anecdotal evidence suggests that 2 to 4 hours may be sufficient for a planning session.

There is a counterargument that asks what happens if 1 day of planning and analysis is not enough to identify a full calendar month's worth of work with sufficient certainty. In this case, the project is exposed to a risk. The risk may lead to waste because the initial analysis was not sufficiently thorough. The only way to assess the impact is to measure it. If a team found that they were creating waste due to unforeseen but not unforeseeable uncertainty, it may choose to extend the analysis period in future Sprints. The great advantage of Agile methods is the opportunity for learning through fast feedback.

Release

A Release is an agreed set of Sprints, that is, a multiple of 1-month iterations. Ideally, 3 months would be a good release period, but longer periods are possible, for example, 6 or 9 months. A Release caps the inventory of tasks and limits the investment in requirements. Shorter releases will release Throughput to the paying customer more often.

Scrum, through its use of Sprints and Releases, reflects basic RAD principles. It minimizes the effect of uncertainty by fixing the delivery date—the element with the most certainty—and varying the scope—the element with the greatest uncertainty. Scrum limits and caps the inventory in the system and releases that inventory as Throughput to the customer as often as practical. Scrum produces frequent, tangible, working results.

The Sprint Goal Commitment

At the beginning of a Sprint, the Sprint team analyzes and agrees to the Sprint Backlog from the Release Backlog. It is a team consensus decision, because the team is making a team commitment. This is very important. It plays to the psychological factors of software development. Because the full team committed to the Sprint Backlog, it will feel joint ownership of the commitment.

The psychological effect is that the team will work together to meet the commitment. There is team pride at stake if it cannot meet its commitment. If team members accepted more requirements than could be comfortably delivered in the 30-day period, they will feel obliged to work extra hard to deliver their commitment. The Sprint Goal Commitment exploits and elevates the developers and testers as a capacity constrained resource by encouraging them to make every conceivable effort to meet their commitment.

The Scrum Meeting

The daily Scrum meeting is another tool designed to maximize the exploitation of the developer as a capacity constrained resource. Scrum can probably be credited as the first documented Agile method to use a daily meeting. The Scrum meeting allows progress on backlog tasks to be reported. Developers can request more tasks, or they can request help on a tricky problem. The daily meeting allows the maximum exploitation of developers as a capacity constrained resource by keeping them busy and keeping development moving forward.

The Scrum meeting allows developers to report completion of work and receive instant recognition from their peers. Being recognized for work completed reassures the developer and makes her feel good about working. A happy developer is a productive developer. The daily Scrum also creates peer pressure on members to pull their own weight. They are all expected to perform and maintain the team pride by ensuring that the team meets its Sprint Goal Commitment.

Team Size

Scrum recommends small teams for each Sprint, both to minimize the communication overhead and to facilitate effective Scrum meetings each day. More than 10 people would make the meetings difficult. So a team size of seven is recommended. This allows interteam communication to be done verbally, quickly and effectively.

A team of seven is optimal because it maximizes the momentum that can be achieved whilst minimizing the communication overhead. In TOC terms, a team size of seven people is contributing to the exploitation of the developer as a capacity constrained resource.

Team Composition

Scrum also recommends that each Sprint team have at least one highly experienced engineer who can mentor the rest of the team. This echoes the surgeon role from the Harlan Mills' surgical team model [Brooks 1995]. The mentor is available to help other team members. If they report issues or challenges with which they need help at the daily Scrum meeting, the mentor can volunteer to assist them. Adding an experienced mentor helps to increase the exploitation of the developer as a capacity constrained resource, avoiding downtime by solving problems quickly.

Working Environment

Scrum says developers should have all the working space and tools they need to get their job done because by far the biggest overhead in software development is the OE for staff salaries. If the team members need a war room space, meeting room, or quiet reading room, they should have it. If they want to arrange their cubicles or desks so that they can sit as a whole Sprint team, pair off, or divide into two teams, they should be allowed to do so. The team should be allowed to self-organize its work environment.

If a team gets push back on making some facilities changes, it is almost certainly the result of a cost accounting analysis that shows an increase in cost per developer. A manager can fight back by using the Throughput Accounting measures described in Section 1—argue that office space and other overheads are fixed costs rather than marginal costs.

Scrum recognizes that developers in the thick of the action will know best how to optimize their time. Allowing developers to arrange their own environments and giving them enough space will exploit the developer as a capacity constrained resource. DeMarco and Lister have suggested that 100 square feet per developer is the optimal amount. To fail to provide this space may reduce Operating Expense, but it will do so at the cost of reduced Throughput. It does not require much reduction in Throughput to completely invalidate the cost saving of providing smaller accommodation—assuming that there is any cost saving, that is, the space would be used for something else or sublet to another tenant.

Provision of good tools is also designed to maximize the exploitation of the developer as a capacity constrained resource. If the developer needs to spend $7,000 on a state-of-the-art integrated development environment, then the Throughput per developer only needs to increase by $7,000 to pay back the investment. Investment in better tools elevates the developer as a capacity constrained resource by increasing the Throughput potential of any given developer.

If the Scrum Master is monitoring the inventory levels and lead time and calculating the cost per item of Product Backlog, he will know how many more items from the Product Backlog are needed to repay an investment in tools. Therefore, it is possible to deploy a tool on trial and monitor the effect on the Production Rate (R) over a single Sprint and perhaps a second Sprint. With 60 days of data, it ought to be possible to determine whether the tool increases Throughput and by how much.

It has been suggested that elevating constraints by purchasing the latest tools for those working in the CCR may result in deviant behavior—human nature being what it is. Teams who want new equipment might masquerade as a constraint in order to justify the expense.

One defense against this is the openness of the operations review. Everyone should understand why an investment to elevate a constraint was made. Also, anyone attempting to construct an artificial drop in production to appear as the constraint will need to explain to the whole business at the operations review why productivity has fallen. A spirit of openness, as discussed in Chapter 13, is essential to maintaining a healthy Agile development system.

The Sprint Review

The Sprint Review takes place at the end of each 30-day Sprint. It serves several purposes. It allows functionality to be demonstrated to the customer. It may also allow for delivery. If it is purely a demonstration, it helps to build customer confidence. If it is a delivery, it releases inventory and generates Throughput for the system. It can also double as the operations review, documented in Chapter 14. The operations review only requires 1 to 2 hours.

The Sprint Review allows the team to learn lessons from the last 30 days and use those to improve on the next 30 days. It is a formal event that encourages an environment of continuous improvement. Members analyze what was done and look for opportunities to improve. They identify constraints, and they discuss and agree on how to maximize the exploitation of the constraint or how to elevate it through improved techniques or new tools. The Sprint Review formalizes the opportunity and encourages the team to constantly seek improvements in production rate.

The Sprint Review also allows the development team to take pride in its achievement. It is important to have reflective periods when team members can look back and admire the fruits of their labors. This psychological effect is important for team morale. Because happy developers are productive developers, the Sprint Review helps to exploit the developer as a capacity constrained resource.

Engineering Practices

Scrum does not define any engineering practices, which advocates maintain is one of its great strengths. It certainly classifies Scrum as a management technique rather than an engineering technique. It also significantly reduces the barrier to entry.

Scrum is based on a notion that a significant improvement in productivity can occur simply by reorganizing the people doing the work—without interfering with the techniques used for working. This view is consistent with De Luca's First Law, "80% psychology and 20% technology." Scrum focuses on organizing around how humans interact with each other and does not try to dictate how they achieve the results. In this respect, Scrum is the ultimate in self-organizing process control.

chapter 30

RAD Process Elements Explained

RAD processes are built on the principle that a date is set in the calendar and will not move. The development effort is then tailored to the available period of time. Delivery dates are often set at regular intervals, such as monthly, every 6 weeks, every quarter, and so forth. The intervals are usually short—otherwise it wouldn't be called "rapid" application development.

Principles of RAD

The foundations of RAD can be explained in TOC terms. RAD sets the delivery date, or project timeline, as the system constraint. With the delivery date as the constraint, everything else is then subordinated to it. Hence, the other main constraints in the system must be protected and exploited to meet the delivery date constraint.

RAD methods correctly identify the scope as the constraint with the greatest uncertainty and unpredictability. Thus, the choice is made to protect the schedule constraint, which is predictable, and to subordinate everything else, including the scope, to that decision.

RAD methods limit the scope to be deliverable within the available time, that is, subordinate it to the delivery date. A wise RAD project manager will buffer the scope and leave some slack to absorb any uncertainty that might jeopardize the delivery date.

The development resources must then be subordinated to the delivery date and the agreed scope. Hence, RAD methods require that the project is staffed to meet the delivery date and agreed scope. The alternative is that the scope must be contained within the bounds of the delivery date and the available manpower.

Inventory Cap

By setting a steady heartbeat for development cycles, RAD methods effectively cap the inventory in the system at any given time. This allows the costs to be carefully controlled and planned. Capping inventory also allows the manpower level to be fixed, which should reduce or eliminate dependence on temporary staff augmentation. Capping inventory allows OE to be tightly controlled and provides a much better opportunity to accurately calculate the ROI for the software engineering organization.

Lead Time

A second benefit of setting a steady heartbeat for releases comes from absolutely defining the lead time for development. With RAD methods, the lead time is set as the constraint and cannot be varied. Everything else is subordinated to it. By fixing lead time, a development organization makes promises that it can honor and that provide a predictability to the market. Fixing lead time as a short, rapid period is likely to reduce waste because it should reduce change requests through reducing the opportunity for the customer to change its mind or for shifts in the market to occur.

Operating Expense

Due to the inventory cap and the fixed Lead Time (LT), it is possible to tightly control the OE of a RAD organization. However, Operating Expense is at risk from uncertainty in the estimating process and failure to correctly analyze the complexity or risk in the proposed functionality. Such failures may lead to a requirement to add staff to meet commitments. This may have caused a temporary increase in OE.

Limits of RAD Methods

RAD recognizes the basic constraints in software engineering and chooses to subordinate them all to the schedule constraint. RAD says little about software development as a human activity. It fails to recognize that 80% of the problem is psychological rather than technological.

RAD methods do provide agility. They provide for rapid delivery, and through those rapid cycles they provide the ability to accept and cope with change in the requirements or project scope. RAD methods have Agile attributes but aren't really Agile methods, as defined in the Agile Manifesto.

RAD can be seen as a forerunner to Agile. It does allow delivery of software faster, better, and cheaper. However, it fails to go far enough. Agile methods learn all the lessons from RAD and take them further. By recognizing the humanity of developers and the human element in the development of software, Agile methods seek to exploit and elevate the human as part of the software development process. Hence, Agile methods should produce a greater Throughput than simple RAD on its own.

My own experience—working on a global RAD project for a Fortune 100 PC manufacturer in 1996 and 1997 and on a large-scale FDD (Agile) project from 1997 through 1999—provides anecdotal evidence that this premise can be validated through experiment. I watched firsthand as FDD produced a significantly higher production rate than a classic RAD system. The difference was the queuing and buffering in FDD. FDD knows how to exploit the developer as a capacity constrained resource. With RAD projects, there isn't enough emphasis on this. Deciding to subordinate everything else to the time-box decision doesn't go far enough.

RAD was seen as a significant improvement over the Waterfall method. Global organizations building large systems with the Waterfall method noticed huge improvements when they moved to RAD. The driver for moving to RAD was the arrival of the Internet and the world wide web around 1995. Suddenly executives were talking about running on "Internet time," that is, every quarter was like a year previously. Internet time was a fourfold increase. RAD seemed to provide that fourfold increment required to live on Internet time. In TOC terminology, RAD appeared to produce four times more Throughput than Waterfall. Actually, what it was doing was releasing inventory to the market more often and that was producing a greater value for the customer.

Comparison of Methods

No one approach to management can be a panacea. It is unlikely that a single method will be acceptable for all situations. It is, therefore, necessary to question the application of Agile methods.

It is always attractive to polarize a debate. It forces people to choose. Which side are you on? Our political systems work that way. In the United States, you are either a donkey or an elephant, or you choose to opt out of politics.

There has been a similar tendency in the Agile community to polarize the debate as in traditional heavyweight methods versus Agile lightweight methods—the former being bad and the latter good.

Such a polarization is naïve, and wise business leaders will see it as such. It is necessary to examine the applicability of Agile methods and consider the spectrum of problem domains in which they might be applicable and those in which other approaches may still be better.

Different methods have different scope and scale, and consequently there are times when each is best applied. Even traditional, non-Agile methods have their place. Section 3 seeks to explore issues of applicability. The discussion is not meant to be conclusive, but rather to open up the debate. It puts a few stakes in the ground and makes some suggestions. Doubtless these suggestions will be debated by some, refuted by others, and agreed upon by a few. In any event, this debate needs to take place in the industry if software engineering is to move on and realize its potential.

chapter 31

Devil's Advocacy

Capers Jones has collected data on over 7,000 IT projects over more than 15 years [Constantine 2001]. He has several conclusions from analysis of his data that show which factors are important in producing a higher production rate:[1] Code reuse is by far the best way to improve the rate of Function Points delivered;[2] teams that conduct peer reviews by far outperform those that don't; teams with specialists outperform those with generalists; teams with a specialist maintenance and performance tuning function outperform teams that use mainline developers for this task.

Traditional Metrics Versus Agile Principles

All four of these conclusions are in conflict with the philosophies of most Agile methods. Extreme Programming, Test Driven Development, and Scrum all advocate the opposite, although Feature Driven Development does encourage code reuse through architecture and code reviews for improved quality.

The Capers Jones results cannot be denied or ignored. With such a body of data, they must be correct. Yet this evidence suggests that traditional software methods using specialists with a high degree of quality should perform best. What is wrong here?

This text has shown that Agile methods do produce better financial results. However, Agile methods promote the use of techniques shown to be less effective by Jones' data. There is a fundamental conflict, and the Theory of Constraints says that such a conflict is not possible. One or the other pieces of data must be founded on a false assumption. Both conflicting ideas cannot possibly produce a win-win, unless there is a false assumption.

In the toolbox of Thinking Processes, TOC provides a mechanism known as the Evaporating Cloud diagram to help resolve the conflict. In-depth explanation of TOC Thinking Processes and Evaporating Cloud diagrams is beyond the scope of this book.

---

[1] Jones measures production rate using Function Point Analysis and Function Points delivered, in a fashion similar to that described in Chapter 17.

[2] Refactoring rather than design for reuse has been popularly advocated by some Agile methodologists, for example, Fowler speaking at JavaOne 2002.

Here is a typical problem describing the conflict between specialists and generalists:

> In order to prevent costly rework, it is necessary to detect faults early. It is necessary that development not be started on a system that falsely assumes a certain functionality is possible. For example, consider the design of a system for use on mobile phones. It is desired to push a message to the phone that asks the user to visit a web page for an update on her account information. There is an assumption that the mobile phone has the ability to invoke the web browser from the messaging system. What if development started and then it was discovered that this functionality didn't exist in many of the target handsets? Suddenly, the whole project would be in jeopardy. Does this sound far-fetched? Do such slipups never happen? Perhaps this scenario sounds real enough because it does happen.

What went wrong? The answer is simple. The problem wasn't thought through sufficiently before the project was started. Most Agile methods advocate the use of developers early in the process to prevent this type of mistake. The developer is by implication a generalist. They are required to work on the requirements to ensure that the requirements are technically possible, feasible, and of minimal risk. The use of generalists is in conflict with the Capers Jones result that says teams of specialists will produce more Throughput. How is this conflict resolved?

The Evaporating Clouds diagram for the conflicting evidence is shown in Figure 31–1. On the far left, the goal is stated—catch the mistake early and correct it before it costs a lot of money. Then the two conflicting paths are drawn to the right. The diagram can be read like this, "In order to catch the fault early, improve Throughput, and reduce cost and waste, the analyst (specialist) must trap the problem. The analyst must engage early in the process. The analyst is a specialist. Alternatively, the developer must trap the problem. In order to trap the problem early, the developer must be engaged early in the process. By implication, the developer is now a generalist. The specialist is in conflict with the generalist."

Several Agile methodologists claim that the top branch of the diagram doesn't work. This is based on the assumptions that the specialist analyst cannot (or does not) think the problem through and the problem is not uncovered until later in the process when the developer tries to write the code. The Agile answer is to use developers. TOC would contend that there must be a false assumption underlying this conflict between Capers Jones' data and the Agile experience. The Evaporating Cloud process suggests that such assumptions must be exposed and challenged. The assumptions are shown on the diagram: Only the developer can think the process through because the developer has to write the code and must iterate through several levels of detail; the analyst cannot or does not think the problem through to sufficient depth. Can these assumptions be challenged?

The assumption about the developer seems safe. If the developer is to maintain employment, he must be competent and capable of thinking a problem through to sufficient depth. What about the assumption that the analyst cannot do this? Is this valid? Does the analyst set out to do bad work, sloppy work, insufficiently complete work? Probably not! People do not naturally set

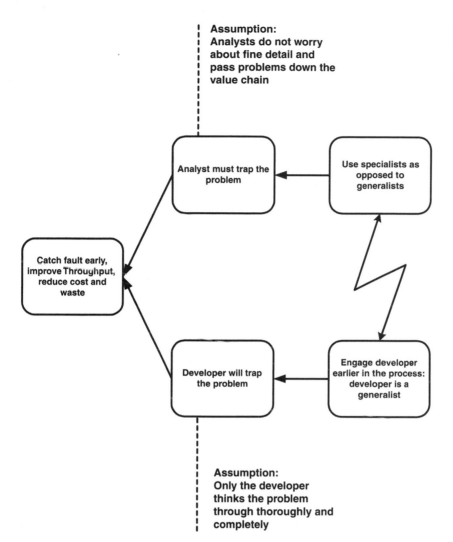

Figure 31-1
Evaporating Cloud
for specialist versus
generalist.

**Assumption:
Analysts do not worry
about fine detail and
pass problems down the
value chain**

Analyst must trap the
problem

Use specialists as
opposed to
generalists

Catch fault early,
improve Throughput,
reduce cost and
waste

Developer will trap
the problem

Engage developer
earlier in the process:
developer is a
generalist

**Assumption:
Only the developer
thinks the problem
through thoroughly and
completely**

out to do bad work. Their personal pride and self-esteem prevent them. They naturally try their best. So what is wrong with the analysts?

There could be two possible and plausible explanations: The analyst does not see it as his job to think the problem through in sufficient depth, perhaps because of policy (or process) decisions in the organization; or, the analyst is locally incentivized to complete his piece of the project as quickly as possible.

The Evaporating Clouds Thinking Process says that an idea must be "injected" to evaporate the cloud—to remove the false assumption and collapse the diagram. If the problem has insufficient depth of thought due to policy or adopted process, the policy must be changed and the processes rewritten. The analyst must see it as his job to think problems through. The analysis must be thorough. If the problem is a local focus on the analysis phase, this is easily fixed. The governing rules from Chapter 12 must be changed to measure the

Devil's Advocacy

analyst based on the Throughput of the entire system. The analyst must not focus on the local efficiency. Localized efficiency in analysis does not improve the performance of the system. In fact, it may degrade performance due to poor quality. The analyst must hold the correct mental model for the whole system and must understand the consequences of his actions. Carmine Mangione, an Agilist now living in San Diego, CA, has suggested an elegant solution to this problem. The analyst must also write the acceptance test case for the analysis. This forces the analyst to realize the cyclic nature of the system and the consequences of poor quality in the forward path.

Therefore, there is a plausible explanation to the conflict between Capers Jones' observation that specialists should outperform generalists and the Agile methodologists' contention that generalist developers will be better. Jones is clearly measuring organizations that employed specialists who were motivated and controlled by processes that led to good quality at every stage in the process. The Agile methodologists are clearly reacting to their environment. They are assuming that it is impossible to fix the systemic issues with analysts and both quality and performance can be improved by eliminating them.

Perhaps the final conclusion is that an Agile team of generalists will outperform a badly organized, badly incentivized, poorly skilled team of specialists following a traditional method. However, a good team of specialists, measured by properly set governing rules and focused on quality, should outperform the team of Agile generalists. Hence, the Agilists and Capers Jones are not in conflict, the Agilists are basing their beliefs on differing assumptions.

Scott Ambler has suggested the ultimate solution to this problem [2003]. He calls them generalist specialists. These are software engineers with specialist in-depth skills in a few areas but adequate skills across a breadth of other areas. The generalist specialist is probably the ideal member for an Agile team. Such a team of generalist experts using an Agile method would probably perform even better. Unfortunately, data for such teams is not available for consideration at the time of writing.

Adding More People Makes Projects Later

Fred Brooks argued that adding more people makes a late project later [Brooks 1995]. This would appear to be in conflict with the constraint theory that recognized constraints should be elevated. With software development such a labor intensive process and recognition that the available labor is a constraint, surely the constraint must be elevated through addition of more manpower. This appears to conflict with Brooks' conclusion. How can this be?

The answer lies in the effect of making a change. All improvements are changes, though not all changes are improvements [Goldratt 1990b, Ch. 2]. When a change is made, it causes disruption. The effect of this disruption is referred to as the J-curve effect. The J-curve specifically refers to the production rate (R). R will decline when the change is initially introduced. The graph of production rate will dip. If the change is truly an improvement, the system will learn to use the improvement properly and the production rate will rise again. It will rise beyond the original production rate before settling down at some higher level. This is the J-curve effect, illustrated in Figure 31–2.

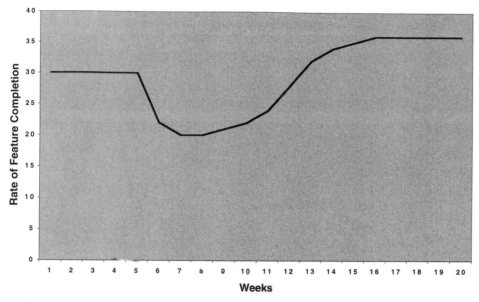

Figure 31–2
J-curve effect.

Brooks observed that the software production rate decreases when more manpower is introduced. The main reason for this is the communication burden on the existing developers to educate the new developers. It is reasonable to think, though not guaranteed, that once the new developers are up to speed, the production rate should be higher than before. However, the increase will not be a linear improvement. The new production rate will not have risen linearly with the increase in labor force.

Brooks' observation that a late project will be later when more labor is added is a reference to the J-curve effect. Brooks is saying that the time it takes to come out of the bottom of the J and repay the lost production from the introduction of the new labor is longer than the remaining time on the project as illustrated in Figure 31–3. This seems to be based on the assumption that early warning on a late project is not available. Hence, by the time the project manager is aware that the project is truly late, it is already too late to add more manpower.

Brooks suggests that the way to elevate the labor constraint on production rate is to use overtime to complete the project. Overtime is used to increase the production rate by temporarily removing the policy constraint of an 8-hour day. What this clearly indicates is that the choice of method for exploitation and elevation of a constraint is important. That choice will vary depending on the circumstances.

It is worth restating here Eli Goldratt's observation that all improvements are changes, but not all changes are improvements. All changes are an improvement if they result in increased Throughput (or production quantity) within the bounds of other constraints. A change is not an improvement if it results in reduced Throughput within the bounds of the other constraints.

Figure 31-3
J-curve fatally
impacts production
rate.

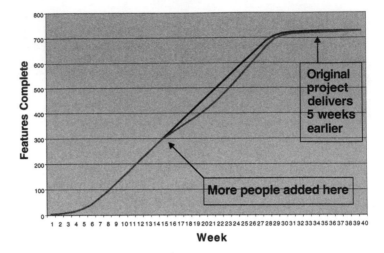

In this specific case, the other constraint was the project timeline. The delivery date was a constraint. When a change was introduced, the production rate was temporarily reduced. If the change does not produce a net improvement within the bounds of the delivery date constraint, it was not a worthwhile change. It was not an improvement.

chapter 32

States of Control and Reducing Variation

In supporting Scrum, Beedle and Schwaber have argued that all software development is empirical and, therefore, cannot be planned with accuracy, is not repeatable, and cannot be easily classified [Schwaber 2002]. They have argued that Agile methods address this through continual assessment and feedback. The term "empirical" has been widely used amongst Agilists[1] including Highsmith [2002]. It is debatable if the true meaning is accurately reflected.

"Empirical" means "based on observation." For example, it was observed that the sun came up yesterday and that it came up again today. It could be further observed that the time difference between each sunrise is 24 hours. A guess could be made, based on empirical evidence, that the sun will rise tomorrow, 24 hours after it rose this morning. Until the science of physics explained why the sun came up every morning, humans had only empirical evidence to work with. However, the empirical data was very dependable and not prone to much variation. The sun always came up. There was no chaotic behavior.

The point is that processes that can only be observed empirically are not necessarily chaotic. They may be predictable. What is important about empirical processes is whether they are continuous or discontinuous (sometimes referred to as convergent or divergent). Henceforth in this chapter, the term "empirical" is used only to mean "based on observation." Such empirical processes are most likely predictable and continuous. The term "chaotic" refers to discontinuous processes, often called "empirical" in other Agile texts.

It has been suggested that all Agile methods must rely purely on feedback (reaction) rather than planning (prediction) [Schwaber 2002]. This implies that all software development lives on the edge of chaos. However, some science can be brought in to this question, specifically the Statistical Process Control techniques pioneered by Walter A. Shewhart and W. Edwards Deming. As described in Chapter 1, their work created the Quality Assurance movement that led to the advances in Japanese manufacturing in the second half of the 20th century. The Deming influence was a key to the development of Japanese quality processes.

---

[1] It is considerably debated on the Scrum Development list at Yahoo! Groups.

Figure 32–1
A Control Chart
showing low and
high tolerance levels.

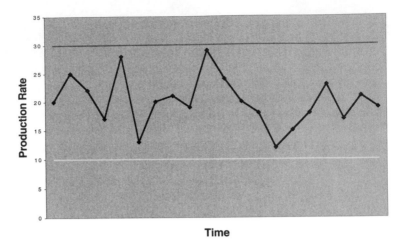

Figure 32–2
Wheeler's four states
of control.

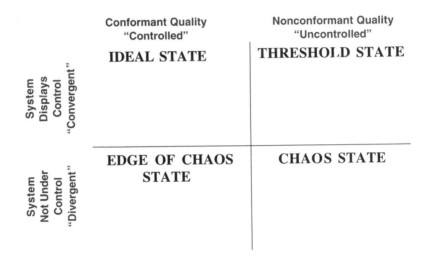

Shewhart states that a process is "in control" if it can be regularly measured within some bounds. So, "in control" means that a process is convergent, that is, it does not exhibit chaotic behavior and stays within some agreed-upon bounds. His graphic method for reporting this is known as a Control Chart, shown in Figure 32–1. Don Wheeler later classified four states of control based on Shewhart's work as shown in Figure 32–2 [Wheeler 1992]. He calls these the Ideal state, the Threshold state, the Edge of Chaos state, and Chaos.

The process is stable over time. The natural spread of the process (the variance in the output) is within the tolerance specified for the product as shown in Figure 32-1. The process is acted upon in a stable and consistent manner. The process is not changed arbitrarily. The average Throughput of the process is known and can be set and maintained. In the Ideal state, a process will produce no or negligible errors.

Traditional software engineering lifecycle methods have tended to assume that software development can be held in the Ideal state. The problem with this is how do you know, if you cannot measure it accurately? Errors can be measured very easily and intuitively. Everyone knows that, in software development, bugs are common and certainly greater than negligible. Hence, software development is rarely or never in the Ideal state.

In this state, a process appears to be reasonably statistically controllable. Variances outside an agreed tolerance are rare. The number of errors due to variance is small, predictable, and manageable.

To bring a Threshold state process towards the Ideal state, the specifications can be changed, that is, the tolerance can be relaxed or some change can be made to the process to reduce variation. The latter approach is that of Six Sigma—reducing variation, then taking a single action to eliminate specific problems.

With FDD, the specification for a given release could be changed by adjusting the Feature List. The number of bugs permitted in the release could be relaxed. Other Agile methods would permit this kind of tampering with the process. However, other Agile methods assume that software development is not in the Threshold state, but at the Edge of Chaos.

With FDD and the 5-point weighting scale for each Feature, it is possible to measure very accurately the level of control in the software development process. FDD allows tracking of errors per Feature as well as the time taken per Feature, and both can be compared against an estimate. The estimate is based on the 5-point weighting scale. How often the 5-point weighting was accurate can be tracked, and the scale can be adjusted if a trend towards inaccuracy is detected.

This ability to estimate FDD accurately based on an objective weighting scale that can be applied repeatedly suggests that FDD can be used to keep the software development process in the Threshold state and gradually move it toward the Ideal state as a team of developers matures and becomes better at executing on the activities of FDD.

Therefore, the foundation of FDD and what enables it to exist in the Threshold state is the technique for first classifying the raw material—the language for describing a Feature: **<action> <result> <object>**. This language coupled to object oriented analysis techniques such as the Domain Neutral Component, that enables a close mapping between the system design and the language used to describe the requirements has enabled FDD to obtain a high level of repeatability.

With FDD Features, the **<action>** is the method to be coded by the developer. The **<result>** is the return value from the method. The **<object>** is the class that will contain the method. Subsequent clauses in the sentence tend to contain parameters for the method. Hence, an FDD Feature leads directly to a single UML Sequence Diagram. It is this structured method for describing small pieces of client-valued output that has enabled FDD to achieve the Threshold state for a software development process.

The effect of the Feature template and the 5-point weighting scale for assessing Feature complexity provides a rigorous framework for empirical measure. This improves the certainty that something is measured or assessed accurately. By implication, uncertainty is reduced, and the net effect is that planning and prediction are possible. Other Agile methods have tended to take an analysis and design agnostic posture. This puts them in the Edge of Chaos state.

The Edge of Chaos State

In this state the process is out of control, even if it is producing conforming products. Most Agile methods assume this, Edge of Chaos, and aim to deliver conforming products despite it. The assumption is that a process in this state suffers from random, unpredictable, severe noise, which will force it out of the acceptable tolerances. In other words, a chaotic event, something that could not be predicted and is out of tolerance with the normal predictive measures, will occur during the process—perhaps many times. If chaos is truly present, prediction and planning are ineffective because they will result in error.

Agile methods such as Scrum and XP cope with this through the use of fast feedback, empirical knowledge, and experience of the developers. There is no recipe for coping, and no way of describing how to cope. The advice is to get people who have experience and can self-organize themselves to cope with each situation that takes the project into chaos.

The advantage of fast feedback is that management knows a situation is unusual, that is, chaotic, very quickly—before it becomes a big problem. This allows compensatory action to be taken to correct the problem before it impacts the agreed delivery.

Chaos

In the state of Chaos, a process is not producing conforming products and is not controllable. This may sound familiar to many software developers.

Comprehending the Known Universe

Wheeler's diagram can be recast as a continuous two-dimensional space, as shown in Figure 32–3. The x-axis will measure process maturity. The y-axis will measure the comprehension of the known universe. It is a measure of the current model versus reality.

In physics and chemistry, the analysis model is highly developed. It allows both to be considered effect-cause-effect sciences. The known chemical properties of substances can be used together with the current mental model for how chemical compounds interact. This allows a prediction about the qualities of a new material under development. For example, a scientist tasked with developing a new sports fabric with water-resistance, light weight,

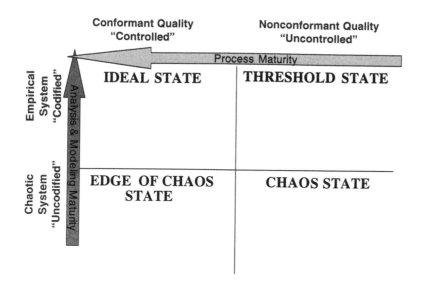

breathability, high strength, and a shiny appearance can use what is known about chemistry to predict a solution. There is less exploration involved because the model of the domain is well developed.

As many of us learned in high school, chemistry has developed over hundreds of years, and during this time, the model has changed. As more is known about the topic, the model is improved, and results based on the old model have to be rethought.

Figure 32–3 revises Wheeler's chart, by labeling the y-axis to reflect the maturity of the conceptual model. The implication is that it is impossible to produce a converging system if you do not know how to describe it or measure it. The y-axis is called "analysis and modeling maturity." This can be thought of as the maturity of the conceptual model of the philosophy of software development—the number and accuracy of the concepts in the model of how software works.

Most Agile methods assume that software process control is impossible because the underlying elements of software development are unknown and unknowable. They base this on the assumption that some previous models have failed. For example, Use Case driven development and all its associated artifacts in UDP could be considered too heavyweight to be useful. As a result, questions have been raised about the flexibility and maintainability of the software delivered. Hence, an argument could be made that the Jacobson model for the software universe was wrong.

Agile methods based on the view that such models have failed assume that it is not possible to improve. They are based on the belief that software cannot be measured because it is never repeatable. In other words, because Jacobson's model was incomplete (or wrong), Boehm's model was incomplete, Constantine's model was incomplete, and so on; there is an underlying

**Improving
Analysis and
Modeling
Maturity**

assumption that attempts to understand the basic nature of software development should be ignored.

However, there is work that is gradually revealing the true model of software. Particular favorites are Coad [1999] (Features, Archetypes, Domain Neutral Component), Palmer [2000] (extending Archetypes and Domain Neutral Component), Mayfield and Nicola [2001] (Pattern Players and Collaboration Patterns), Fowler [1996] (Analysis Patterns), Hays [1996] (Data model patterns and the Universal Data model), Horrocks [1999] (Statecharts applied to user interface), and Constantine [1999] (Task Cases for user interface).

Looking specifically at construction of user interfaces [Horrocks 1999] using the Type-II MVC architecture for a web application using the Statechart design technique, it can be shown that there is very little that is chaotic. A Statechart model gives a very precise description of the code to be implemented and yet can be precisely mapped to the design. This allows for accurate empirical measure of the complexity and level of effort required for user interface development.

My experience is that development of controllers, which process events, and views, which process states, tend toward a very statistically consistent level of effort. Therefore, I believe from experience (empirical observation) that UI design and development can be accurately defined, that is, it is not chaotic, and through careful empirical observation of these defined elements can be accurately predicted, that is, it is repeatable.

Peter Coad's work with Features can be examined in a similar light. Features relate directly to business requirements and are comprehensible by business owners. Coad has also shown that they map directly to object-oriented design and UML sequence diagrams. Chapter 21 showed that Features can be classified into categories. Within each category they behave in a statistically repeatable fashion.[2] In other words, Features development can be accurately predicted, within a given tolerance, through empirical observation.

In conclusion, both user interface and business logic development is repeatable and controllable. It is not "unknown" or "unknowable"—or chaotic.

Improving the Process Maturity

Switching to the x-axis on the graph, the process maturity improves as the arrow moves to the left. The process improvement shown is Agile process improvement. That is to say, it is a self-organizing, human-centric, psychologically aware process. Using more traditional language, it is constraint driven, leadership oriented, and highly delegated. Regardless of the take on Agile methods, process improvement will drive the system of software

---

[2] I have empirical data from 13 projects over a 4-year period that demonstrates the repeatable nature of Features estimated using the 5-point complexity rating. The incredibly low standard deviation was initially a considerable surprise. However, having collected data from three teams in three different locations across more than 10 projects, I believe that a sufficient statistical sample exists to claim that Features are statistically repeatable.

development left on the chart. Moving left on the chart means that the system of software production delivers with better quality. Quality implies, with agreed function, within a given tolerance of defects and schedule.

However, it is folly to ignore the other dimension on the chart. If the process can move up the y-axis, the ability to control and predict is being improved. The ability to measure and track what is happening is improving because there is a better clarity over what to measure and what to track. Moving up the y-axis improves the ability to plan with accuracy.

Seeking to use best-of-breed methods for understanding the true model of the domain—these things that have been generalized as "ideas" for software—enables developers to estimate, plan, measure, and track more accurately. With more accuracy, there is more control.

Most Agile methods claim to be analysis or design method agnostic. In many cases, it is implied or explicitly assumed that the analysis and design method is unimportant as long as there is fast feedback and the ability to react. By choosing not to prescribe such techniques, and occasionally proscribing them on the basis that they are traditional and by implication "failed," some Agile methods are confined to a single dimension—the x-axis on the Wheeler chart. This limits these methods to the Edge of Chaos State. It also leaves the manager of a professional, mature organization with the question of whether a purely reactionary feedback mechanism is good enough for her organization or whether some degree of planning and predictability is expected.

There is no doubt that the use of Agile methods will improve the state of control of the software development process and can elevate it to a point where it is manageable and will produce desirable results.

However, not all software analysis and design is chaotic or unpredictable. It is possible to reduce the noise down to a level where the development process can be performed in a predictable fashion within agreed levels of tolerance. The up-front work approach and the "right first time" principle with FDD coupled with its architectural partitioning of the work to be undertaken are aimed at reducing noise and unpredictability during the Design and Build stages. FDD seeks to eliminate the unknowable piece of a systems development during the Modeling and Architecture stage. As a result, the Design and Build stages exist in the Threshold state.

FDD differs from other Agile methods because of its emphasis on up-front analysis for predictive planning. Stephen Palmer calls this JEDI (Just Enough Design Initially).[3] The use of the Domain Neutral Component modeling technique developed by Palmer, Coad, and others has produced very repeatable results with low variance. Rules of thumb such as "1 week of modeling results in 12 weeks of development" have proven remarkably accurate. There is empirical evidence to correlate the result.

FDD Focuses on Variance as Well as Quality and Inventory

[3]"Jedi Masters" Feature Driven Development Community Website, February 2003, http://www.featuredrivendevelopment.com/node.php?id5507.

If the goal is to run a business making investment decisions based on accurate predictions, then such predictions must be accurate within a given or agreed tolerance. FDD can deliver this when executed correctly. Some other Agile methods do not offer or promise this. Rather, they take a pragmatic approach. They reverse the problem and ask the business how much risk it is willing to take. They say, "Give me a little money and a little time, and I will deliver you something. I cannot say exactly or with certainty what that 'something' will be. But, it will be useful, and you will not be unhappy with the result."

Hence, there appears to be a difference between FDD and other Agile methods. FDD seeks to bring the process under control through underlying improvements in technique and understanding of the mechanisms of software development. Some other methods seek to cope with the assumption that software development defies Descartian deconstruction and cannot be controlled in the conventional sense. Instead, they offer to minimize the risk for the business. In this respect, FDD appears more like a traditional software method, which has led some Agilists to refer to FDD as "less Agile." By implication the term "agile" is used to imply that such processes are entirely reactive control systems.

In contradiction to this, Lean Production methods do make use of "right first time" approaches and do make use of predictive control techniques. FDD may be "less Agile," but it might be "more Lean." FDD is a process that has an additional focus on reduction of variance, as well as quality and inventory. As such, FDD may be more suitable than other Agile methods for Six Sigma companies.

XP Focuses on Quality and Short Lead Times

XP methodologists deify the notion that XP is a method that tames chaos. In early writings it appears to be a method that promises conforming product from the chaotic, unpredictable, empirical (sic) nature of software development. Yet, close examination of its best practices, including small stories written on cards, broken down and prioritized based on business value, assessed for risk and complexity, and estimated for level of effort, suggests that XP is a process with all the core metrics for controllability. The recent trend in XP towards shorter iterations of 1 day initially and 1 week (rather than 2 weeks) suggest that Kent Beck is trying to leverage the advantage to be gained from predictive control based on empirical experience.

It seems possible that by using all of XP's best practices an XP process can be brought into the Threshold state and produce control results comparable with FDD. This will require a codification for writing of Stories* in a repeatable fashion and the widespread use of Story Points for complexity, risk, and size assessment.

---

*At the time of writing Mike Cohn is undertaking authorship of a book which seeks to define a repeatable method and codification of stories in XP. http://www.userstories.com/.

Table 32–1

Management theories and their focus areas.

Theory	Focus	Control
Scrum	Lead Time & Expediting	Feedback
XP	Quality & Lead Time	Feedback
FDD	Inventory, Lead Time, Quality, & Variance	Feedback & Feed-Forward

It is worth revisiting Table 1–1, which examined the process focus of Lean, TOC, and Six Sigma. If we were to draw a similar chart for Agile methods, such as Table 32–1. It would highlight some of the differences among them. FDD is a more elaborate process with more concepts. It uses feedback as well as feed-forward control. It addresses quality, inventory, lead time, and variance. Some other Agile methods are simpler and arguably easier to implement. XP, for example, focuses on lead time and quality and exclusively uses feedback. A side effect of fixing lead time is that it constrains WIP Inventory. Scrum is even simpler because it is purely focused on lead time and elimination of expediting. It shares the XP side effect of capping inventory based on lead time. Scrum relies entirely on feedback control

It is, therefore, worth noting that announcing adoption of an Agile method is not enough to indicate an improvement. The system is probably still in the state of Chaos State. However, proper use of an Agile method will quickly produce system maturity. A method that elevates quality and subordinates the system to it, such as XP, will quickly move an organization left across the graph to the Edge of Chaos State. To reach the Threshold state, a system must be doing all the best practices in the methodology and adopting methods of analysis and design that reduce the unpredictable nature of software and bring it to a point where empirical observation is possible. The latest practices in XP, which seek to formalize or codify the method in detail, appear to be addressing this.

Ultimately, Agile methods appear to recognize that there must be something beyond purely reactionary control. They are seeking to move up the y-axis on the graph. They recognize that this improves controllability. In control engineering, predictive controllers produce better results than purely reactive controllers. Hence, processes that can be predicted should produce better results than processes that rely purely on reaction to past events. Without process control which delivers accurate metrics, management will struggle to make proper investment decisions. Poor investment decisions are reflected in an underperformance in the ROI financial metric. Good process control is a direct requirement for superior financial results.

chapter 33

Comparison of
Production Metrics

"Measure the smallest thing you can measure. . .
Because it gives you fast feedback."

Seth Godin

The manageability of a software development process can be compared and predicted through a study of the available management metrics for Throughput. Shewhart's work on Statistical Process Control and Wheeler's classification of the states of control provide some clues. Essentially, the output from the process—the pieces of client-valued functionality being delivered in the system—must be measured. The variance in the system must also be measured against a set band of acceptability. The smaller the unit of measurement in comparison to the size of the output, the more feedback is being provided. The more feedback provided, the greater the sensitivity of the measurement. This greater sensitivity of measurement leads to more sensitive adjustment of the process and better feed-forward predictability.

FDD measures the Features completed every day, week, month, and quarter. Features are very fine grained,[1] very easily assessed for complexity, and very repeatable. A typical 3-month-long web development project with 10 developers may have around 500 Features, including User Interface, Business Logic, Data Management, and System Interface Features. A typical programmer may produce 5 Features per week. Each Feature is estimated to an input scale of 4, 8, 16, 32, 48 (or more) man hours (without local safety). In a project that will take 65 calendar-week days with a need to deliver 500 Features, this translates into an average of more than 7 Features per day.

FDD

Each Feature can be measured to ensure that the overall delivery rate is on target, the weighting of the Feature was accurate, and the elapsed development time for its Feature weighting was within an acceptable tolerance of the standard allowed time. Features are tracked at each of six stages of transformation. In other words, each day on an FDD project with only 10 developers,

---

[1]"Features are tiny," Jeff De Luca.

up to 40 or 50 data points are obtained. These can be used to assess the state of control of an FDD project. Within a few days, it is possible to know whether the project is in the Threshold state or the Edge of Chaos State. This allows the project manager or development manager to take action to bring the project back from the Edge of Chaos State, into the Threshold state.

Extreme Programming

The unit of control for XP is the Story Point. Stories represent a measure of client-valued functionality and can be used as a measure of inventory. The Tracker on an XP project should be able to provide daily data on Story Points queuing to start, in-progress, and completed. Data on Story Points passing the tests within an XP iteration should be available on a daily basis—or at worst a weekly basis. The total Story Points for the Stories completed can be calculated on a daily basis. XP teams use the term "velocity" to measure the rate of Story Point completion. Velocity is equivalent of production rate in this text.

However, there isn't (at the time of writing)[2] enough definition around the method for writing a Story to treat them as normalized for comparison across teams. As a team matures, the style of Story writing will converge. This will allow guidelines to be set based on "velocity" and people to expect this measure is accurate.

With XP[3] it is easier to show product conformance than the rate of production. Given that Stories are subject to irregular definition, it would be better to try to control whether or not a Story passes the tests or not. This would measure the quality and establish whether quality is under control. As quality is directly related to production rate, the quality metric is valuable as a health check.

XP may not provide the same number of data points as FDD. XP Stories appear to be bigger than Features. There is also less visibility into the stages of transformation due to the extreme nature of XP. It may be possible to track tasks relating to given Stories. These tasks may relate to the stages of transformation. If this data is available, then XP will produce a similar number of data points to FDD.

Scrum

Scrum provides certainty of measurement at the end of each Sprint (30-day cycle). Some degree of objectivity is possible within the Sprint through the daily Scrum meeting. However, reports at Scrums are essentially subjective and are based on developer opinion. The Sprint has an objective to complete an agreed set of tasks from the Product Backlog. The task descriptions in

Agile Management
for Software
Engineering

288

[2]As of January 2003, some XP methodologists are working to standardize the method of Story definition. There appears to be a wider recognition that reducing variance in Story writing produces better predictability.
[3]Again, this is a direct result of the state of the art in Story definition at the time of writing. This statement will cease to be true in the future when a more repeatable Story template is available.

Scrum look a lot like Features in FDD and use similar language. However, there is no documented method for defining and weighting tasks. Tasks are probably not as fine grained as Features because they are not formed from any formally described analysis. They are less likely to be repeatable and more likely to be prone to variability.

For a web project lasting 3 months, it seems reasonable that several hundred tasks could be completed from the Product Backlog by 10 developers. Within a Sprint, task completion is measured using the burn-down chart. The burn-down chart typically measures the level of effort for tasks and, hence, is measured in hours. For a team of 10 developers, approximately 80 hours of work are being recorded daily. This is very fine grained.

When the project exists at the Edge of Chaos State due to noise, uncertainty, and variance in the software development process, Scrum provides a reliable method for managing projects empirically based on feedback. Prediction and planning are not encouraged due to the lack of predictable metrics that could be used for feed-forward control.

The unit of control for structured methods is the Function Point. Function Points represent a derivative measure of client-valued output and can be used as a proper measure of inventory. Function Points are very small. They are very similar to Features in FDD although their original motivation was structured analysis and design whereas FDD's Features were motivated by object-oriented analysis and design. An SDLC project run thoroughly using FP metrics and tracking should provide a similar degree of control to an FDD project. It should exist in the Threshold state and approach the Ideal state.

Traditional Methods— Function Points

Jacobson's OOSE (Object Oriented Software Engineering) provides the basis of the most commonly used instance of Unified Process, a traditional method. It seems less readily controlled.

Traditional Methods— UDP

Measuring a UDP project in terms of the client-valued output involves examining the requirements. UDP produces the requirements analysis in the form of Use Cases. There is very little uniformity in the method for writing Use Cases. Numerous authors have argued for different approaches and different degrees of refinement. This lack of uniformity in Use Cases, as compared to Features in FDD or Function Points in structured methods, introduces noise, uncertainty, and variance, which almost immediately places a UDP project in the state of Chaos.

However, within a given software development organization, following the specific advice of one Use Case author, Use Cases may be more predictable.[4] The process of writing the Use Cases is better than chaotic, perhaps in the Threshold state.

---

[4]This is rarely achieved as the analysts hired to write the Use Cases have varied backgrounds and education. The likelihood that they all trained in the same style of Use Case authoring is slim.

Considering again a 3-month-long web development project with 10 developers, it might be reasonable to have 35 Use Cases for such a project. I have heard estimates of between 7 and 100 Use Cases for projects of this size, but I have seen several projects that produced around 35 Use Cases for such a project.

Requirements Use Cases are hard to map to specific classes and functional programming work. It is, therefore, difficult to precisely declare a Use Case to be designed or to map specific interim steps, such as design review. Some projects are run this way, but it often leads to suboptimal procedural code. Hence, Use Cases are often mapped through several interim artifacts, including system-level Use Cases and other design documents. Tracking the precise state of the client-valued output becomes more difficult.

In the example, it takes 65 calendar-week days to produce code for 35 Use Cases. If the only tracking available for Use Cases is "started" and "finished," at best there will be one or two data points every 2 days. The Use Case driven approach to quantifying production produces data that is two orders of magnitude less than the finer grained approaches using Features or Function Points. The estimate of the state of control of the project must be two orders of magnitude less certain. In common language, there is greater uncertainty, whether or not the process is in control.

Summary

Systems of software production are reliant on feedback for management and control. The granularity of the feedback is important. The finer grained the measurements, the better the control should be. In general, Agile methods focus on fine grained frequent measurement. This makes them good reactive control mechanisms. As explained in Chapter 32, those methods, such as FDD, that use measurements with a low variability will also be good feed-forward predictive control mechanisms.

chapter 34

Applicability of Agile Methods

It really isn't sufficient to suggest that Agile methods are better and leave it at that. It really isn't acceptable to suggest that you can pick any Agile method and you will see the correct results. Some Agilists might like to suggest a one-size-fits-all approach, but most experienced managers will tell you that such a suggestion usually implies a management fad rather than a real trend and improvement [Miller 2002]. As I genuinely believe that Agile methods are a genuine trend and are truly better for many software businesses, it is necessary to consider when Agile methods may not be applicable.

Figure 34–1 divides the project space into a 2 × 2 grid. The rows divide software projects into those that can be easily partitioned into smaller pieces and can be delivered incrementally and those that must be delivered as a whole to have value. It is easier to think of the latter projects in a physical sense, such as the Boeing 777, the Space Shuttle, or the Tacoma Narrows Bridge. There is not much value without the whole thing.

Dividing up the Process Space

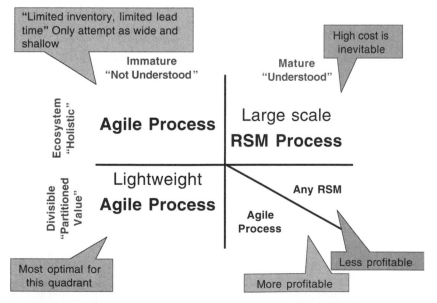

Figure 34–1
Problem domain versus process map.

Such projects have to be delivered holistically. It was not possible to deliver the wings of a 777 and test them in production without the rest of the plane. Equivalents of such projects exist in the software world. They include: air traffic control; ambulance dispatch; large-scale operating systems; algorithmic software (for example, cryptographic systems, DNA sequencing, fraud detection systems); government systems, (tax collection and vehicle licensing); and systems tied to physical objects (digital camera software, vehicle engine control, embedded mobile phone software). In general, any kind of system in which the vast majority of features are must-have and/or are mandated by government regulation should be seen as a holistic system for delivery of Throughput.

The columns on the grid divide the space into domains that are mature and understood and those that are immature and not understood. For example, air traffic control is a mature and understood domain in which the requirements ought to be clear before the project is undertaken. However, an operating system for wireless telephony Internet data services is not currently a mature and understood problem. Hence, requirements for such a system are likely to change often.

This two-dimensional analysis gives us four quadrants. Both Agile methods and traditional software methods could be used in all four quadrants. However, I believe that success in the upper right—mature, holistic—can only be achieved by large-scale Rigorous Software Methodologies (RSM).[1] This is very much the quadrant for CMM Level 3 through 5. In this sector, domain uncertainty is low, but scope must be delivered in full—only a whole system has Throughput value. Hence, the traditional project management model of scope-budget-schedule appears most appropriate. There is no need for incremental or iterative delivery common in Agile methods though use of iterative incremental development may help to reduce risk.

Success in the upper left quadrant—holistic, immature—can only be achieved using Agile methods. The reason for this is simple: such projects must seek to build out breadth rather than depth in order to obtain coverage of the whole problem domain. To do this and avoid continual rework from changing requirements, the project must be agile. It must exhibit short lead times and small inventory levels, due to the risk that the inventory will go stale as a more mature understanding of the space emerges.

In the lower half of the graph, I believe that you could employ either RSMs or Agile methods. However, using an RSM in the lower left quadrant—divisible, immature—is likely to lead to failure. Why? Once again, it is known that the requirements will be fluid. It is known that there is excessive risk and uncertainty attached to the requirements. Hence, it would be foolish to pursue a project management model that fixed the scope and varied the schedule. It is essential to tackle such problems with short lead times and low inventory levels. This is best achieved with a very lightweight Agile method using fixed time-boxes, such as Extreme Programming, or the XP/Scrum hybrid, XBreed.

As a general rule, Agile methods will outperform RSMs in the lower half of the graph because they will successfully deliver results, and incur lower costs and lower investment to achieve the same output. With divisible prob-

[1]Rigorous Software Methodology is the term coined by Jim Highsmith to encompass all traditional (SDLC) software development processes [2002].

lems that can be incrementally delivered, covering most software development domains, Agile methods will produce the best business results.

Agility would normally be defined as "an ability to cope with change." In a Darwinian sense, agility is "genetic fitness." Genetic fitness is a measure of a species ability to cope with a changing environment and to evolve and avoid extinction.

Most Agilists do not define agility in this manner. They prefer the notion that Agile methods put the human side of software development first and treat development as a largely chaotic (unknowable) emergent genetic phenomena. Often, this is used to mean that Agile methods should not seek to plan or control, but should allow emergent self-organizing behavior focused and measured on an overall goal. The goal is always to deliver working code.

In fact, this is just an observed behavioral way of stating that Agile methods are able to cope with change. They are able to cope with change because many of them do not use planning in the traditional sense. They allow the "developer on the spot" to make decisions. They are tactical in nature. Hence, they are able to cope with change. There is no plan to throw away!

I would like to suggest a more expansive expression of agility. Not just that Agile methods are able to cope with change, but that they are particularly good at coping with a particular type of change—expedited requests.

Agility as Ability to Expedite

An expedite request is one made with top priority, and by its very nature all other work must be subordinated to it. In simple terms, expediting is queue jumping. Requests for expediting are more likely in immature markets or with immature organizations. Regardless of the software development method being used, it will always be possible to expedite a request. However, I believe that Agile methods cope with such requests better. What do I mean by "cope"? I mean that Agile methods will incur less impact to the overall goal of the organization—to make more profit—than any RSM will for the same expedite request. Or stated another way, Agile methods will incur a smaller increase in work-in-progress inventory, a smaller increase in investment, a smaller reduction in production rate, and a smaller increase in overall lead time due to the expedite request. Once again, using the metrics laid out in this book, such a supposition can be easily measured and tested.

Figure 34–2 lays out a possible measure of the ability to expedite with different development methods.[2] The diagram shows that requests to expedite are more likely in less mature, more dynamic markets or in exploratory problem domains. The diagram then seeks to map several methods against these criteria.

---

[2]In this diagram, RUP indicates a typical OOSE derived instantiation of UDP. It is recognized that UDP could be used to implement a more Agile method (spiral, iterative). However, it is likely that most UDP shops around the world are using a Use Case driven derivative of OOSE or Objectory, as generally taught by the consulting group at Rational Corporation.

Figure 34–2
The agile expedite
spectrum.

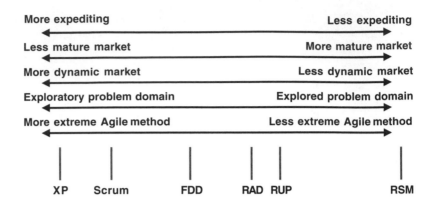

This diagram suggests that Extreme Programming is really "serial expediting." In other words, Extreme Programming is most appropriate in a world where there is almost no stability. The requirements arrive pretty much every few weeks, and the desire is to turn around a working system in short order. With iterations of 1 or 2 weeks, the latest, most important requests are always being built with less than a 2-week delay. Other requests get deprioritized and wait for a future iteration. In this model, an Extreme Programming team can be thought of as the short-order restaurant for code production.

Scrum, on the other hand, excludes expedite requests during the current Sprint. The request must wait until the next Sprint. This implies that the average lead time for an expedite request in a Scrum shop is 6 weeks.

FDD tends to be used on larger projects with teams of 10—or more. The iterations tend to be quarterly or longer. There is a change control process available. Hence, FDD can accept changes. However, there could be significant work-in-progress and winding it down in order to facilitate the expedite request is likely to be more costly than in either an XP or Scrum project.

Scale Versus Ability to Expedite

The graph "Scale Versus Ability to Expedite," Figure 34–3, seeks to map out the cost of an expedite request in terms of lost inventory production days multiplied by the number of days of increased lead time. This two-dimensional metric is hard to envisage, but gives a truly balanced view of the impact of an expedite request on both reduced production and increased lead time. Increased lead time is of negative value to the client and adds risk because requirements can atrophy and waste levels will increase. Reduced production is a direct hit to profitability. Hence, both must be considered when viewing the impact of an expedite request.

In Figure 34–3, the y-axis shows the number of developers employed on a project. This could equally be mapped to the OE burn rate of a project. The x-axis shows the inventory lead time days, that is, number of days of WIP Inventory in the system multiplied by the number of days for the lead time through the system. The areas delineated for each process attempt to show the spectrum of cost for an expedite request on the normal on-going produc-

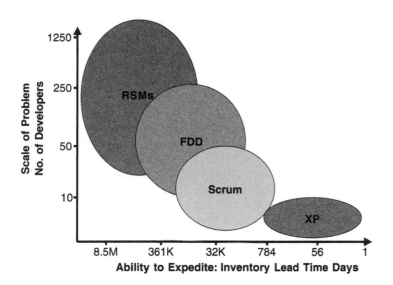

Figure 34–3
Scale versus ability
to expedite.

tion of software. Note that cost is measured in longer lead time through the system and increased inventory in the system. Expediting causes inventory to increase, which incurs a greater carrying cost in terms of risk and uncertainty to the project. Longer lead times carry risk from greater uncertainty and change as well as the potential for lost Throughput due to delay. Hence, there is a benefit in minimizing the potential cost of expediting.

Looking again at Wheeler's four states of process control, it may be possible to map Agile methods and RSMs against the four quadrants. The results would probably look something like Figure 34–4.

The rows show the difference between repeatable methods with low variance measurements and methods that use poorly defined or uncodified, subjective approaches to measurement. The columns show quality in relation to conformance with an acceptable standard, for example 1 bug per Feature, 0.25 bugs per Function Point. Note that poor quality of written code against test scripts would lead to a drop-off in production rate. Hence, as discussed in Chapter 33, it is preferred to measure conformance against a production rate, although conformance against an agreed quality standard would be roughly equivalent.

As the system moves towards the upper left of the chart, there is both process maturity and an increased understanding of the underlying elements—the "natural philosophy of software"—of the work being undertaken. As in other sciences such as physics, until there is an understanding of the basic building blocks of the universe, the measurements are only as good as the knowledge of what to measure. An improved understanding of the underlying philosophy provides an improved understanding of what to measure.

XP has been placed below the *y*-axis to indicate that explicit analysis, modeling, and planning are not a focus in XP and that consistency of Story

**Statistical
Process
Control and
Agile
Methods**

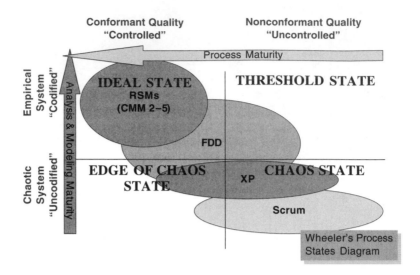

Figure 34–4
Mapping methods onto Wheeler's four states of control.

definition is still emerging. Kent Beck will argue that XP involves modeling "every day." However, there is no recommended approach, and the method chosen is unrelated to the XP process itself or any "smells" (metrics) for XP. Hence, modeling is not a part of the control process of an XP project.

XP claims to deliver what the customer asked for every two weeks.[3] This would imply that a good XP team would be operating in the left-hand column, that is, they are delivering conformant quality.

Scrum is positioned lower on the *y*-axis because its advocates shun codification and modeling. Schwaber even states modeling may be a "waste of time" [2002]. Scrum does, however, help to make sense out of chaos and deliver conformant quality every month. From a process control perspective, XP and Scrum look very similar.

On the other hand, FDD is very different. It is grounded in advanced codification schemes: Features, Feature Sets, Subject Areas, Archetypes, Domain Neutral Component, and Statecharts. With FDD, the metrics to be measured are highly defined. FDD starts in the Threshold state, providing the team is fluent in the conceptual model and codification scheme employed. A good FDD team will improve its processes and move into the Ideal state.

RSMs used in teams that have achieved SEI SW CMM Level 2 or better should in theory only ever appear in the Ideal state. By definition, they can deliver conformant quality, that is, the precise scope on schedule. This meets the basic CMM Level 2 qualification of "repeatable." Any process based in the PMI/ISO/SEI model of scope-budget-schedule must be accurately estimating and delivering on time to be delivering conformant quality. To be repeatable, a team must have conformant quality and a high degree of codification to facilitate empirical measure. Anything other than the Ideal state is CMM Level 1. This highlights the high barrier to entry of a typical RSM and why the CMM model may be insufficient for practical use.

³Possibly every 1 week by the time this book is published.

The process control map suggests that there is a large universe that is normally referred to as CMM Level 1—Chaos. It also suggests that it is not completely chaotic, but can be split into three distinct areas. Further, it suggests that Agile methods help to make sense of these areas. Hence, Agile methods can be used to produce significant improvements without having to jump the barrier to entry of an RSM at CMM Level 2—no need for superhuman ability to accurately predict an uncertain future.

It also suggests that through Agile methods there is a potential maturity progression that can be undertaken by an immature organization. This progression could be mapped against the growth and maturity of a start-up organization.[4] In the early life of the business, it makes sense to build very quickly to be able to expedite very easily and to show customer-valued working code very often. This suggests that Extreme Programming is the correct choice for this early-life business.

As the business matures and begins to adopt more of a product lifecycle approach, moving away from a customer-chasing organization to a product-driven enterprise, it may make sense to introduce longer iterations and use techniques mostly found in Scrum—wrapping the XP approach with Scrum.

As the market matures yet further and it is no longer necessary or desirable to release software every month, it makes sense to adopt FDD. FDD introduces a number of more advanced concepts, and the barrier to entry is higher. A more mature business needs to be able to predict the deliverables in a release. There is a lead time involved in communicating product features to the sales and marketing and customer support organizations. In more mature businesses, the engineering organization must be able to deliver on its promises. FDD helps to do this because of the advanced analysis methods and the resultant reduced uncertainty and its predictability of planning.

Finally, if the market demands it, it may be necessary to mature into the use of full RSMs. This would happen if legal and regulatory conditions were introduced that required rigorous traceability and attention to detail beyond that offered in Agile methods or the domain-required holistic delivery of larger systems where the scope was fixed by legal or regulatory demands.

Lapre and Van Wassenhove published the results of a study into repeatability of process improvement initiatives in manufacturing [Lapre 2002]. By repeatability, they meant that a process improvement could be taken from one location or department in an organization and successfully replicated in another. This is a critical factor if a process is to scale across a large enterprise.[5] They mapped their results into a 2 × 2 matrix. They divided the space into two dimensions: conceptual learning and operational learning.

**What Does
This Mean?**

**Transferable
Quality
Improvement**

---

[4]Jim Highsmith [2002] provides coverage of this topic when he maps the Agile methods against Geoffrey Moore's Market Adoption curve and the phases of early market, chasm, bowling alley, tornado, and main street.

[5]How to achieve enterprise scalability of process is a current area of research amongst Agilists. There were two workshops held at the annual OOPSLA conferences in 2001 and 2002. There is likely to be a lot more published with respect to scaling Agile methods across enterprises over the next 2 years.

Figure 34–5 attempts to map various Agile methods and RSMs onto the Lapre and Van Wassenhove diagram. Conceptual learning has been interpreted as closely related to the notion of a natural philosophy of software development. The more concepts involved and the more those concepts are proven, understood, and repeatable, the higher on the y-axis the method would appear, that is, the same y-axis as Figure 34–4.

Conceptual learning implies that a method has the ability to evaluate and improve the use of its concepts. For example, in Feature Driven Development, the discovery of a fifth Archetype for UML modeling would represent learning in the concept of Archetypes. Discovery of improved methods for determining batch sizes for the design stage such as FDD Workflow[6] would be another example of conceptual learning.

The columns represent the operational learning. This has been interpreted as meaning an ability with the process practices normally associated with Agile methods, that is, this is really a two-dimensional measure that includes both the psychological human aspects of process knowledge and the metrics and measurements discipline demonstrated throughout this book.

Lapre and Van Wassenhove classified the four quadrants of the charts as Fire Fighting, Artisan Skills, Unvalidated Theories, and Operationally Validated Theories. Fire Fighting implies little conceptual understanding of how to bring a process under control and little operational concept of how to achieve such control. Artisan Skills implies that practitioners have a strong knowledge of how to produce good quality results, but struggle to explain why this is possible because they have a poor vocabulary of concepts with which to describe

Figure 34–5
Repeatable process improvement.

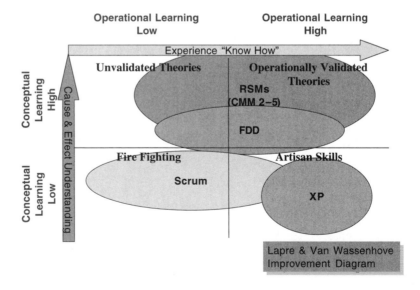

[6]FDD Workflow is an area of active research in the FDD community. It is likely more material on this topic will have been published between the time this book went to press and the publication date.

and explain their technique. Unvalidated Theories is self-explanatory. In this case, there is lots of conceptual conjecture. But, it is not possible to prove them by cause-effect analysis, and correlation has not yet been obtained through empirical observation. Finally, Operationally Validated Theories imply that a process is well understood using a conceptual model that maps well onto the reality and has been shown to work in operation.

This gives us some slightly different results from the earlier views. Extreme Programming tends to shun conceptualization, and most of its practitioners would agree that XP is craftsmanship—the craft of writing code. This places it firmly in the Artisan Skills quadrant.

Scrum was placed across the Fire Fighting and Artisan Skills quadrants because Scrum has a very low barrier to entry. In fact, to get Scrum under way, all you really need is an agreement to time-box iterations at 30 days, a list of tasks to represent the Sprint Backlog, and a daily stand-up meeting (Scrum) to keep track of progress. Scrum advocates boast that it can be taught in a single day. It is, therefore, very light on concepts. In comparison, FDD (including UML Archetypes and DNC) takes several weeks of mentoring to teach to a typical team.

FDD has a much higher barrier to entry. It involves many concepts, several of which represent the state of the art, particularly in object modeling for business processes and Statechart modeling for user interface interaction. With beginners new to these concepts FDD is not usually executed properly. The individuals have to go through several iterations before they truly understand the concepts in FDD and can start to use them to formulate further improvements.

RSMs are heavy on concepts and heavy on process discipline. They have by far the highest barrier to entry. Hence, they belong in the upper right quadrant when they are being executed by a team of experienced practitioners well grounded in the concepts and their use. However, due to the high barrier to entry and steep learning curve, most organizations using RSMs are really operating in the Fire Fighting quadrant. There is a poor comprehension of the concepts, and they are poorly used. As a result, learning is low.

Lapre and Van Wassenhove set out to show how transferable process improvement knowledge can be across different organizations. FDD advocates refer to this as "repeatability," that is, the ability to transfer the knowledge from one project team to another and achieve similar results without having to actively mentor with and mix in individuals from an existing, experienced team. Lapre and Van Wassenhove have shown in manufacturing that only organizations that operate in the Operationally Validated Theories quadrant are successful at transferring knowledge to other plants and operational units.

Their results, mapped to Agile methods, seem to suggest that Agile methods are hard to transfer. In fact, a common complaint about published material on many Agile methods is that it is hard to repeat because the descriptions of what to do are so vague. One Agilist I know paraphrased writing on XP as "a bunch of guys who all knew each other well, had worked together for years, and were all experienced coders, who got together and decided to write high quality unit tested code in pairs, whilst showing each other mutual respect and leaving their egos at home." It is easy to see why the claimed results are hard to transfer.

The true value of the Lapre and Van Wassenhove chart is that it indicates how much word of mouth and direct knowledge transfer is required to develop proficiency with Agile methods. In many ways Agile methods are crafts, and crafts have to be learned by apprenticeship with a master. This makes Agile methods hard to scale across an enterprise with any great speed.

The Lapre and Van Wassenhove results suggest that Scrum may be easy to pick up, but the results will be limited and the knowledge gained will be impossible to transfer because there is no conceptual model on which to map the learnings. XP is also hard to transfer. It does have some concepts,[7] and there is a lot of experience-based knowledge encapsulated. However, it will transfer best when a member (or members) of an existing team actually teach a new team how to do it and teach the undocumented craftsmanship techniques.

FDD has a much more developed conceptual model and is documented in a way (ETVX process definitions) that is designed to be transferable. However, the concepts can prove difficult for many engineers, and some mentoring by an expert in FDD is preferable. However, once a team is up to speed with FDD, they have a strong conceptual model on which to map improvements, and transferring knowledge of improvements to other groups should be straightforward.[8]

With RSMs, assuming a basic level of competency on the teams involved, transferring knowledge should be straightforward providing the learning can be explained using existing concepts and does not require the introduction of any new concepts. The problem has been scaling the training. For example, counting Function Points is not a widely adopted skill, despite the many years that the technique has been available.

Summary

Craft techniques are hard to scale across large organizations quickly. They require an apprenticeship program that rarely exists in software development. The book learning approach that is possible with RSMs is easier to scale across large organizations. However, history has shown that the results can be very poor.

---

[7]The number of concepts in XP is growing every year. Some XP advocates are already complaining that there are too many new concepts and the method was better when it only had 12 core principles.

[8]I have seen this process in action with three teams over the last 4 years. Learning typically kicks in around the 6-month stage—learning is often restricted to the chief programmers who are usually the smartest and most conversant with the concepts involved.

Bibliography

Ambler, Scott W., and Jeffries, Ron, *Agile Modeling*, John Wiley & Sons, 2002.

Ambler, Scott W., Specialist Generalists, *Isn't That Special*, January 2003.

Anderson, David J., *Extending FDD for UI—Implementing Feature Driven Development on Presentation Layer Projects*, *http://www.uidesign.net/2001/papers/fddui.html*, uidesign.net, 2001.

Anderson, David J., *Morning Roll Call*, The Coad Letter, October 2002.

Astels, David, Miller, Granville, and Novak, Miroslav, *A Practical Guide to Extreme Programming*, Prentice Hall, 2002.

Auer, Ken, and Miller, Roy, *Extreme Programming Applied—Playing To Win*, Addison Wesley, 2002.

Beck, Kent, *Extreme Programming Explained—Embrace Change*, Addison Wesley, 2000.

Beck, Kent, and Fowler, Martin, *Planning Extreme Programming*, Addison Wesley, 2001.

Proceedings of XP Universe 2002—August 6th, 2002, *Lean Manufacturing*.

Object Mentor wiki, *http://monet.objectmentor.com/cgi-bin/openspace/wiki.py?LeanManufacturing*.

Boehm, Barry, *Software Engineering*, IEEE Transactions on Computer, Vol. 12, No. 25.

Boehm, Barry W., *Software Engineering Economics*, Prentice Hall, 1981.

Bousfield, W. A., and Cohen, B. H. The occurrence of clustering in the recall of randomly arranged words of different frequencies-of-usage, J. Gen. Psychol., 1955, 52, 83–95.

Bousfield, A. K., and Bousfield, W. A., Measuring of clustering and of repeated constancies in repeated free recall, Psychol. Reports, 1966, 19, 935.

Brooks, Frederick P., Jr., *The Mythical Man Month*, Addison Wesley, 1995.

Christensen, Clayton M., The Innovator's Dilemma, *Harper Business Review*, 2000.

Clark, Kim B., and Wheelwright, Steven C., *New Product and Process Development*, Harvard University Press/Simon & Schuster, 1992.

Coad, Peter, Mayfield, Mark, and North, David, *Object Models: Strategies, Patterns & Applications*, 2nd Ed., Prentice Hall, 1996.

Coad, Peter, Mayfield, Mark, and Kern, Jonathan, *Java Design: Building Better Apps and Applets*, 2nd Ed., Prentice Hall, 1998.

Coad, Peter, Lefebvre, Eric, and De Luca, Jeff, *Java Modeling in Color with UML: Enterprise Components and Process*, Prentice Hall, 1999.

Cockburn, Alistair, Re-examining The Cost of Change Curve—Year 2000, *http://www.xprogramming.com/xpmag/cost_of_change.htm*, XProgramming.com, 2000.

Cockburn, Alistair, and Williams, Laurie, The Costs and Benefits of Pair Programming, Humans and Technology Technical Report, 2000, *http://members.aol.com/humansandt/papers/pairprogrammingcostbene/pairprogrammingcostbene.htm*.

Cockburn, Alistair, *Agile Software Development*, Addison Wesley, 2002.

Constantine, Larry L., and Lockwood, Lucy, *Software for Use*, ACM Press/Addison Wesley, 1999.

Constantine, Larry L., *Beyond Chaos—The Expert Edge in Managing Software Development*, ACM Press/Addison Wesley, 2001.

Constantine Larry L., Process Agility and Usability: Towards Lightweight Usage-Centered Design, *Proceedings of* OOPSLA 2001.

Corbett, Thomas, *Throughput Accounting*, North River Press, 1998.

De Luca, Jeff, *Using The FDD Trend Report*, Nebulon Pty Ltd, 2002. *http://www.nebulon.com/articles/fdd/trend.html*

De Luca, Tom. Getting flexible with planning,*Feature Driven Development Newsletter*, January 2003, *http://www.featuredrivendevelopment.com/node.php?old=508*.

DeMarco, Tom, and Lister, Timothy, *Peopleware—Productive Projects and Teams*, 2nd Ed., Dorset House, 1999.

DeMarco, Tom. *Slack—Getting Past Burnout, Busywork, and the Myth of Total Efficiency*, Broadway Books, New York, New York, 2001.

De Meyer, Arnoud, Loch, Christoph H., and Pich, Michael T., Managing project uncertainty: From Variation Chaos, MIT *Sloan Management Review*, Winter 2002.

Descartes, Renee, *Rules for the Direction of the Mind*.

Farson, Richard, and Keyes, Ralph, The failure tolerant leader, *Harvard Business Review*, August 2002.

Fowler, Martin, *Analysis Patterns—Reusable Object Models*, Addison Wesley, 1996.

Gerstner, Louis V., *Who Says Elephants Can't Dance?*, Harper Business, 2002.

Godin, Seth, *Survival Is Not Enough*, Free Press, 2002.

Goldratt, Eliyahu M., and Cox, Jeff, *The Goal*, 2nd Rev. Ed., North River Press, 1992.

Goldratt, Eliyahu M., *Theory of Constraints*, North River Press, 1990.

Goldratt, Eliyahu M., *The Haystack Syndrome—Sifting Information Out of the Data Ocean*, North River Press, 1990.

Goldratt, Eliyahu M., *Theory of Constraints Journal*, 1990, 1(2).

Goldratt, Eliyahu M., *It's Not Luck*, North River Press, 1994.

Goldratt, Eliyahu M., *Critical Chain*, North River Press, 1997.

Goldratt, Eliyahu M., Schragenheim, Eli, and Ptak, Carol A., *Necessary But Not Sufficient*, North River Press, 2000.

Habraken, N. J., and Teicher, Jonathan (Eds.), *The Structure of the Ordinary: Form and Control in the Built Environment*, MIT Press, 2000.

Hays, David C., *Data Model Patterns—Conventions of Thought*, Dorset House, 1996.

Highsmith, James A., *Agile Software Development Ecosystems*, Addison Wesley, 2002.

Horrocks, Ian, *Constructing the User Interface with Statecharts*, Addison Wesley, 1999.

Jacobson, Ivar, et al., *The Unified Software Development Process*, Addison Wesley, 1998.

Johnson, Steven, *Emergence: The Connected Lives of Ants, Brains, Cities and Software*, Penguin, 2002.

Jones, Capers, *Software Assessments, Benchmarks and Best Practices*, Addison Wesley, 2000.

Kim, W. Chan, and Mauborgne, Renee, Fair process: Managing in the knowledge economy, *Harvard Business Review*, January 2003.

Koskela, Lauri, and Howell, George, *The Underlying Theory of Project Management Is Obsolete*, Project Management Institute, 2002.

Kruchten, Philippe, *The Rational Unified Process—An Introduction*, 2nd Ed., Addison Wesley, 2000.

Lapre, Michael A., and Van Wassenhove, Luk N., Learning across lines: The secret to more efficient factories, *Harvard Business Review*, October 2002.

Larman, Craig, *Applying UML and Patterns: An Introduction to Object Oriented Analysis and Design and the Unified Process*, Prentice Hall, 2001.

Lepore, Domenico, and Cohen, Oded, *Deming and Goldratt*, North River Press, 1999.

Magretta, Joan, and Stone, Nan, *What Management Is*, Free Press, 2002.

Maxwell, Katrina D., *Applied Statistics for Software Managers*, Prentice Hall, 2002.

Mayford Technologies, *Extreme Programming—Introduction*, Mayford Technologies, 2002. *http://www.mayford.ca/download/xp_overview.pdf*.

McGrath, Michael E., *Product Strategy for High Technology Companies—How to Achieve Growth, Competitive Advantage and Increased Profits*, McGraw-Hill, 1995.

Meyer, Managing project uncertainty: From variation to chaos, *Sloan Management*, (Winter) 2002.

Miller, Danny, and Hartwick, Jon, Spotting management fads, *Harvard Business Review*, October 2002.

Nicola, Jill, Mayfield, Mark, and Abney, Mike, *Streamlined Object Modeling   Patterns, Rules & Implementation*, Prentice Hall, 2001.

O'Connor, Joseph and Ian McDermott, *The Art of Systems Thinking—Essential Skills for Creativity and Problem Solving*, Thorsons, London, England and San Francisco, California 1997.

Ohno, Taiichi, *Toyota Production System: Beyond Large Scale Production*, Productivity Press, 1988.

Palmer, Stephen R., and Felsing, John M., *A Practical Guide to Feature Driven Development*, Prentice Hall, 2002.

Patrick, Francis S., *Program Management: Turning Many Projects into Few Priorities with* TOC, 1998. *http://www.focusedperformance.com/articles/multipm.html*, Focused Performance.

Poppendieck, Mary, Lean programming, *Software Development Magazine*, Pt. 1, May 2001/Pt. 2, June 2001.

Poppendieck, Mary, and Poppendieck, Tom, *Lean Development—An Agile Toolkit*, Addison Wesley, 2003.

Reinertsen, Donald G., *Managing the Design Factory—A Product Developer's Toolkit*, Free Press, 1997.

Royce, Winston, W., *Managing the Development of Large Software Systems*, Proceedings of the IEEE WESCON 1970.

Sackman, H., Erikson, W. J., and Grant, E. E., Exploratory experimental studies comparing online and offline programming performance, *Communications of the ACM*, 1968, 11(1).

Schwaber, Ken, and Beedle, Mike, *Agile Software Development with Scrum*, Prentice Hall, 2002.

Schwaber, Ken, Scaling Scrum to the large, *IEEE Transactions on Computing*, July 2003.

Senge, Peter M., *The Fifth Discipline—The Art & Practice of the Learning Organization*, Doubleday, 1990.

Shingo, Shigeo, *A Study of the Toyota Production System from an Industrial Engineering Viewpoint*, Rev. Ed., Productivity Press, 1989.

Smith, Adam, *An Inquiry into the Wealth and Causes of the Wealth of Nations*, Modern Library, 1994.

Taylor, Frederick Winslow, *The Principles of Scientific Management*, Dover Publications, 1998.

Tayntor, Christine B., *Six Sigma Software Development*, Auerbach, 2002.

Ogunnaike, Babatunde A., and Harmon, Ray W., *Process Dynamics, Modeling and Control*, Oxford University Press, 1994.

Weaver, Richard G., and Farrell, John D., *Managers as Facilitators*, Berrett & Koehler, 1997.

Weinberg, Gerald M., *Quality Software Management Volume 1—Systems Thinking*, Dorset House, 1997.

Weinberg, Gerald M., *Quality Software Management Volume 2—First Order Measurement*, Dorset House, 1997.

Weinberg, Gerald M., *Quality Software Management Volume 4—Anticipating Change*, Dorset House, 1997.

Weinberg Gerald M., *The Psychology of Computer Programming: Silver Anniversary Edition*, Dorset House, 1998.

Wendorff, Peter, An essential distinction of Agile Software Development Processes based on Systems Thinking in Software Engineering Management, *Transactions of XP 2002. http://www.agilealliance.com/articles/articles/EssentialDistinction.pdf*

Wheeler, Donald J., and Chambers, David S., *Understanding Statistical Process Control*, 2nd Ed., SPC Press, 1992.

Wiegers, Karl E., *A Software Engineering Culture*, Dorset House, 1996.

Wiegers, Karl E., *Peer Reviews in Software—A Practical Guide*, Addison Wesley, 2002.

Womack, James P., Jones, Daniel T., and Roos, Daniel, *The Machine that Changed the World*, Harper Perennial, 1991.

Womack, James P., and Jones, Daniel T., *Lean Thinking—Banish Waste and Create Wealth in Your Corporation*, Simon & Schuster, 1996.

International Function Point Users Group, IT *Measurement—Practical Advice from the Experts*, Foreword by Ed Yourdon, Addison Wesley, 2002.

Index

K

Kanban Approach, 4, 6
Knowledge Management System (KMS), use of, 93, 199
Koskela & Howell's three-dimensional model for project management, 57

L

Labor, implications of adding additional, 274–276
Late start, 65–66
"Late" status, 68
Lead time (LT)
  estimation of, 63
  in Extreme Programing (XP), 228
  in Feature Driven Development (FDD), 185
  reduction of, 135
  in Scrum, 254, 285
  in Software Development Lifecycle (SDLC), 164
  and software production metrics, 53
  in Unified Development Process (UDP), 173
Lean production, 5–6, 284
Learning Organization Maturity Model
  goals of, 105
  Stage 0-Analysis Ability, 105
  Stage 4- Anticipated ROI and the Failure Tolerant Organization, 107
  Stage 1-End-to-End Traceability, 106
  Stage 2-Stabilize System Metrics, 106
  Stage 3- Systems Thinking and a Learning Organization, 106–107
Level-of-effort (LOE) estimate, 50, 186–188
Lifecycle methods, software engineering, 18
Lifetime revenue per subscriber (LRPS), 150
Line of code (LOC), 50
Little's Law, 53
Local safety considerations, 44–46, 219

M

Management accounting for systems
  complex development systems, 18–20
  emergent properties, 14
  operating expenses (OE), 15
  systems thinking, and, 14–15
  throughput accounting, and, 15–17
  value added, and, 16
Management roles and rules, 73–76, 109, 112
Manufacturing Resource Planning (MRP), 95
Marketing Requirement Document (MRD), 171
Maturity progression, 297
Morning roll call, use of, 213–215
Multitasking, role of, 218

N

Net profit, 21–22, 24, 179, 244
Net profit for services (NPBITDA), calculation of, 152

O

Object Oriented Analysis, 8
Object Oriented Software Engineering (OOSE), 289
Offshore development and process maturity, 121–122
One-dimensional model of project management, 57
On-going investment, role of, 142
On-site customer, role of the, 240
"On Time" status, 68
Operating expense (OE)
  in Extreme Programing (XP), 244
  factors of, 146
  in Feature Driven Development (FDD), 222–223
  importance of, 27
  operating expense for services (OEBIDA), calculation of, 151
  reductions in, 135
  in traditional methods, 178–179
Operational learning, 297–300
Operationally validated theories, 298
Operations review
  attendees, 123
  financial information, presentation of, 124–125
  information, presentation of, 124–128
  minute taking, 128
  production metrics, presentation of, 125–126
  program management metrics, presentation of, 127
  project management metrics, presentation of, 127
  purpose of, 123
  timing, 124
Option theory, 234
Outsourcing decisions, 120–122
Overtime, effectiveness of, 81

P

Pair programming, use of, 236–237
Parallel paths, definition and identification of, 64–65
Peer reviews, use of, 210
People constraint, protecting the, 37–38
Perishable requirements, 32

TEST-DRIVEN DEVELOPMENT:
A Practical Guide

by DAVID ASTELS • **Foreword by RON JEFFRIES**
©2004, Paper, 592 pp., 0-13-101649-0

Test-Driven Development: A Practical Guide enables developers to write software that's simpler, leaner, and more reliable...Now, there's a TDD guide focused on real projects, real implementation challenges, and real code. Dave Astels shows TDD at work in a start-to-finish project written in Java and using the JUnit testing framework. You'll learn how "test first" works, why it works, and what obstacles you'll encounter and how to transform TDD's promise into reality.
- Relentlessly practical! Full of downloadable code examples, hands-on exercises, and a fully hyperlinked version of the "resources" appendix.
- Introduces powerful TDD tools and techniques including key JUnit extensions, presented by their creators (Scott Ambler, Tim Bacon, Mike Bowler, Mike Clark, Bryan Dollery, James Newkirk, Bob Payne, Kay Petacost, and Jens Uwe Pipka).

AGILE MANAGEMENT FOR SOFTWARE ENGINEERING:
Applying the Theory of Constraints for Business Results

by DAVID J. ANDERSON • **Foreword by ELI SCHRAGENHEIM**
©2004, Paper, 336 pp., 0-13-142460-2

"A tremendous contribution to the literature in the field. This should be required reading for all development teams going forward."

— JOHN F. YUZDEPSKI
VP & GM, Openwave Systems

In *Agile Management for Software Engineering*, David J. Anderson introduces a break-through approach for managing projects based on agile methodologies. Drawing on the proven techniques of the Theory of Constraints and Lean Production, Anderson shows how to go Agile while inspiring the confidence of senior executives in Fortune 1000 companies. Whether you're a development manager, project manager, team leader, or senior IT executive, this book will help you achieve all four of your most urgent challenges: lower cost, faster delivery, improved quality, and focused alignment with the business.

A PRACTICAL GUIDE TO ENTERPRISE ARCHITECTURE

by JAMES McGOVERN / SCOTT AMBLER / MIKES STEVEN / JAMES LINN / VIKAS SHARAN / ELIAS K. JO
©2004, Paper, 256 pp., 0-13-141275-2

In *A Practical Guide to Enterprise Architecture*, six leading experts present indispensable technical, process, and business insight into every aspect of enterprise architecture. Written for every working architect and every IT professional who wants to become one, this classic handbook goes beyond theory and presents strategies that are based on experiences within organizations across multiple industry verticals. Behind each opinion, technique, and principle is a wealth of knowledge provided by some of the best-known industry thought leaders today.

FROM PRENTICE HALL PTR • www.phptr.com

PRENTICE HALL PTR

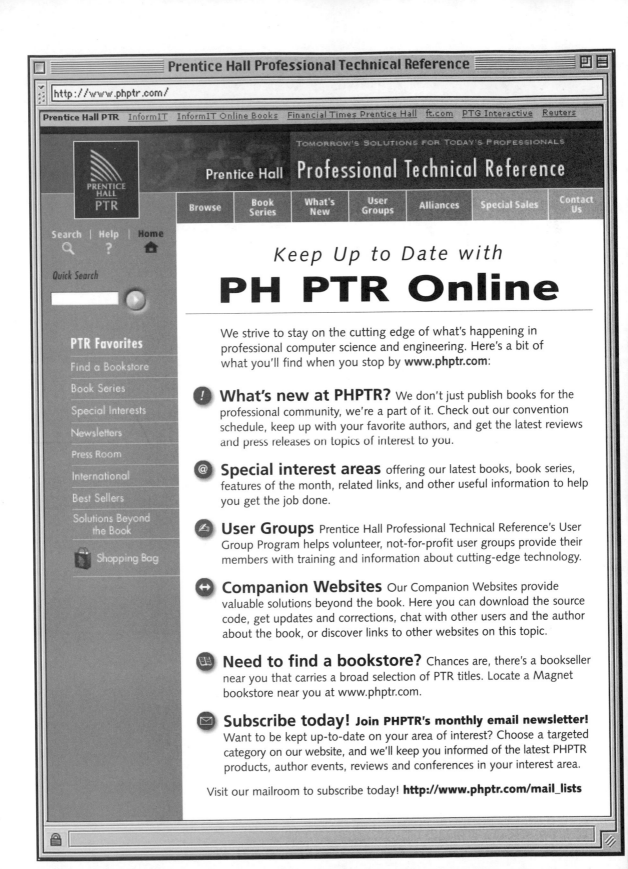